T0316926

Development Without Aid

Development Without Aid

The Decline of Development Aid and the Rise of the Diaspora

DAVID A. PHILLIPS

ANTHEM PRESS
LONDON · NEW YORK · DELHI

Anthem Press
An imprint of Wimbledon Publishing Company
www.anthempress.com

This edition first published in UK and USA 2013
by ANTHEM PRESS
75–76 Blackfriars Road, London SE1 8HA, UK
or PO Box 9779, London SW19 7ZG, UK
and
244 Madison Ave. #116, New York, NY 10016, USA

Copyright © David A. Phillips 2013

The author asserts the moral right to be identified as the author of this work.

All rights reserved. Without limiting the rights under copyright reserved above,
no part of this publication may be reproduced, stored or introduced into
a retrieval system, or transmitted, in any form or by any means
(electronic, mechanical, photocopying, recording or otherwise),
without the prior written permission of both the copyright
owner and the above publisher of this book.

British Library Cataloguing-in-Publication Data
A catalogue record for this book is available from the British Library.

Library of Congress Cataloging-in-Publication Data
A catalog record for this book has been requested.

ISBN-13: 978 0 85728 303 0 (Hbk)
ISBN-10: 0 85728 303 0 (Hbk)

ISBN-13: 978 0 85728 623 9 (Pbk)
ISBN-10: 0 85728 623 4 (Pbk)

This title is also available as an eBook.

CONTENTS

LIST OF ACRONYMS

3ie	International Initiative for Impact Evaluation
AECID	Agencia Española de Cooperación Internacional para el Desarrollo
AFD	Agence Française du Développement
AFFORD	Africa Foundation for Development
AGOA	Africa Growth and Opportunity Act
BSF	budget support fund
CCT	Conditional Cash Transfers
CDI	Commitment to Development Index
CGAP	Consultative Group to Assist the Poor
CGD	Center for Global Development
COD	cash on delivery
COMESA	Common Market for East and Southern Africa
DAC	Development Assistance Committee
DDI	Diaspora Direct Investment
DFID	Department for International Development
EBRD	European Bank for Reconstruction and Development
EC	European Commission
EIU	Economist Intelligence Unit
EPA	Economic Partnership Agreement
FDI	foreign direct investment
FTI	Fast-Track Initiative
GAVI	Global Alliance for Vaccines and Immunisation
GDP	gross domestic product
GFATM	Global Fund to Fight AIDS, Tuberculosis and Malaria
GNI	gross national income
GPG	global public good
HPIC	heavily indebted poor countries
HTA	hometown association
IADB	Inter-American Development Bank
IBRD	International Bank for Reconstruction and Development
IDA	International Development Association
IEG	Independent Evaluation Group
IFAD	International Fund for Agricultural Development
IFC	International Finance Corporation

IFI	international financial institution
IMF	International Monetary Fund
IOM	International Organization for Migration
IT	information technology
KFW	Kreditanstalt für Wiederaufbau
LDC	less-developed country
MBA	masters in business administration
MCC	Millennium Challenge Corporation
MCF	Millennium Challenge Fund
MDG	Millennium Development Goals
MDRI	Multilateral Debt Relief Initiative
MFI	microfinance institution
MIDA	Migration for Development in Africa
MPI	Migration Policy Institute
NBER	National Bureau of Economic Research
NGO	non-government organization
ODA	official development assistance
OECD	Organisation for Economic Co-operation and Development
OED	Operations Evaluation Department
OPIC	Overseas Private Investment Corporation
PBF	performance-based funding
PEPFAR	President's Emergency Plan for AIDS Relief
PRSP	Poverty Reduction Strategy Paper
PSD	private sector development
QUODA	Quality of Development Assistance
RIE	randomized impact evaluation
SADC	Southern Africa Development Community
SEZ	special economic zone
SIDA	Swedish International Development Agency
SME	small and medium enterprise
SSA	Sub-Saharan Africa
TiE	The Indus Entrepreneurs
UNHCR	United Nations High Commissioner for Refugees
USAID	United States Agency for International Development
USTDA	United States Trade Development Agency
WDI	World Development Indicators
WFP	World Food Program
WHO	World Health Organization
WTO	World Trade Organization

ACKNOWLEDGMENTS

This book would not have been possible without the support of Nadya who has always been there for me, to deal with moments of both doubt and euphoria; the distractions of Joshua and Josephine who have never quite understood what I do with my time; and the moral support of Jacqui and Caroline from further away.

In writing the book I would also like to thank a number of anonymous referees for the extremely valuable and detailed comments they made on the draft, and to many others with whom I had conversations about where I was heading. In particular I would like to acknowledge Professor John Weiss, the University of Bradford in the UK, and Professor Kenneth Reinert, George Mason University in the US, for the time they spent trying to decipher my arguments and suggesting improvements. Finally I would like to thank Tej Sood, Janka Romero and Rob Reddick at Anthem Press who guided this project through. Of course, all remaining errors and omissions are solely my responsibility.

Finally I would like to acknowledge the extensive and invaluable sources of information that are readily available through the papers and seminars of the Center For Global Development in Washington DC under the energetic leadership of Nancy Birdsall, many of which I have read or attended during the course of writing this book; the Migration Policy Institute, also in Washington; and the extensive resource of informal, and therefore up-to-the-minute, working papers and bulletins of the World Bank and the IMF which often act as leading indicators of the direction of thinking on development.

Chapter 1

INTRODUCTION: MOTIVATION
AND PERSPECTIVE

International development cooperation has achieved many positive results. When we met in Monterrey a decade ago, we recognised that increases in volumes of financing for development must be coupled with more effective action to generate sustainable and transparent results for all citizens. Our dialogue in Busan builds on the foundations laid by previous High Level Fora, which have been proven to remain relevant, and which have helped to improve the quality of development cooperation.

"Partnership for Effective Development Cooperation,"
Fourth High Level Forum on Aid Effectiveness,
Busan, South Korea, 1 December 2011, par. 6

Development aid, far from being necessary to rescue poor societies from a vicious circle of poverty, is far more likely to keep them in that state.

Peter T. Bauer (1993)[1]

A Starting Point

This book is ultimately a personal reflection rather than an academic treatise, and so, while as far as possible remaining objective and supported by evidence, it is in the end as much advocacy as argument, at times taking the risk of verging on the polemical. It aims to open up perspectives as much as analyze facts. It is about the development of poor countries, not the principles of how societies and economies develop but the narrower canvas of development assistance to poor countries, its effectiveness and whether there is a different way to achieve its objectives. It aims, in fact, to help move the perception of the path to development in poor countries squarely beyond development assistance and beyond the discussion of its architecture, design and practice. It also asks for a partial suspension of belief that only rigorously evidence-based statements are admissible while judgments based on experience are not. Evidence is a wonderful thing; but conclusive evidence on how to succeed in development aid is almost unobtainable, and it is wholly predictable that much of the current effort to obtain it will in the end provide no better basis for action than experience.

Nearly US$4.0 trillion (in today's currency) has been disbursed in net official development assistance (ODA) to developing countries (after repayments) since 1960, or an average of about US$70 billion a year at today's prices, according to the Organisation for Economic Co-operation and Development (OECD).[2] During all this time foreign aid, or foreign assistance,[3] has been the subject of extensive attention – books, papers, films, concerts, pamphlets, investigative reports and advertising campaigns, produced overwhelmingly by outside governments, organizations and individuals. The British Library lists over 250 new books on "economic development assistance" published during 2010 to 2011. There are 300 or so internationally recognized journals focusing on development, including development aid, and many others that deal intermittently with the subject.[4] One might well question the value of another work on how to strategize, design, appraise, negotiate, implement, procure, manage, monitor, evaluate, scale up, reform, reinvent or move beyond foreign aid, written by another outsider, when what is now clearly called for is an upsurge, an outcry, from indigenous thinkers themselves, especially those from the poorest and most affected countries, about how to handle foreign aid. Those indigenous thinkers are emerging but seemingly there are still too few of them.[5] In the meantime I offer two reasons why I should be entitled to speak up both for myself and for them.

The first reason is that I am not entirely an outsider. I was brought up from infancy in the "colonies" – that is to say, in the countries known then as Nyasaland and Southern Rhodesia in Central Africa that were once part of the British Empire. So what, one might ask. That life has gone with the wind and we have all said good riddance to a historical era that featured the nineteenth-century "Scramble for Africa" by the rival imperial powers. The gone-with-the-wind allusion is however important. From my viewpoint I did not much like the idea that the world of my childhood had vanished without trace, nor did I enjoy leaving behind forever the country of my earliest memories and experiences.

The fact of being from a transitory component of African society living a relatively privileged life did not mean that my childish sense that Nyasaland was my *country* and my *home* was more unreasonable than those of another child, whether of a farmer, a trader or a government official, indigenous or alien. I was the son of a colonial government official, and colonial officials tended to have a lesser sense of ownership than farmers and traders, even foreign ones, who invested in the country. Nevertheless as children our feelings about being part of the place were quite natural even if our parents tended to see themselves more on a temporary mission for his or her Britannic Majesty. Many of us after all were actually born there, or in my case nearly so, arriving at less than 1 year old. We were not on any mission. We belonged to the place. And in a sense we remain a part of the Nyasaland, now Malawi, diaspora, because those of us who left still retain some residual, if distant, allegiance to the country, while a few of us stayed on.[6]

Many of us also grew up to think of Nyasaland as different from other colonies. The country surely had the usual ethnic and class anomalies of a colony. Some of us would experience a vague sense of guilt at being waited on by a retinue of servants; it didn't seem to make sense that people who were deputed to look after me, my sister and brother, some of whom were themselves parents, should treat our own parents with exaggerated respect and be treated in turn with exaggerated, albeit institutionalized, disrespect. But I lived with it and so did they, apparently without too much trouble. The big difference was that the country did not have the gold, diamonds and other high value minerals that caused overt social trauma among neighbors like the Congo or South Africa, and it did not have the same toxic race relations. The country's exportable offerings were largely tobacco and tea rather than minerals. It had a few towns, scattered villages and the beautiful Lake Nyasa (now known within the country as Lake Malawi) "discovered" for Europe by David Livingstone.

It was generally a quiet place, termed quaintly a protectorate according to the nomenclature of that era, a status that distinguished it somewhat from the settler colonies around it. In 1960, its population was only 3 million. The British colonial authorities invented a beautiful national crest consisting of a leopard standing on a rock before a rising sun. The leopard disappeared after independence and only the less beautiful, but more relevant, rising sun remained. Pity about that leopard. At the base of the crest was the Latin motto "*lux in tenebris.*" I was rather fond of the motto as well, but later understood that it was not a reference to the delights of Nyasaland but rather to a subtext about the illumination of a dark continent. In that apparently quiet country,[7] the emergence of African nationalism in the late 1950s came as a surprise to both colonial parents and colonial children, though perhaps less in the case of the latter.[8]

My home for most of my childhood was a place called Zomba. In 1964, just prior to independence, the town of Zomba was hardly more than a village. Its population was about 3,000 made up almost entirely of Africans, Indians and Europeans. The British colonial population numbered a few hundred administrators, military and police officers, a few settlers and businessmen, and their children. The town had a long main street with a narrow strip of asphalt on top of gravel, lined in places by blue jacaranda trees. There was a cluster of small stores owned mainly by Indian migrants, various legislative, administrative and judicial buildings scattered across the town, a couple of churches, a temple and mosque, the occasional inn and bar, schools and small hospitals (ethnically selective), a Freemason's hall (my first school), a couple of sports and social clubs (also ethnically selective) and an airfield boasting two flights a week by a single-engine "Beaver" airplane. The town was located on the lower slopes of a mountain that looked out over a broad plain to another higher mountain (called Mlanje) and to a lake (called Shire) on the horizon. This was the country's capital under the British colonial administration.

Elevated as it was and reasonably cool, Zomba was a beautiful place in the rugged manner of Africa. Our house was a little way up the mountain, according to a pecking order among the colonial cadre based on altitude. I grew up imbued with the sights, colors, smells and sounds, the plains, rivers, woods and mountains, plants and animals, tropical rain and heat, big skies and quiet solitude of small town Africa just as did the son of an African farmer or trader, even though they eked out a much more precarious existence than mine.

And that leads to another thought. Not only did I see this as my country but I sometimes thought that had I had the opportunity I could probably have worked more determinedly for my country to try to help it to prosper than the first of a stream of technical advisers that started to arrive as Nyasaland became independent of the British Crown in 1964, when my family and I had to leave. These newcomers really seemed to think that they knew more about what to do about my country than we colonial types, but I in my simple way felt they knew rather less. Certainly they knew less than us in terms of the history, geography, people, languages, cultures, realities and opportunities of my country, and some would agree that that was an important consideration, even though our knowledge had been gained within a social system that was incompatible with national aspirations. And, by the way, they also seemed to live in more comfortable circumstances than my family had ever done even as part of the colonial ruling class, protected by the assistance agency that sent them to this remote and risky place far away from civilization, a place with which we colonial teenagers in contrast were very familiar and saw as neither remote nor risky.

This idea of "my country" and questions about the meaning of national identity have remained with me ever since. I have no doubt that it remains today one of the keys to understanding the intractable problems that have beset foreign assistance to the poorest countries, especially in Africa, and have been extensively debated with little conclusion for 50 years, pretty much ever since the first technical advisers set foot in the former colonies of Britain, France, Portugal, Spain, Holland, Belgium and others. These are problems which, one suspects, have something to do with the present-day equivalent of the "quaint protectorate" system under which foreign aid is currently dispensed to the poorest countries, especially in Africa.

But there is a second reason why I think I am entitled to write a book on how to deal with foreign aid even though I don't belong anymore to a country that is being aided. This is because I think that the era of foreign aid, as it is currently understood and practiced in the poorest countries, should be brought to a close, and this is an issue which concerns the donors as much as the recipients. I am in a very good position to talk about this because it has to do with the rich country which is now mine and its own policies. In other words, I am not presuming to tell anyone else in another country what to do.

In the meantime I have been employed in various parts of the world, in Africa, the Former Soviet Union and Asia in the foreign-aid business, for national and international organizations, for academia and as an independent "expert," since the time that my family left Africa for what then seemed to us a rather remote and risky country known as Britain. My formative years in Africa led me to want to explore and work in and for other countries. But during these times, and since seeing the first foreign advisers arrive in Malawi, this experience has led me to a simple, perhaps simplistic, conviction. If after 50 years of extensive practical and theoretical effort, and several trillion dollars spent, we are still heatedly debating the main issue – how and whether foreign aid can be effective – it is extremely probable that in its present form it is, for the most part, not effective.[9] Perhaps therefore we should be focusing not on trying to reinvent it but on alternative ways than foreign aid for poor countries to achieve the beautiful goal of ending poverty.[10] Such alternative ways of thinking, of course, has to be led by the leaders and people of those countries themselves, not by outsiders.

This assertion is not intended to imply that none of the assistance that has been provided to poor countries has ever done any good, so immediately I have to temper such a sweeping proposition. And the "aid problem" largely applies to a group of countries with about a billion inhabitants (15 percent of the world's population) that have, despite particularly large amounts of aid, remained in especially severe poverty up to now. It cannot be so easily applied, almost by definition, to those who have started to emerge from poverty even though emerging countries like China and India still contain large numbers of very poor people. And even in the poorest countries there are numerous examples where aid has in fact helped. Plenty of perfectly well-conceived and executed assistance projects have been delivered. After all, how can we say that roads and bridges, immunization programs, medicated mosquito nets, clinics, training of nurses, technicians and software engineers, or the provision of advice to finance ministers, hospitals, schools, farmers, businesses and banks by genuine experts have not added genuine value? Equally, numerous individuals and institutions involve themselves in foreign-aid work with the best of intentions, and sincerely strive to be effective.

In principle, properly conceived and in the right conditions, all outside advisory assistance can be valuable wherever it is given, both to rich and poor countries. Indeed, major international consulting firms worldwide who provide development advice to poorer countries do the large majority of their business in their home countries where markets are highly competitive and quality is essential.

Following the Paris donor conference of 2005 a renewed and extensive effort was launched by the international donor community to determine how to achieve effectiveness in development assistance through upgraded evaluation methods, in order to support the continuation of these programs. The declaration of the Busan conference 6 years later, from which I quote above, bears witness to these efforts.

Nevertheless, and despite the renewed efforts to understand how to improve assistance, as we shall see during the course of this story the results in the particular conditions of the poorest countries have been questionable. This is because the intrinsic quality of the assistance is not necessarily related to its ultimate effects. Thus, when it comes to assistance from the richest countries to the poorest countries *quality is not necessarily the same thing as impact*. This makes it difficult for even sophisticated evaluation methods to identify the reasons why assistance succeeds or fails. What is as, if not more, important is the environment in which that assistance takes place, whether advice, training, management or something else. It is not the quality of advice or training that has necessarily been defective but rather it is the broad social, economic and institutional context that has been inimical to its success, at least in the poorest countries, of which my first country remains one. It lies as much within the political and social dynamics of these countries and the relationship between the donor and the recipient societies. It is this aid relationship, the "aid model," that has not worked.[11] It is the old "quaint protectorate" syndrome but now perhaps worse. Yet the time and opportunity may have now arrived in which this aid relationship could start to be abandoned and replaced by something else. This is what much of this book is about.

Another qualification is in order. Aid is not a homogeneous commodity. Rather, it consists of multiple types of activities with different types of objectives, different methods of achieving such objectives, backed up by different levels of resources and commitment.[12] Accordingly, emergency and humanitarian aid is not what I am talking about. Aid for tsunami, earthquake, drought or conflict victims, or epidemics such HIV/AIDS will always be needed and justifiable, although even this has to be provided in a sensible way.[13] Nor am I talking about military and security-related assistance. What I am talking about is aid for longer-term social and economic development – *development aid*, which accounts for the bulk (around 90 percent) of the total amount of official development assistance (ODA) given each year by donor governments, the gross total of which rose to US$130 billion in 2010, supplemented by at least US$25 billion in grants from international foundations and charities and other non-government organizations (NGOs). Such sums represent no more than 0.4 percent of the total 2008 gross national income (GNI) of the donor countries but much larger shares of the GNI of the recipients.[14]

Development aid has evolved over 50 or more years, since the first colonial countries became independent, through a series of what might be called ideological life-cycles – conceptions, materializations, maturations, disillusionments, die-offs and resurrections – as aid policy makers have attempted to find new approaches. This diverse product also takes different deliverable forms. One distinction is between what might be called "soft aid" and "hard aid." Hard aid provides the hardware, that is, tangible goods such as factories, warehouses, roads, schools, hospitals, dams and power stations, mainly capital projects. Soft aid provides the software, the services – for policy advice, technical advice, and knowledge, skills, capacity and institution building. These two categories currently account for about an equal share of the funds for development aid when everything is categorized and counted up.

According to the World Development Indicators if we exclude humanitarian or emergency assistance the share of the total going to "development projects, programs and other resource provisions" in 2008, just before the recent financial crisis, was about 56 percent. Most of this expenditure was for hardware, or capital aid, but a proportion was also for technical assistance or software. Another third of the non-humanitarian assistance went to technical cooperation and the administration costs of the aid agencies themselves (which took about 8 percent). If the software component of aid is averaging close to 50 percent of the total (down from a higher proportion in past years), this means that currently about US$65 billion a year of advice and consulting services is going into poor countries. Software remains important. Despite an increasing realization of the urgency of refurbishing poor country infrastructure, the World Bank still allocated more of its lending in 2009 and 2010 to public administration and finance, which are heavily institution-building oriented than to transport and energy which are heavily capital oriented.

Nevertheless, the indications are that the emphasis of official aid funding is returning to capital projects, especially to infrastructure where it started its journey 50 years ago. The World Bank adopted an Infrastructure Action Plan in 2003 under which its infrastructure projects were re-launched. Large numbers of infrastructure funds have been set up in Asia and Africa over the past few years. This type of foreign assistance activity could be relatively well justified in that the public sector has an important role to play. But most assistance by value is outside infrastructure.

Hard aid and soft aid involve different kinds of assistance dynamics, which in turn probably have different implications for effectiveness. But the performance of foreign assistance for both hardware and software as a whole has received poor ratings in a multitude of studies over many years. Since this has been clear for a long time it is important to understand why such an enormous amount of effort is expended on it. What are the mechanisms at play? Exactly *why*, for example, do host governments not make good use of the advice of aid donors? Exactly *why* is responsibility and accountability lacking when it comes to implementing aid programs/building institutions, etc.? And *why* cannot the aid donors understand why accountability is lacking? In 2009, I wrote a book about how to reform the World Bank. I ended the book as follows:

> As well as having an ambiguous effect on economic growth, foreign aid is at best quite marginal to the world's economic activities. Its resource flows are dwarfed by the impact of import tariffs and controls, agricultural and industrial subsidies within the rich nations, indebtedness, and even by the level of personal remittances by migrant workers…
>
> [F]oreign aid is limited by its own internal anomalies, which go along with its grant-based, publicly subsidized, and politicized nature. It also consumes to dubious effect an enormous amount of human resources worldwide, remarkably and disproportionately highly educated, devoted to teaching, research, writing, governance, administration, consultancy, implementation, management, monitoring, and evaluation.

This book explores further the implications of these rather sweeping and perhaps half-baked statements. It is mainly about the scale, nature, composition and direction of the financial and resource flows between rich and poor countries and their social and political significance for development.

Aid or Trade? Preliminary Thoughts

The focus of the rest of this story will therefore be principally on aid and resource flows, and how they have been, could be or should be used to accelerate development. However, these are, as suggested in the quotation above, by no means the only factors affecting the economic development of the poorest countries. Before getting to the main focus of the book it is important to try to clear the ground a little by first talking about one of the anomalies referred to, one that is in fact an impediment to the flow of resources. This impediment is trade protection, sometimes conceived in the form of three pillars of protection – market price support through trade barriers, production subsidies and export subsidies.[15]

Trade barriers have had a very important impact on the development of poor countries.[16] Over the period 1970 to 2000 the share of 49 very poor countries in world trade fell from an already tiny 2 percent to less than 1 percent, still concentrated into a few sectors despite years of diversification effort.[17] Part of this problem has been due to broadening non-tariff protection (sanitary and phyto-sanitary measures, rules of origin and so on), which have tended to replace tariffs but are similar in their barrier effect. The 2000 UN Millennium Development Goals (MDGs) called on rich countries to provide duty-free, quota-free access for poor countries.[18] However, despite some progress, according to the World Bank OECD producers still received direct or indirect protection worth about US$336 billion per annum over 2005–2007 in the form of market price support (tariffs and subsidies), technical support and transfers. US$336 billion was about four times the amount of worldwide official aid provided by the OECD nations during that period, and about 1.3 percent of their GDP. Of this total amount more than half was estimated to be directly trade distorting.[19] In Europe and the US, much of this support was also provided to those living in rural areas that comprised only about 3.5 percent of their own population.[20]

Protection puts all primary producers at a disadvantage including high- and middle-income countries like Australia, New Zealand or Brazil. If all protection was dropped it is these wealthier and more competitive countries who would stand to gain the most, but overall the poorest countries would also stand to gain substantially.

Trade negotiations have proceeded very slowly. In 2006, the poorest countries were finally given access to rich country markets for 97 percent of their exports free of duties and quotas; but 3 percent of products that were excluded were also those that were the most important, and estimates of the impact of moving from 97 percent to 100 percent showed that these countries could increase their welfare significantly, with minimal effects on production in OECD countries.[21] Malawi, for example, stands to gain significantly from moving from 97 percent to 100 percent, although this would largely require the freeing of the tobacco trade. The EC has tried to alleviate the problem by entering into bilateral Economic Partnership Agreements (EPAs) but these have been criticized for impeding economic integration and forcing poor countries to adopt complex trade rules (such as for intellectual property). To make things more difficult progress on trade reform came to a halt in 2008 when the Doha Round of global trade negotiations collapsed.

Several countries still retain high levels of protection for "sensitive" products, such as sugar in the case of the US, and rice and other agricultural and fishery products in Japan. Generally, high tariffs have remained on sectors in which poor country exports specialize – agricultural products, textiles and garments, footwear, and light manufactures, and these barriers have only been partly offset by trade preference programs such as the United States Africa Growth and Opportunity Act (AGOA).[22] Tariff escalation is a further problem: developed economies impose higher tariffs on processed and finished goods than on primary products in a particular sector, thereby discouraging poorer exporting economies from moving along the production value chain. The garment sector has been particularly sensitive to remaining tariff impositions. In Bangladesh and Cambodia, which are major garment producers, most exports receive no preferential treatment. In 2006, these countries paid tariffs to the US worth seven times more than the value of development assistance they received from the US. The elimination of "tariff peaks" on specially protected products alone would substantially increase the poorest countries' exports.[23]

Production subsidies also impede trade, although they are less important than tariff barriers and if they were removed it is again the most competitive producers such as Brazil, Australia and Thailand who would gain the most.[24] However, the effect of subsidies is still significant for specific industries in the poorest countries. For example, cotton subsidies have been estimated to cause the loss of up to US$250 million every year in West and Central Africa where an estimated 10 million people rely on cotton. In the sugar industry from 1999 to 2001 support to OECD countries' producers averaged just slightly less than the value of developing country sugar exports, increasing the share of rich country exports while that of poor countries declined.[25]

Aid for Trade?

Partly to diffuse the pressure for removal of barriers the so-called Aid-for-Trade Initiative was launched in 2005 to help low-income countries by building the capacity and infrastructure that they need to implement and benefit from World Trade Organization (WTO) agreements and to maximize the benefits of trade and investment opportunities.[26]

Several countries had previously been hesitant to espouse the WTO rules because of concerns about preference erosion, loss of tariff revenue and lack of capacity to gain from foreign market access opportunities under WTO agreements. To address this the idea was that aid money would encourage WTO trade liberalization[27] and would help to improve trade systems through establishment of trade corridors and regional economic communities. Thus, significant amounts of aid money were not only directed towards the software of trade such as trade facilitation, but also to the massive transport and communications infrastructure required for trade. However, while repairing the road to the border is essential it still does not deal with the difficult policy actions of dealing with the duties, quotas and controls that prevent you shipping your products when you get there. Furthermore, there has been a tendency of some donors to "re-label" general infrastructure and trade assistance that was already ongoing as aid for trade, which has increased skepticism about the value of the initiative.

According to the launch document of the WTO Task Force on Aid for Trade the initiative would "enable developing countries, particularly least developed countries (LDCs), to use trade more effectively to promote growth, development and poverty reduction and to achieve their development objectives, including the Millennium Development Goals (MDGs)." There is an element of disingenuousness in this declaration since it is understood that the fastest way to increase trade is to increase import demand for goods by lowering the remaining barriers.[28] Thus the initiative avoids the main problem while providing customary capacity building for strategies and negotiation, support to investment in export sectors and assistance to soften the impact of tariff reductions, as well as the more important capital assistance for roads, ports and telecommunications.

The success of the program is self-assessed every 2 to 3 years by the donors. At the Global Review of July 2009, the donors agreed that the most effective programs consisted of the usual array of soft aid. That is, trade policy analysis, negotiation and implementation through training and workshops; trade facilitation, such as simplification of customs procedures and improvements to port authorities; and competitiveness promotion programs such as the Banana Special Framework of Assistance for supplies, teacher training and export diversification through support to pilots and strategy making.

Aid Effectiveness: Preliminary Thoughts

What is the significance of trade barriers and subsidies for foreign assistance and for the rest of this book? Taking account of the various estimates that have been made of welfare losses resulting from trade impediments in the poorer countries, the economic cost of barriers and subsidies significantly exceeds the value of foreign assistance to those countries. The large scale of the barriers to trade flows compared to the scale of aid flows is part of what justifies the assertion that foreign aid is marginal to the economic development of the poor world. The overwhelming effect of trade and production barriers contradicts claims about aid effort and is a major example of what is called *policy inconsistency*.

But it is not only that development aid has been marginal in terms of its overall scale within the world economy. It is that those countries that have had the most marginal amounts of assistance relative to the size of their economy have been the most successful in escaping poverty, i.e. in East and parts of South Asia, and increasingly South America. In many cases, assistance has been proportionately tiny compared to the overall GDP of these emerging economies and has hardly affected their aggregate public or private investment. In China, with one-fifth of the world's population and where more than 200 million still very poor live on less than US$1.25 per day, the total amount of assistance each year over the past decades has been tiny in relation even to the value of the *annual increase* in the country's GDP. Where assistance has been such a minor factor, the governments of recipient countries have not been overwhelmed by it and have been able to be selective about the type of assistance that the country needs, so the effectiveness of the aid provided may have been good. On the other hand, those countries that have become bound to aid, receiving very large, non-marginal doses of foreign assistance relative to the size of their economies and budgets, especially in Africa and a few countries in Asia and Latin America (comprising a sixth of the world's population), have mostly not moved out of poverty. Some have got worse, while much of their population still subsists on little more than US$1 a day. These are countries where foreign aid has become quite dominant, significantly interfering with perceptions about what might be beneficial for the country's development, while bearing a questionable impact on the welfare of the population.

My first country, Nyasaland, was not a focus of much development attention by the British authorities; in fact, it tended to remain in severe poverty, ignored in relation to the mineral-rich or more geopolitically sensitive countries around it. Things did not get better afterwards either. During the post-colonial era the country's living standards have remained at a dismal level with minimal income growth per capita, even during the recent period of faster growth in Africa.[29] It still relies heavily on tobacco and tea exports, while its population has risen from 3 million in 1960, to 15 million today. Its dependence on aid has furthermore grown to historic levels at which nearly $1 of national income in every $4 is donated from outside, a total of nearly US$1 billion a year in development assistance.[30] At the same time, its population of foreign advisors in the present day is enormous compared to the size of the colonial administration.[31]

Thus, on the one hand, development assistance that is a minor factor within the economy and society of the countries who received it might well have been beneficial, but on the other hand, when development assistance is a major factor within the economy and the society of the countries who received it, in many cases it appears to have largely failed.

The weak or non-existent impact of large-scale assistance on the overall economic performance of the poorest countries does not, however, prove that assistance has not helped them at all. The direction of causation could be ambiguous or reversed. For example, it may be that it is because these poorest economies have been so incapable of moving out of poverty that aid has been poured in in an attempt to make a difference. If that were the case then large amounts of aid would inevitably be associated with minimal progress but could still have been partially effective.[32] Development economists have discussed this possibility.[33] But even if there is some truth in this, it would probably make little difference to the inference that assistance to these countries has not worked or has only worked very poorly. Certainly, it would not change assumptions that aid has produced *very little benefit in relation to its high cost* of which much, as we will see, is not even counted.

Take Malawi. It is of course possible that the quarter of the country's gross national income that has consisted of foreign aid has been an essential input over the decades, without which Malawi would be in an even worse state. But is this really believable? The catalogue of poor results from hundreds of foreign-aid projects and the continuing dismal state of the economy simply does not add up to the product of an effective long-term, large-scale assistance input. The downside of this effort, disempowerment through aid dependency, may well be the more believable situation; this is a possibility that we will be looking at more closely.

The catalogue of problems that have faced aid to the poorest suggests that the complex, tortuous, frustrating and mysterious process of reinventing foreign aid to make it more effective in such countries in anything like its present form, whether it be through arduous scaling up of individual projects, payment by results or injecting large resources into villages, is not worthwhile. Even leaving aside the issue of trade barriers, there remains the array of other impediments that suggest that foreign aid as it is currently practiced cannot ever succeed in the poorest countries. The extent to which this conclusion is justified and what alternative dynamic might replace aid is the subject of the rest of this book, returning us again to the question of "whose country?".

Organization of the Book

I have organized the book into nine chapters. In Chapter 1, the introduction, I have explained my background as a child in the British colony that became Malawi, and how that has influenced my perceptions; I have reviewed the nature of foreign aid; and I have dealt with a preliminary important issue – the impact of rich country trade barriers and production subsidies on development – to clear the ground for the main focus: foreign aid flows.

In the next chapter, I carry out a rapid survey of foreign aid, looking at its typology, evolution, size and structure; its motivations and other important features; and then set up the question about its effectiveness. Chapter 3 examines the extensive literature on aid effectiveness coupled with my own experience, from the macro and micro perspective, reviewing highlights of its performance across sectors and exploring some of the evidence from World Bank evaluations. I conclude that on balance it has not been effective, especially in the case of non-capital aid, i.e. advisory assistance, and that it cannot achieve its central object of poverty reduction. Chapter 4 investigates the reasons for its relative failure – historical, geographical and economic structural. It focuses on the inheritance of a dysfunctional power relationship between recipients and donors. It explains features of this relationship, the alienation of aid recipients, and argues that general aid ineffectiveness is a result of systemic factors that cannot be identified or resolved through the project evaluations that are the current focus of attention but are part and parcel of the overall system of relationships. The next chapter looks at what may be a historic opportunity created by changing development dynamics that has seen the emergence of the diasporas as a powerful quasi-indigenous economic and social force, as a source of skills, experience, entrepreneurship and various sources of financial flows. Chapter 6 considers whether the contribution of the diasporas could constitute a new pathway out of poverty, and how a path to growth could evolve using the help of the diasporas and geographical concentrations of economic power. In Chapter 7, we step back once more to look at New Aid, i.e. the array of aid instruments that have been introduced in recent years to try to improve effectiveness by addressing some of the systemic problems, and examine how far they might be able to succeed given the central problem of power relationships between rich and poor. Chapter 8 outlines conditions and features of an aid exit strategy for poor countries. Finally, Chapter 9 provides, by way of a postscript, end thoughts on one of the poorest countries, Malawi, and the conclusions to be drawn.

Chapter 2

WHAT IS FOREIGN AID, WHO DOES IT, WHY AND HOW MUCH IS THERE?

The Fourth High Level Forum on Aid Effectiveness in Busan, Korea follows meetings in Rome, Paris and Accra that helped transform aid relationships between donors and partners into true vehicles for development cooperation.
    "OECD 50" Development Cooperation Directorate website, 22 August 2011[1]

SIR – The parlous state of the public finances in Britain provides the perfect opportunity for British taxpayers to end their half-century-long experiment with "development aid," which has, since its inception, stunted growth and subsidised bad governance in Africa. As Africans, we urge the generous-spirited British to reconsider an aid programme they can ill afford, and which we do not want or need. A real offer from the British people to help our development would consist of the abolition of the Common Agricultural Policy, which keeps African agricultural exports out of the European marketplace. It is that egregious policy, combined with the weight of regulations, bad laws and stifling bureaucracy, subsidised by five decades of development aid, which prevents Africans from lifting themselves out of poverty. Andrew Mitchell, the Secretary of State for International Development, speaks about a "moral imperative" to combat poverty around the world. We could not agree more. The British have a unique opportunity to cut the deficit and help Africa: please, ask your new government to stop your aid.

Andrew Mwenda Editor, *Independent* newspaper, Uganda
Franklin Cudjoe Executive Director, IMANI Center for Policy and Education, Ghana
Kofi Bentil Lecturer, University of Ghana and Ashesi University, Ghana
Thompson Ayodele Executive Director, Initiative for Public Policy Analysis, Nigeria
Temba Nolutshungu Director, Free Market Foundation, South Africa
Leon Louw Law Review Project, South Africa
    "What is the best way to help the world's deserving poor?"
    Daily Telegraph, 22 August 2010[2]

What Is Development Aid?

Official development assistance (ODA) is formally defined by the Organisation for Economic Co-operation and Development (OECD) Development Assistance Committee as follows: financial flows, technical assistance and commodities that are (1) designed to promote economic development and welfare as their main objective (excluding aid for military or other non-development purposes); and (2) are provided as either grants or subsidized loans or conversion of past loans to grants, and the costs that donors incur to administer their own programs.[3] To qualify as aid the funding from government and government agencies for the economic development of poorer countries has to have a "grant element" of 25 percent or more. With this grant element payment made for the assistance services is equal to or less than 75 percent of the value at market prices in the origin country over the period in which they are provided.[4]

The list of activities considered to promote development and welfare has been widened substantially over time. *Inter alia*, the cost of refugees in donor countries, imputed costs of students from developing countries, internally paid interest subsidies, promotion of development awareness and recording of debt forgiveness on military debt and other non-ODA debt have all been added to the list. There is still an ongoing debate on the inclusion of expenditures for conflict prevention, peace building and security activities.

Year by year, total net ODA (after repayments) has grown. After dipping down in the 1990s partly as a result of the ending of competitive assistance inspired by the Cold War, its relatively rapid rise since 2000 to almost US$130 billion in 2010 was the result of renewed commitment following the series of key donor conferences between 2002 to 2008 in Monterrey, Rome, Paris and Accra. Much of the rise has, however, been debt relief and emergency aid rather than core economic aid. The overall total currently represents a little more than 0.3 percent of the national income of the donor countries.[5]

About 70 percent of the ODA comes through bilateral organizations such as USAID or DFID (Britain), AFD (France) or KFW (Germany), and 30 percent through multilateral organizations such as the World Bank (IBRD), Asian Development Bank and the African Development Bank. The share of bilateral in total ODA has remained relatively stable since the mid 1970s,[6] with the exception of 2005 when debt relief and the inclusion of donor administrative costs increased it. The largest multilateral providers are the European Commission, the United Nations and the World Bank (IDA), although the Bank's share has declined from 40 percent in the 1970s to about 20 percent during the first decade of the 2000s.

Most ODA is in the traditional form of soft loans and grants for specific assistance programs and projects. However, increasing proportions have been "fast disbursing." This includes the older structural adjustment loans and, more recently, what are known as budget support and sector programs. The poorest countries have also received another type of budget support, debt relief, as a result of policy changes by the donors since the 1990s leading to programs known as the HPIC and the MDRI.[7] The estimated value (in today's prices) of all annual aid flows over the past 50 years is shown in Figure 2.1.

Over 50 years, the net amount of ODA (in today's US dollars) that has been provided for developing countries is nearly US$4 trillion, an annual rate of about US$70 billion (gross ODA is over US$4 trillion). The definition of the volume of aid in terms of money does not, however, explain very much because as we have noted, aid is not in practice a homogeneous monetary resource. It consists of a large number

Figure 2.1. ODA ($ billion, 2009 prices)

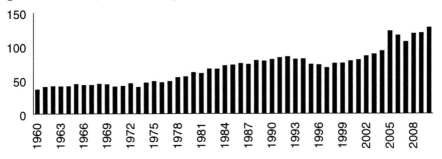

of different types and approaches of assistance, from the provision of food to the provision of economic advice, from mobilization of local resources to the provision of foreign products, from building factories to building institutions. There are various ways that it can be categorized depending on what we want to know about it.

In the last chapter, we categorized aid into "hardware" and "software," where hardware consisted of goods and software consisted of services. Goods provision may be easier to evaluate and less prone to ideological interpretation. Projects to build bridges, roads, dams, power stations, factories, schools and hospitals are tangible additions to the economy. Tangible additions can still be subject to poor, politically driven decisions. Bridge and road projects can fail because they have been built in the wrong place to satisfy ideologies or political interests; new factories can produce uneconomic products or subsidize products and services that undercut existing local suppliers. Hospitals can reflect an ideology of curative (expensive, top down) as opposed to preventative (inexpensive, bottom up) health care. Roads can be built to excessively high specifications or with advanced technology that make them difficult to maintain with locally available resources, or they can be under-specified (perhaps due to fraud) so that they fall apart quickly. However, the economic successes and failures of projects that provide hardware are relatively transparent, while the issues of how to deal with them are less ambiguous and opaque. Often the most important issues are practical problems of project implementation and management.

Software aid, on the other hand, is less tangible and more difficult to value. It is formally defined to include the funds spent on the administration of the donors' own programs which may or may not be worth doing. It includes advisory services for international issues such as climate change and financial stabilization; economic management and reform, agriculture, private sector development, education, health or social policy; and the development of democratic institutions. It may involve institution-building services, such as help to draft laws and regulations, or capacity building, such as fortifying the civil service or regulation and enforcement. Such assistance is more difficult to assess because it is not valued in the market place and its effects may be non-transparent, difficult to identify and measure, and long term. Ideas, information, skills and knowledge transferred by external providers also reflect not only technical knowledge but the ideology embedded in that knowledge and may reflect a relationship of donor to recipient embedded in the style in which the knowledge is transferred. Top down, externally driven strategies and programs may imply an assumption of innate superiority of judgment on the part of the provider, whereas participatory bottom up programs imply a greater trust in local decision makers.

The different assistance dynamics of hardware and software aid also, we can say, involve different levels of domestic ownership or empowerment. One aspect of this is the extent of external presence in local decisions and actions within a project or a project-related transaction. We can refer to assistance that involves a greater domestic role with less intrusive, non-systemic, effects on local values, capacity and initiative as "type-A" assistance. We can refer to as "type-B" assistance that would involve a more systemic, significant external agency presence, probably of a longer-term nature. The significance of external presence results from a) the method of transferring information and knowhow, and b) the values embedded in the information and knowhow transferred. The planning and implementation of capital projects such as roads or power may require less intrusive presence at the strategy, policy and general capacity level. Road building generally would involve type-A effects especially if contracts are locally tendered. Long-term advisory projects may involve type-B effects.

There are various other ways in which aid has been categorized, for example in terms of project aid and program aid. This definition is also important for aid dynamics. Whereas project aid involves the decentralization of effort and a multiplicity of initiatives, program aid tries to rationalize projects by situating them within a broader framework, perhaps as part of a sector plan or at national level. The ultimate version of a framework approach was the so-called Comprehensive Development Framework proposed by James Wolfensohn at the World Bank in 1999, which aimed to coordinate multi-donor assistance.[8] Project aid can be more effective in terms of results on the ground, but program aid can be more effective in terms of the smaller demands made on capacity of a government or implementing agencies to implement projects.

Somewhat related to this there has been a recent renewal of interest in the relative merits of the macro and the micro approaches to development assistance. That is, on the one hand, the "big plans" approach (of which currently the biggest is the Millennium Development Goals initiative) which devolve down from above in generalizations about what works; on the other hand, there is the small projects method which scales up on the basis of the assessed effectiveness of smaller projects into wider programs.[9] The funding for these alternatives is also different. Big plans and programs are funded by structural or sector adjustment loans and grants, budget support loans and grants, poverty reduction or program loans and grants and the like. Individual projects are funded by specific allocations of funds for physical goods and services to individual projects, or by multi-project investment or social funds or credit lines.

But even though recognizing the diffuse character of assistance and some of its inherent dynamics may provide general indications of the conditions under which aid is effective, it is still not necessarily much use in terms of discerning the more fundamental reasons why foreign assistance succeeds or fails. In this respect, another categorization might be proposed: all types of foreign assistance, whether they are at the big top-down plan level or the small bottom-up project level, and even with inherently different transparency levels and ideologies, result in *a need for more capacity to be dedicated by the recipient country to process and utilize foreign services and less capacity to be dedicated by the recipient country to process and utilize domestic services.* This definition is not about funding modalities, or program versus projects. This is about the inherently weak link between the use of foreign assistance and the strengthening of domestic capacity, and of domestic ownership. One way of thinking about it is in terms the extent to which there is "alienation" of domestic capacity and what its implications are. Perhaps it could justify another definitional dichotomy: *"alienative"* and *"non-alienative" assistance.*[10] Using the code proposed above, less alienative projects would be associated more with type-A effects and more alienative projects would tend to be associated with type-B effects. This type of definition is one that we will consider further.

A Rapid Review of the Evolution of Aid Strategy

Development assistance can be traced back to the nineteenth century and before. Towards the end of the colonial era, systematic efforts were made to organize assistance. For example, the British under the Colonial Development Act of 1929 gave small amounts of money for development of colonies which until that time had been expected to be self-financing.[11] But in its currently recognizable form, assistance dates back about 50 years to the independence of the countries which were once ruled by the European colonial powers. These powers included primarily Britain, France, Belgium, Netherlands, Portugal and Spain.

At the risk of oversimplification development assistance has gone through a series of phases. We can get some idea of this phasing by looking at the activities of the World Bank because many of the official aid donors have tended to either follow its lead or act with reference to it. The date of foundation of the World Bank, or International Bank for Reconstruction and Development (IBRD), in 1944 at Bretton Woods also predates serious efforts at development assistance. The World Bank was thus in at the start and was in the lead in thinking about how to do it.

Initially the IBRD acted as a post-war European reconstruction agency alongside the US Marshall Plan, making its first loan of US$250 million to France in 1947. As it diversified in the 1950s, lending to poorer countries such as Chile and India, reconstruction objectives came to be replaced by broader aims of reducing savings and investment shortage, eliminating poverty traps and providing a big push to achieve a critical mass of investment for economic growth, involving large investments in infrastructure and industry.[12] There followed a period during the 1960s in which the big capital investment push was broadened out into a wider effort incorporating technical assistance to expand the skills base of poorer countries.

But by the late 1960s it was concluded that large investments were failing to reach down into the poor rural and urban areas to reduce poverty. From the 1970s, direct poverty targeting through projects in agriculture, health, education and urban development, as well as the environment, emerged, promoted particularly by the World Bank under Robert McNamara.

Continuing difficulties, such as the apparent failure of some of the McNamara-inspired multi-sector agricultural and rural development projects in the 1970s then led to a perception that the impediments were not primarily to do with the lack of capital or skills, either in urban or rural areas. This perception was reinforced by the OPEC oil price increases of 1973 and of 1979–80, which brought to the forefront the potentially adverse macroeconomic conditions under which projects were operating. The oil price shocks highlighted the vulnerability and inflexibility of poorer economies resulting from high levels of protection, exchange rate misalignments, impediments to exporting, fiscal imbalances and accumulating debt.

The 1980s assistance paradigm was thus dominated by the issues of debt and adjustment. There was a concerted move away from project lending towards macroeconomic reform and program lending, an approach that became known in the late 1980s as the "Washington Consensus."[13] While international debt was a dominant issue at this time, it did not any longer imply a pure capital constraint. Rather, indebtedness was seen as a function of excessive borrowing and inattention to macroeconomic management.

From 1980 and over the following 15 years most of the world's poorer economies were put through Structural Adjustment Programs by the World Bank and IMF, supported by many major donors and in particular by the US under Ronald Reagan, whose internal economic policies were now dominated by ideas about liberalizing markets rather than supporting producers. But by the late 1980s structural adjustment was itself being seriously questioned because once again the reforms in many countries, even if justifiable in principle, were not by themselves achieving satisfactory progress on the ground in terms of a supply response by the producers, nor were they alleviating poverty.

The IMF's original conception of a transitional adjustment lasting 3 to 5 years to stabilize and redirect troubled economies was forgotten. In many countries there was failure to adjust despite multiple adjustment loans. Easterly cites the case of Côte d'Ivoire, which received 26 such loans in a 20-year period.[14] By 1999, the World Bank and IMF were responsible for three-quarters of new foreign lending to that country. Yet 37 percent of Ivoirians were in poverty in 1995 compared to 11 percent in 1985. Paul Collier writes in a similar vein that "the Government of Kenya sold the same agricultural reform to the Bank five times in 15 years."[15] It was not as it turned out just a matter of liberalizing markets or "getting the prices right" and good things would happen. Much more was required to restructure a poor economy.

Furthermore, as the 1980s debt problems were resolved the private banks resumed lending to the developing world. While capital market cycles still created intermittent need for international public institution financing, generally the international capital market was substantially larger than it was in 1945. At the turn of the millennium, funding of investment, per se, remained a core rationale only in the poorest economies, and here increasingly it was in the form of grants linked to capacity building.

In the 1990s, the focus moved to a new set of ideas: the problems of development and poverty alleviation in the poorer countries were not primarily those of capital shortage, nor skills shortage, nor price and exchange rate mismanagement. Rather they were to do with failure to develop stronger institutions in the public and the private sectors and the associated weak governance resulting from that. So from the 1990s into the 2000s, institutional development and capacity building became regarded by donors as central to achieving the beautiful goal of ending poverty. Aid money went to capacity building within organizations and to the development of legal and regulatory systems. Capacity building was differentiated from the "technical assistance" of the 1960s and 1970s because the latter was thought to be too narrowly focused on filling skill gaps with outside experts whereas capacity building meant holistically addressing the weaknesses of an organization as well as filling the gaps. For several years large proportions of World Bank funds went towards shoring up public financial management, civil services, banking systems and judicial institutions, and to promote market institutions like credit bureaus and trade associations. Indeed, in 2009 and 2010, finance, public sector governance and law, areas that are heavy with institution building, were still the largest sectors of its lending.[16]

But holistic institution building has proved to be a daunting challenge – indeed in some areas an unachievable task for an alien organization with limited time or understanding of local cultures, capacities and incentives, and their influence on how institutions actually develop. Aid donors transferred their attentions to capacity building in finance and public administration partly because of lack of success in direct production sectors such as agriculture, but the problems of public administration may well be just as intractable, only less easy to identify or measure. Whereas the discredited technical assistance tended to be targeted, shorter term and less intrusive, associated more with what I have referred above as "type-A" effects, capacity building on the other hand tended to involve extended and more intrusive outside intervention associated with "type-B" effects. There were years of repeated, externally sponsored reforms of the civil service in various countries, including Malawi, with little to show for the efforts.

In the first decade of the 2000s yet another inconvenient truth dawned: the years of attention to structural adjustment, capacity and institution building had neglected the very obvious fact that the roads and power systems of many of the poorest countries were in a terrible state. Even in the event that the donors could actually help build decent, and credible, market-based institutions to tight timetables in other people's countries while at the same time creating democracy and fighting corruption, the producers in those countries still had to produce the goods and get them to the market, especially to the export market. The transport and energy capacity for doing that was in very bad shape, so much so that even in relatively prosperous countries such as Kenya all larger firms had to use their own power generators. Consequently new donor initiatives were launched such as the World Bank's Infrastructure Action Plan and the Aid-for-Trade Initiative in 2005 under which roads came back on to the agenda to speed the goods to market. Spending on roads and electricity started to catch up once again with spending to support the civil service, bank supervisors and the judicial system.[17]

The preoccupation with governance, institutions, capacity, and associated problems of corruption (the pervasive concern of the aid community triggered by James Wolfensohn's state-of-the-world speech in 1996) had not only disguised a neglect of roads, but an even more startling neglect of agriculture.[18] Despite its centrality in the alleviation of poverty the World Bank's 2008 World Development Report was the first one to focus on agriculture for 26 years. But while agriculture is back on the donor's rhetorical agenda there is a long way to go in terms of action. In 2009 and 2010 agriculture still took a historically low share of World Bank lending. About three-quarters of the world's poor still depend on agriculture and the need for a renewed focus has been continually made, but without much result. The USAID administrator Natsios asked at a Capitol Hill forum in 2003: "how can we possibly deal with the problem of poverty in the developing world without dealing with agricultural productivity?" In 2007, a report by the World Bank evaluators on agricultural assistance in Sub-Saharan Africa stated: "a major drag on Africa's development is the underperformance of the agriculture sector. This is a critical sector in the region, because it accounts for a large share of gross domestic product (GDP) and employment."

Simultaneous to the return of large infrastructure funding has been the re-emergence of a version of the 1950s vintage "big push" as exemplified in the 2000 UN Millennium Project. While the focus on institutions and adjustment, and on individual projects, has continued, to some extent we have gone full circle and returned to the idea of the poverty trap and the need for a critical mass of investment. While the original poverty trap was one in which poor economies faced savings and capital shortage, the modern version of the trap involves economic and institutional failures caused by poverty, which justify large injections of technical and monetary aid.[19] The "big push" is at the heart of the UN Millennium Development Goals and one initiative under this program, the so-called "Millennium Villages Project," applies the push even at rural level, that is, the "village push."[20]

The lending history of the World Bank reflects some of the changes in fashion. As Figure 2.2 shows, in the last few years energy and transport lending (hard aid) from the World Bank has resumed after falling to a low level. In the mid-1970s this sector had accounted for an average of 38 percent of total bank lending. Between 1992 and 2001 it declined steeply from 31 percent to a low of about 18 percent, climbing back only during the first decade of the 2000s. During the intervening years public governance and finance sector assistance increased to 35 percent of the total. Agriculture, which averaged 28 percent of total World Bank lending in the mid-1970s, fell to 15 percent in the mid 1980s, and then continued a long and steep decline to a pitiful 5 percent and below from 2008.

This pattern of assistance has been to some extent mirrored across all agencies. OECD Development Assistance Committee (DAC) figures show that between 1990 and 2010 "social infrastructure" aid to Africa increased steadily from 20 percent to 45 percent of total gross ODA while aid to economic infrastructure declined from 21 percent in 1990 to 10 percent in 2005 before partially recovering. In the case of DAC bilateral aid the power and transport sectors in 2008 took as little as 8.5 percent. Within social infrastructure aid to "government and civil society" peaked in 2005 at 15 percent and has remained higher than either education or health. Aid to agriculture fell from about 19 percent in 1990 to about 8 percent in 2008 out of all sector-allocable aid.

The most recent aid policy reversal has occurred in industry assistance. The World Bank has started to reintroduce "industrial policy" after about 25 years in which support to industrial development per se came to be regarded as an unnecessary activity, one that should be addressed through macroeconomic management, laws and regulations, rather than through actual knowledge of how industries worked.[21]

Figure 2.2. World Bank: Sector lending shares (%)

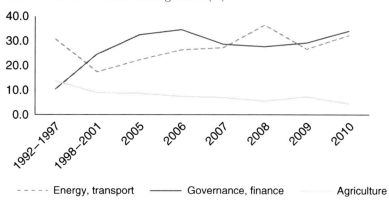

What is to be made of these ideological life-cycles of development assistance, entirely conceived and directed by external agencies? The unfortunate truth is that for all the certainty that accompanied every new idea, from the big push to rural development to structural adjustment to capacity building to institution building, and back to the big push, none has turned out to be the answer for the poorest countries and the questions about how to eradicate poverty in Sub-Saharan Africa and the poorest countries of South Asia, and Latin America remain essentially unresolved, at least by the aid community which has been responsible for the evolution of development thinking on behalf of its client countries.

The Motives for Giving Aid

Development aid policy is obviously critical to its effectiveness, but the process of aid giving is equally so. One aspect of this is aid motivation. Motivation has a major influence on the possibilities of improving aid performance. Without taking into account the motivation of aid givers and its effects on delivery, the search for the factors determining aid effectiveness tend to get channeled into preoccupations with the problems on the recipient side – institutions, capacity, economic management, corruption and so on, when in reality they may have more to do with the givers. Indeed the search for effectiveness that is enshrined in the evolution of aid policy is of little or no concern to donor governments with purely self-interested motives, and that is a weakness lurking behind the solemn international declarations about improving aid.

It is not necessarily easy to define motivation because development aid agencies, both bilateral and multilateral, operate with a complex of motives. For bilaterals these have ranged from self-interest (national political, diplomatic and security advantages, access to important resources, the maintenance of historic links, expansion of overseas markets) to altruism (diffusing skills and knowledge for the benefit of the world, alleviation of poverty and suffering, including disaster relief and humanitarian support).[22] Aid agencies that espouse developmentally progressive goals are themselves subject to conflicting pressures to account for expenditure by showing effectiveness, to disburse money in order to justify its allocation and to show quick results.

For multilaterals motives are more developmental and less driven by national interests. In practice, however, they still face multiple objectives and they have multiple principals and constituencies, which constrain lending. The political interests of certain countries, notably the US, have also been influential, for example at the World Bank which the US hosts in Washington, DC, and in which it is the largest single shareholder.[23]

Some of the objectives espoused by donors are consistent with improving aid effectiveness. Some are not and may even militate against the main requirements for effectiveness if they are concerned with political influence and commercial gain. If the latter motivations are paramount then the commonly agreed factors that strengthen aid effectiveness such as country ownership, accountability and democracy will not be seriously addressed through some aid programs, and the reform efforts at the donor conferences in Paris, Accra and Busan are in such cases futile.

Motives are also complicated by the long chain of delivery of aid, often through a range of channels from a simple direct private donation to a single individual or project all the way to large-scale multilateral agency-to-government assistance.[24] The larger the scale the more complex the intermediary arrangements need to be. At the largest scale, multilateral and bilateral agencies have the function of intermediating between the government(s) of the donor country, representing supposed voter or tax payer intentions, and the recipient organizations (public and private) in the receiving country, which represent supposed beneficiary needs, in a long chain of principals and agents often complicated because the agents may be outsourced.[25] At the simplest end of the scale the preferences of donor and recipient are reasonably well lined up. At the most complex end, involuntary aid (i.e. via taxation) means that there is no preference alignment at the micro level but instead, at best, a vague interconnection of desire to "give" and "receive."

Another interpretation of the relation between givers and receivers is that the delivery of aid is not a "chain" but a "game" (played by multiple actors such as donors, recipient governments, contractors, civil society, NGOs) whose interrelationships create the incentive structure that will ultimately determine the likelihood of success from foreign intervention.[26] The existence of multiple donors and special interest groups with diverse rules and the easy possibility of corruption effectively impede the achievement of their stated ends. Perverse incentives hinder sustainability and project success.

Few, if any, of the DAC countries run aid programs that are completely free of political and commercial objectives favoring the donor. The conflicting objectives within the long chain of intermediaries are also often combined into the same national aid infrastructure – sometimes deliberately, where commercial objectives and developmental objectives are managed by separate agencies within one administration. Aid activity has also distracted attention from objectives such as removal of subsidies and trade barriers where vested interests ensure that commercial considerations dominate even as other parts of the aid network are working for poverty alleviation.

Strategic and security concerns have been an inevitable force. Aid flows may be a low-cost way of retaining allies, and in this respect they were for a long time dictated by Cold War politics. The US Marshall Plan was partially motivated by the desire to prevent the spread of communism in Europe while aid to India was also to counter the influence of the Soviet Union.[27] A reduction in aid during the 1990s was associated with the ending of the Cold War just as a revival was associated with the 9/11 terrorist attacks and new US alliances with countries such as Angola, Cameroun and Guinea. Yemen lost US aid because it did not vote in favor of the first Gulf War while, US aid increased to countries on the UN Security Council. In the case of multilateral aid where national considerations are relatively damped down, the World Bank still has a political agenda despite a provision in its Articles prohibiting it.[28] In the case of the United States' Millennium Challenge Fund the eligibility criteria were initially strict (in terms of governance and democracy), such that only twelve countries qualified for the program, too few to use up the budget.[29] Political realities ensured that the program was quickly expanded to include countries such as Egypt, which were strategically and commercially important to the United States but not eligible in terms of the US definition of good governance, and thenceforth the selection criteria have become more opaque.

Commercial interests were once reflected in the extent to which aid was tied to the goods of the donor country rather than being available for purchase on the open market. As a result of a series of international agreements over many years, aid tying has been largely eliminated (except in the case of Greece and Portugal and to some extent Italy), although although tying of assistance remains more prevalent for the donor nation's service suppliers, such as consulting firms. However, even if national self-interest has been reduced on this dimension, in many others it has not been. For the average citizen of a donor country such as the US, foreign aid is probably conceived primarily, albeit vaguely, as either a humanitarian operation, or a security operation, or as a support to the donor's own commercial interests, and not at all as assistance to help another country to develop its economy and become a competitor.

Who Receives Aid and Who Gives It – Aid Architecture and Activity

The structure of the foreign-aid sector worldwide has followed national self-interest even if aid policy has in some cases been genuinely altruistic. This is apparent from the rapid increase of national agencies, often several per country. Total numbers are unclear since there are different definitions of what constitutes an agency; according to one estimate, after 50 years of expansion there are over 50 principal national (bilateral) agencies of which 23 are members of the big donors club, which is the Development Assistance Committee of the OECD (DAC). There are several UN system agencies, and 20 global and regional financial institutions.[30] In addition there are at least 100 minor government agencies. Another calculation finds that the number of bilateral donors grew from 5 in the mid-1940s to about 56 today with an increase to more than 230 international organizations, funds and programs including thematic funds.[31] Yet another effort to count up finds that the United Nations alone accounts for close to 70 organizations or special funds dedicated to development – more than the countries that they are supposed to be assisting.[32] In 2008, the United States alone operated across 152 countries with 16 US major and minor aid-providing agencies while there were 31 US agencies altogether providing some measure of foreign assistance.

The 23 main DAC agencies supply most bilateral aid (90 percent) while the multilateral development banks or development finance institutions (DFIs) supply over 90 percent of the multilateral non-concessional and concessional development finance. In absolute terms the US is the largest bilateral donor, followed by Germany, UK and France.

Vested interests build up behind aid structures that may have initially been set up to respond to legitimate international concerns.[33] New institutions have arisen sometimes as a result of perceived deficiencies in existing ones but the existing ones have tended to continue due to vested interests, inertia and non-transparent funding methods. The system has expanded through the arrival of both new non-DAC donors and the increase in the number of channels providing ODA to a given recipient country, with increasing numbers of donor-funded projects. Some of the countries that have recently started aid programs are also aid recipients. The new arrivals include Eastern Europe (Czech Republic, Slovakia, Hungary, Poland and Baltic states), Asia (China, Korea, Malaysia, Thailand and India) and the Middle East (Turkey, Israel, UAE, Kuwait and Saudi Arabia). Between 2004 and 2008 the aid flows of the new group rose from US$3.7 billion to US$9.5 billion, of which Saudi Arabia is the largest provider. New institutions are born every year; they seldom die.[34]

The architecture of the system since the 1990s has also been complicated by "verticalization" through global thematic funds that cut across regions. These include GFATM (the Global Fund for AIDS Tuberculosis and Malaria), GAVI (the Global Alliance for Vaccines and Immunisation), the Global Environment Facility, and the Education for All Fast-Track Initiative, among others. These funds now account for some 4 percent of annual ODA or 7 percent of multilateral aid. The vertical funds expand further the number of donors and projects and introduce new dimensions of negotiation, implementation, monitoring and reporting.

In summary, by 2010 development aid went to about 185 countries from nearly 100 major official aid agencies including in some cases several agencies in one donor country, about 100 smaller agencies, and an average of 26 donors operating in each country. The proliferation of national aid agencies and organizations is paralleled by a similar mushrooming of individual projects. Roodman estimates that from 1995 to 2003 there was a more than 150 percent increase in the number of development projects worldwide, from 10,000 to 27,000, with a very rapid increase in the number of aid missions. By 2002, the total number of client countries of the OECD donors had risen from 37 to 120.[35]

In addition to the expansion of the official aid programs from both DAC and non-DAC governments there has been a major increase in the number of non-government donors, to the tune of many tens of thousands. In India alone some 15,000 organizations are registered to receive foreign funding.[36] Other research finds that from 1980 to 2008, the number of active foundations in the US alone increased from just over 22,000 to almost 76,000, and that between 2001 and 2005 foundations giving to international causes increased by more than 70 percent.[37] Between 2001 and 2005 the number of similar foundations in 13 EU member countries increased by more than 50 percent. Much of this growth has been driven by newly invented corporate responsibility programs in large private firms. International NGOs are estimated to number about 18,000, channeling funds larger than those of the United Nations system. The bulk of funding is concentrated in a small percentage of organizations and tends to be diffused among myriad small projects.

The NGOs include large organizations such as Oxfam, CARE and Save the Children Fund. Private foundations have also become major actors. The Bill and Melinda Gates Foundation has financed a third of world R&D expenditure for HIV/ AIDS vaccines. Net grants by NGOs, as reported by the OECD DAC, have risen rapidly from US$5.4 billion in 1992–93 and reached US$23.6 billion by 2008, an amount that is now not insignificant in comparison with ODA. In the United States, ODA already accounts for a smaller share of total economic engagement with developing countries than private philanthropy.[38]

On the other side of the counter, the top five recipients of ODA in 2008 (apart from the special cases of Iraq and Afghanistan) were Ethiopia, the West Bank, Vietnam,

Table 2.1. Aid recipients: The top 15 ($billion)

1987–88		1997–98		2007–2008	
Indonesia	3.8	China	3.3	Iraq	7.5
Egypt	3.4	Indonesia	3.0	Afghanistan	2.8
India	2.9	Egypt	2.8	China	2.1
Israel	2.9	India	2.7	Indonesia	2.0
China	2.3	Philippines	1.6	India	1.8
Bangladesh	2.0	Thailand	1.5	Vietnam	1.4
Pakistan	1.9	Bangladesh	1.3	Sudan	1.4
Philippines	1.8	Vietnam	1.2	Tanzania	1.3
Tanzania	1.6	Mozambique	1.2	Ethiopia	1.2
Mozambique	1.4	Tanzania	1.2	Cameroon	1.1
Kenya	1.2	Pakistan	1.1	Egypt	1.1
Thailand	1.2	Bosnia-Herzegovina	1.0	Bangladesh	1.0
Turkey	1.2	Côte d'Ivoire	0.9	Mozambique	1.0
Sudan	1.0	Madagascar	0.8	Nigeria	0.9
Ethiopia	0.9	Peru	0.8	Palestinian Adm. Areas	0.9
Total	29.5	Total	24.4	Total	29.5
Total ODA	46.9	Total ODA	57.2	Total ODA USD mill.	125.9

Source: DAC Development Cooperation Report (2010), table 32

Sudan and Tanzania.[39] Of the total of about 185 recipients of ODA, 51 were classified as least developed (LDCs) and a further 21 as low income. The definition for this combined category in 2008 was a maximum of US$745 per capita per annum. A further 45 countries were classified as low-middle income, and 32 as upper-middle income.[40]

Over 1988 to 2008 out of the "top 15" countries receiving aid only three of the now poorest countries have been on every list, i.e. Bangladesh, Tanzania and Mozambique. India and China have been on the list because of the size of their economies. Surprise entrants at various times have been Thailand and Peru. The presence of Israel, Egypt and Turkey, and of course Iraq and Afghanistan, is wholly or partly a response to political pressure, mainly from the US. Surprise omissions on one or more lists have been Sudan and Ethiopia.

Sub-Saharan Africa has absorbed increasing shares of foreign aid. The largest donors in the sub-region are the EU, IDA (World Bank), and bilaterally the US, France and the UK (DFID). By region Table 2.2 shows how ODA has been distributed over the last few years.

The table includes both multilateral and bilateral aid from the DAC and the new donor countries (who provided about US$5 billion in 2010). From the table various notable trends can be identified. The key one is a moderate increase in the share of aid going to the poorest regions – that is, Sub-Saharan Africa from 29.8 percent in the peak year of 2005 to 33.6 percent in 2010 and Central/South Asia from 10.6 percent to 14.0 percent, while most other regions received stable or declining amounts, notably the Middle East. However, ODA per capita overall remains below the average levels of the 1980s despite the recent surge.

Aid Effort

As mentioned, a very long-standing goal of the donor governments has been to achieve a minimum donation of 0.7 percent of their GNI as ODA. The target of 1 percent of all flows was originally proposed by the World Council of Churches in 1958 and during the 1960s all DAC members subscribed to it. But because of the unpredictability of private capital flows the target was limited to official flows. In 1970, the UN General Assembly adopted the declaration of the so-called Second Development Decade, that "each economically advanced country will progressively increase its official development assistance to the developing countries and will exert its best efforts to reach a minimum net amount of 0.7 % of GNP … by the middle of the Decade."[41]

The target has been criticized as being numerically obsolete (as a result of the large increases in savings and income in both rich and poor countries since it was first proposed) and irrelevant (since it assumes that the key problem in poor countries is a lack of savings rather than a lack of capacity and institutional development).[42] Nevertheless it remains a rallying cry that is in use to this day.

The 0.7 percent target has only ever been achieved by the Scandinavian countries, Luxemburg and the Netherlands. In 2005, at the Gleneagles summit, the 15 countries that are members both of the European Union and the DAC announced a renewed but

Table 2.2. Recent trends in foreign aid by region (ODA US$ million at 2009 prices)

Year	2004	2005	2006	2007	2008	2009	2010
Developing countries total	93,591	123,462	119,067	111,472	124,559	126,968	130,038
Europe	4,361	4,735	5,751	4,500	5,251	5,731	5,831
Africa	35,237	40,934	49,309	40,553	43,867	47,808	47,959
North of Sahara	3,772	3,140	3,284	3,523	4,143	2,992	2,671
South of Sahara	30,746	36,925	45,094	35,583	38,462	42,465	43,741
America	8,094	7,735	8,229	7,362	9,071	9,022	10,832
North and Central America	4,100	3,762	3,942	3,656	4,206	4,352	6,773
South America	3,447	3,296	3,708	3,135	3,690	3,773	3,286
Asia	26,770	52,561	36,648	37,917	43,187	38,169	36,069
Far East Asia	6,946	9,605	7,379	7,572	6,734	8,249	7,318
South and Central Asia	10,718	13,090	12,513	14,268	15,561	18,464	18,239
Middle East	8,772	28,640	15,734	15,102	19,634	10,378	9,426
Oceania	1,152	13,42	1,360	1,324	1,482	1,560	1,801
Developing countries, other	17,977	161,55	17,770	19,814	21,702	24,678	27,546

Source: DAC Development Cooperation Review (2012)

lower commitment to reach a minimum ODA country target in 2010 of 0.51 percent of their gross national income. Despite the explosive growth in aid institutions and aid programs total ODA did not, however, come close to this target.

Figure 2.3 shows the share of ODA in the national incomes of the main donor countries over 50 years, according to DAC estimates. It is notable that despite the rise since 2005 the aid effort remains historically low. In 2010 the aid effort was estimated at 0.32 percent of GNI compared to over 0.4 percent on average in the 1960s, which is the independence decade for most former colonies. The aid effort of individual countries is shown in Figure 2.4.

At the top stand Norway and Luxembourg who committed over 1 percent of their GNI in 2010. Almost at the bottom stood the United States, which was the largest single country supplier of aid but which committed just 0.2 percent of its GNI in 2008, itself an improvement from 2007 when it was only 0.16 percent and when the US (with US$79 of official aid per person per year, compared to US$770 in Norway) stood with Japan at the bottom of the rankings of ODA effort.

Charitable contributions put US donations in a slightly better light. In 2007–2008, US NGO donations were equal second with Canada behind Ireland, at 0.1 percent of GNI. This would raise the estimated worth of total official and unofficial US donations to nearly 0.3 percent of GNI, but it would still rank near the bottom of the league at about

Figure 2.3. ODA/GNI (%)

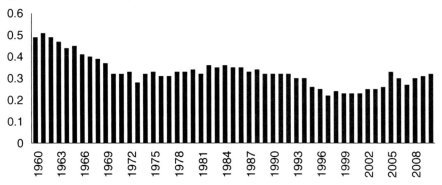

US$120 a head, one-sixth of what Norwegians give through their government alone. An alternative estimate from the NGO industry claims that the US private charitable contributions are significantly higher, US$33 billion out of a total from 14 countries of US$49 billion in 2008, channeled by NGOs, foundations, corporations, religious congregations and universities.[43] Taking into account the totality of charitable donations from all countries if this higher estimate is correct it would probably put the US about half way up the rankings but still well below the Scandinavians, Luxemburg and the Netherlands in terms of total aid effort. But the NGO funding is often for emergencies so including all of it would exaggerate the US contribution to development aid.

Aside from the ODA/GNI measure of aid effort, Easterly and Pfutze looked into the internal performance of 30 bilateral and 17 multilateral agencies in terms of what have come to be regarded as key indicators of aid performance.[44] These included fragmentation, selectivity, types of aid channels and overhead costs. In terms of overhead costs, their tentative findings showed the UN agencies as the most expensive. Australia, Italy, Japan and Norway showed the lowest overhead costs.[45] The overall average of

Figure 2.4. Net ODA (%) GNI by country (2010)

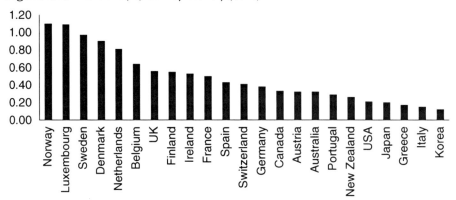

Source: DAC Development Cooperation Review (2012)

overhead costs to official development funding was 9 percent, which is close to the WDI reported result. On all the four indicators the agency with the best practices was found to be the IDA, followed by the United Kingdom as the best bilateral donor. The UN agencies are usually at or near the bottom of the rankings. In terms of aid disbursed per permanent employee bilaterals were twice as productive as multilaterals, and the UN was the lowest, with as little as US$30,000 in aid per employee from the World Food Program (WFP) (less than one professional salary), and US$70,000 from UNHCR compared to Norway and Italy who disbursed more than US$10 million per agency employee.

The study was updated in 2011 when it found that the UK was still best among bilateral agencies, while the US was below average.[16] Greece ranked last overall. The biggest contrast was again between the UN agencies and everyone else. The paper found modest improvement in transparency and effectiveness of aid channels, but no improvement in specialization, fragmentation and selectivity, despite escalating rhetoric. The authors concluded that

> the overall international aid community continues to suffer from many of the problems previously identified. Aid is fragmented among many donors, large and small, and donors do not specialize, splintering aid allocation among many countries and many sectors. Donors continue to allocate aid to corrupt and unfree countries, even taking into account the worthy aim of directing aid to poor countries. In short, the aid community criticizes these practices but continues them anyway.[17]

Another broader approach to performance assessment is the CGD's "Commitment to Development" Index (CDI), which ranks donor countries in terms of their "dedication to policies that benefit the five billion people living in poorer nations."[18] The CDI looks at both organizational performance and elements of effectiveness on seven dimensions: the quantity and quality of foreign aid, openness to developing-country exports, policies that encourage investment, migration policies, environmental policies, security policies and dissemination of new technologies. In 2010 the CGD also launched the Quality of Development Assistance or QUODA index, which was designed to measure something different from the CDI although both indices look at the activities of the donor agencies rather than the recipient countries.[19] The QUODA index scores aid delivery on four main dimensions: efficiency, institution building, administrative cost and transparency/learning. These four dimensions are supposed to match up with the main principles of the Paris Declaration, i.e. results, ownership, fostering institutions and alignment.[50]

Leaving aside the usual issues that can invalidate indexes – such as the choice of weights, the presence of double counting, and uncertainty about how to value different indicators, under the QUODA approach in 2010 of the major donors top came Scandinavia, the Netherlands and New Zealand. Bottom came Japan and South Korea. The UK surprisingly came seventh from bottom, slightly below the US. Sweden's big strength is aid quality with a high score on migration as well. Norway's strengths are the same but it scores very low on trade assistance. A very low score on aid quality pushes the US down the list but the US scores very high on "security." The UK's low score overall comes especially from very low scores for "migration policy" and (surprisingly) "security." Within the US some agencies do better than others in terms of appropriate motivation – the Department of Defense for example would score low on development effectiveness objectives in general and high on security objectives, compared to USAID.

How Important Is Aid in the Finance of Development?

Up to the 1980s development assistance usually constituted a majority of the total value of financial flows to the poor world. Since then, while the ODA proportion has fluctuated, largely because of the volatility of private investment, its share has trended steadily downwards. In the 1980s and up to the beginning of the 1990s it still averaged about 50 percent of total net resource flows of official and private capital to poor countries, but from the early 1990s, at the end of the Cold War, there was a marked decline in the share of ODA. FDI and portfolio equity investment surged while ODA stagnated. As a proportion of worldwide flows ODA has accounted for less than 20 percent in almost every year since 1990, and in 2007, at the peak of the private investment boom, fell to 8 percent, recovering by 2009 as a result mainly of the collapse in private lending during the crisis.

The rapid expansion of officially recorded NGO resources from US$5.8 billion in 1992–93 to US$23.7 billion in 2008 has further diluted the ODA share.[51] As mentioned above one study finds that in the United States ODA already accounts for a smaller share of "total economic engagement" with developing countries than private philanthropy. An alternative estimate of worldwide private development assistance arrived at a figure of US$49 billion of "philanthropic aid" in 2008 from 14 countries.[52]

The falling share of ODA is still more pronounced if another resource, current private transfers, is taken into account. These transfers are counted separately from aid, foreign investment and equity inflows because they are not classified as capital. But it seems that they are in fact to a large extent doing the same job, as we shall see. Within private transfers are workers' remittances, which alone overtook worldwide aid in the 1990s in terms of value, and have even exceeded the estimated value of worldwide trade barriers.

Based on World Bank data in 2007, just prior to the financial crisis, the combination of increased remittances (estimated at US$275 billion) and "total private and official flows" (approximately US$1.0 trillion) would have reduced the share of ODA ($103 billion) to 7 percent of the value of total resources going to developing countries.[53] This recovered to 12 percent by 2009. However, the importance of remittances for the Sub-Saharan Africa region has been less than for the world as a whole. While growing fast they are still to catch up with ODA according to official data. But when likely substantial flows of unrecorded remittances are included they are estimated by many sources to be significantly higher than the ODA going to Sub-Saharan Africa.[54]

In 2007, just before the financial crisis, ODA to Africa was about a third of recorded total private and official flows plus remittances.[55] And with the continuing recovery in remittances and other private flows it is likely that the share of ODA will decline below 30 percent fairly soon.

Clearly the world has reached a stage where ODA is no longer a critical resource in terms of its simple value. Worldwide it is of marginal importance and in Africa it will be a substantially lower proportion than it comprised prior to 2000. It is important to realize, however, that this reduction in the relative size of aid is not because of some strategic phase-out resulting from accumulated aid donor wisdom. On the contrary, it has happened despite a surge in aid and an increase in the number of donors, because the corporate and individual private sector has replaced aid, and this is a significant development.

Beyond the numbers is a further reason for deducing a lesser significance of aid. Generally private capital or capital-like flows consist of cash and credit and some guarantees for defined commercial purposes channeled into both consumption and investment. Official aid flows, however, consist of a mixture of offerings – skill transfer, institutional development and capacity building, as well as funding for power stations, bridges and roads. As we will see later, this mixed bag of services and cash is difficult to value. Even though it is mainly intended for activities with a high public payoff, in practice a significant amount has been spent on programs of low impact; but it is not easy to define what they are actually worth. If official resource flows are not worth their nominal value then they may not be appropriately included as part of the flow of global finance. To add the mixed bag of official "flows" to private flows would be to add up apples and oranges. Furthermore, development is as much about culture, institutions and attitudes as it is about cash. This has been the cry of outside observers from Peter Bauer to Douglas North. This we will return to. In the meantime in terms of impact the place of ODA in total flows is probably in reality less than even the dwindling percentages imply.

The Human Resources Effort

How large is the effort required to deliver the world's complex bundle of aid donations to the poorer countries? While 100 or so national government aid agencies employ about 90,000 international staff, they also probably directly employ some 30,000 consultant and local staff on a regular basis, spending 7 to 9 percent of their budget on overhead administration.[56] For the DAC member countries alone overheads cost about US$10 billion per annum, and probably upwards of US$11 billion for all official donors.[57] Within these totals the World Bank and the principal regional development banks employ a total of about 18,000 staff plus about 5,000 "permanent" consultants and they spend about US$2.5 billion in all on administration. About 100 additional smaller government agencies devoted to international aid and development employ probably 40,000 additional staff members and a further 10,000 local staff and consultants, both short and long term, and probably spend US$4 billion per annum on administration.[58]

Member governments also employ a further large number of staff in foreign, development and finance ministries that oversee the bilateral and multilateral agencies. This means a group of specialized government officials in nearly 200 countries. In the British DFID, a special department is devoted to the task of monitoring the World

Bank and regional development banks. The member countries represented on the World Bank's board (and those on the boards of the other IFIs) each receive the same information and each processes it in parallel, sending it back to parent ministries at home. Thus, instead of channeling specialized information to different corporate functions (for example, lending, finance or strategy), oversight offices based within the World Bank are processing the same information and passing it back to 185 sets of parent ministries who then frequently use outside consultants to interpret it.

Permanent or regular staff, including local country staff and regular consultants working for or on behalf of the aid agencies assisted by home government staff therefore number close to 200,000 and cost in the order of US$12 billion per annum.

Under the present arrangements there is an even larger cohort of recipient government officials dealing with the demands of foreign-aid programs, projects and missions. Recipient countries deploy at least ten central government ministries and a far larger number of semi-government, sectoral and sub-national official agencies, promotional organizations, regulatory bodies, think tanks, laboratories and research institutes in the public sector, to handle components of foreign aid programs and projects, in addition to the personnel of private institutions and organizations that have been brought in to manage programs. The grand total personnel in these areas would certainly amount to a further 200,000.

These personnel are only on the management side of foreign aid – policy making, identifying, planning, negotiating, implementing, procuring, monitoring, reporting and evaluating. In addition to this impressive number there are, of course, the project-level aid workers within developing countries, a large number as would be expected from the figures provided by the OECD for technical cooperation and other advisory programs, which amounted in 2008 to about US$65 billion out of total ODA of US$130 billion.

Anecdotes are available even if no one has added up all the numbers. Riddell cites a finding that there were as many as 100,000 expatriates in Africa in the late 1980s costing more than US$4 billion per annum and amounting to 35 percent of ODA payments.[59] Berg notes that the cost of foreign experts in Tanzania in the late 1980s amounted to twice the cost of the entire civil service payroll.[60] The report's negative assessment of technical assistance led to its phase-out and replacement by "capacity building." Based on US$65 billion of advisory assistance and assuming personnel costs are the bulk of this total then approximately five times the number of aid-management staff are actually working in officially aided projects, and thus we come to a figure of over one million individuals.

Apart from the official aid-agency activities there exists, as stated earlier, an enormous network of private voluntary organizations or NGOs. This sector has surged throughout the rich and poorer countries over the past few years. The largest global International NGO has a paid staff of 46,000 with a US$2.2 billion worldwide budget.[61] The CARE foundation states that it employs 12,000 worldwide. Oxfam has 9,000 staff and 46,000 volunteers. The Gates Foundation employs 1,000 staff. In 2008, the value of total NGO grant aid amounted to at least one-fifth of the value of total ODA and it may be assumed that the personnel engaged approximately correspond.[62]

The estimates of the number of international NGOs in existence have varied very widely. The current Union of International Associations yearbook lists 64,000 civil society organizations worldwide (increased from 21,000 in 2003). One study estimated that the number of active foundations in the US alone was 76,000 by 2005.[63] The number of similar foundations in Europe has also grown rapidly, partly because of the new corporate responsibility programs in large private firms. An online directory of development organizations publishes a list of 70,000 development organizations (although there is duplication) for the purpose of promoting "interaction and active partnerships among governments, private sector and key development organisations in civil society, including NGOs, trade unions, faith-based organizations, indigenous peoples movements, foundations and research centres."[64]

According to the Johns Hopkins Comparative Nonprofit Sector Project, 1.3 percent of a total 40 million paid and volunteer workforce in non-profit organizations work in the international field, amounting to 520,000 individuals about half of which are volunteers.[65]

The wide-ranging data on the number and staff of international NGOs (that is, excluding developing country based NGOs) makes it difficult to guess a number. Including the small number of very large organizations and the myriad small ones, it would probably be reasonable to predict that another 500,000 individuals are involved in managing and administering rich country based NGOs and their projects.

Finally, we could bring into the calculation some of the principal supporting actors, for example those from the academic community who opine about what should be happening in poor countries. A very large number of some of the best academics have spent a significant part of their careers thinking about how to deliver free money to poor countries. Such brainpower could well be doing something else like contributing to the growth of their home economies but, leaving that thought aside, there is indeed an enormous academic enterprise associated with foreign aid. In the US, for example, there are hundreds of institutes and departments with a major focus on aid and development, from the Ivy League across the entire spectrum of colleges, along with think tanks such as the Center for Global Development, Brookings, Carnegie, Cato, the Ford Foundation and many others. In Britain about forty university departments or schools advertise research and teaching through the UK Development Studies Association (and that excludes the generic areas of economics, sociology, gender, social studies and anthropology). Many more are located in colleges and universities in cities across all the OECD countries, and within the large proportion of developing countries themselves whose faculties of development studies and similar schools and centers are often funded by donors and twinned with universities and institutes in the donor countries.

The total amount of academic resources based in rich countries devoted to the study of the economic, sociological, anthropological, political and institutional development of poor countries is remarkable in terms of the numbers of academic departments. The number of world-recognized academic journals is equally so. The British Library for Development Studies lists about 300 journals and e-journals that have a development focus, and approximately 150 in addition with a more general focus that include papers on development.[66] This seems to be a very healthy segment of the 1,800 journals listed by the American Economic Association covering the whole field of economics and related social science subjects including development studies.[67]

Finally, as a footnote, a brief mention of celebrity aid is called for, that segment of the aid business that might be thought of as involving another element of the foreign-aid workforce, low in number but high in net worth. Challenged to comprehend the dynamics and machinations of international agreements between calculating or reluctant parties about what seem to be obvious needs, celebrities emerge intermittently to raise funds, to chastise the rich countries for not paying up or doing enough, and sometimes to stage theatrical events like adopting babies. The 28 June 2010 post on *Aid Watch*, quoted the *Financial Times* headline: "Celebrities urge G8 to make new unkept promises to keep previous unkept promises." The work of individuals like Bono and Bob Geldof has been highly effective in attracting attention and raising emergency funds and there can be no doubt that this has been important at times. But winning charitable funding with intermittent histrionics is not a sustainable solution to the complex problems of poverty nor the way the poorest countries are going to emerge from it, as might be deduced from a look at the activities of the pop star, Madonna.[68]

Some Preliminary Conclusions from Simple Facts

Before digging deeper into meaning, rationale and effectiveness there are a number of conclusions that can be drawn about the nature of development assistance just from a cursory examination of the facts laid out so far. Firstly, it delivers a complicated mix of goods and services through a very large number of public and private providers across the world, through multiple channels each of which inevitably has its own delivery mechanisms and rules according to the requirements of legislators and is therefore likely to demand significant time from both givers and receivers.

Secondly, despite the steadily falling share of ODA in world financial flows the number of donors has increased rapidly along with the number of agencies and projects, both in the public and the non-government sector, resulting in likely dilution of effort. Thirdly, because of the large number of donors operating simultaneously there is likely to be duplication of types of service and consequently there is likely to be inefficiency and waste.

Fourthly, development effectiveness is in doubt because the motives for provision of assistance are diverse and never simply altruistic or developmental in character despite declarations of intent about poverty alleviation, while sometimes they are directly in the interest of particular donor nations. Fifthly, regarding policy, even where genuine efforts have been made to address developmental concerns, ideas about how to assist poorer countries develop have themselves changed frequently over time with likely limited improvement in developmental result and possible worsening.

Sixthly, the aid industry delivers through large numbers of unconnected civil service bureaucracies, even within the same country, without workable efficiency norms or operationally applicable performance criteria. Seventhly, complementary to the extensive fragmented aid bureaucracy there is a similarly fragmented academic community monitoring what the aid bureaucracy is doing which is part of the total picture of extensive and unfocused resources expended in the task of critiquing the provision of free money to poor people.

Finally, show business has taken an interest. The life of the world's poorest who still live in conditions that could not be countenanced by most of the inhabitants of the rich world seems to be part of a world theater on which, with some worthy exceptions, ultra-wealthy publicity seekers demonstrate their lack of familiarity with the real world.

These facts do not suggest a well-oiled machine, nor a resource that can be brought to bear efficiently on the problems of the poorest countries. On the contrary, without digging any deeper or attempting to separate the judgments from the facts it could easily be concluded that, regardless of the best of intentions, there are many problems of aid delivery and implementation that render effectiveness very unlikely and provide scant hope of it being able to accelerate emergence from poverty. But in case these conclusions are unwarranted the rest of this book will take a closer look both at the results and the alternatives.

Chapter 3

HOW FAR HAS DEVELOPMENT
AID BEEN EFFECTIVE?

We, Ministers of developed and developing countries responsible for promoting development and Heads of multilateral and bilateral development institutions … resolve to take far-reaching and monitorable actions to reform the ways we deliver and manage aid … we recognize that while the volumes of aid and other development resources must increase to achieve these goals, aid effectiveness must increase significantly as well to support partner country efforts to strengthen governance and improve development performance.

Paris Declaration on Aid Effectiveness (2005)[1]

Foreign aid can thus do no more for development than to reduce somewhat the cost of a resource (capital) which is not a major factor in economic development.

Peter T. Bauer (1984)[2]

The bare facts about foreign aid give few grounds for expecting much in the way of achievement. The effectiveness of aid has indeed been a continuing and controversial issue for 50 years and an entire literary genre is devoted to it. As mentioned earlier, the first decade of the 2000s saw unprecedented energy aimed at assessing its value. The Paris conference of 2005 singled out improving effectiveness as the principal objective of aid reform, followed up with further declarations in Ghana in 2008 and Busan in December 2011 which have in turn led to extensive evaluation efforts. Major international conferences on aid evaluation such as one in Mexico in June 2011 are being held with increasing frequency.[3]

There is considerable ambiguity within the development assistance community itself about its ability to achieve effectiveness, with opinions falling firmly on both sides of the fence. Commentators, whether academics or practitioners, often set out merciless critiques and then back away from them, in effect losing their own argument. One emphatic statement goes as follows:

[T]he criticism is that aid has produced a culture of dependency, that it feeds corruption in the recipient countries, and that [it] stifles domestic production and distorts market forces. Also aid is frequently misplaced, supports poorly planned projects and is intended for political reasons based on the best interest of countries rather than the recipients. These are some of the major criticisms and I think they are to a large extent valid.[4]

Two paragraphs later the same commentator continues: "without foreign assistance however it is clear that Africa would be far poorer and that its people would live shorter more painful lives with greater disease hunger and human misery." If the first statement is to true then it is very unlikely that the second would hold, but for some reason the writer does not pursue his own withering critique to its logical conclusion.

Riddell is challenged by a similar ambiguity. "Donor efforts in many countries have produced little to show in terms of sustainable country capacity," he writes, "but this should not lead one to conclude that they cannot work. Indeed, we already know a great deal about when they are likely to work."[5] These unsuccessful efforts have continued for 50 years and the conditions required to make them work tend not to exist in the poorest countries and indeed that is what the problem is all about. Finally, Altaf, a Pakistani economist, commenting on the conclusion of a 2011 report by the Center for Global Development entitled *Beyond Bullets and Bombs: Fixing the US Approach to Development in Pakistan*, writes,

> Even here the report manages to suggest a way around its own recommendation; … an alternative reading of the report would suggest that the problem is not with aid in general, but with governance in Pakistan. It is not aid that needs to be fixed, but the governance of the country. The report makes it quite clear that it is not aid that will do so and acknowledges it may be worsening the problem. Yet it proceeds to make the case for aid. And that is what makes *Beyond Bullets and Bombs* almost beyond belief as well.[6]

The many examples of such difficulty with drawing simple conclusions from the evidence suggest ultimately that a conflict of interest exists that prevents conclusions being drawn from evidence. This conflict surely affects development academia (who understandably wish their departments, posts and research grants to survive) just as much as it affects what academia loves to dismiss as the conflicted "bureaucrats" of foreign aid (who understandably wish their organizations and jobs to survive). Both groups conform to rules that characterize bureaucracy. But leaving that aside it is more useful to look at some actual results than to question motives.

Aid and Growth: Macro Evaluation

For the past 20 years, economists have been trying to trace the economy-wide impact of aid on growth. The origin of this endeavor was a laudable effort to get beyond anecdotes and to take into account the effects that would impact whole economies if aid was doing a good job. William Easterly, who was one of the main researchers involved in this effort at the World Bank, writes that it was hoped that the new growth literature that arose in the early 1990s could at last empirically find the answers.[7] However, after extensive effort it has found too many results and too few answers.[8] One meta-study reported on 68 individual studies between 1968 and 2004 with 541 estimates of aid effectiveness. By 2008, the number of reported estimates re-doubled to 1,217.[9]

Initial cross-country research found an overall negative correlation between aid, investment and growth. Easterly showed such a weak link between aid and investment that of 88 countries over the period 1965–95 about 50 showed a *negative* relationship between foreign aid and investment and only 6 showed a significant positive relationship including Hong Kong and China who received very little aid in relation to income.[10] Tunisia, Morocco, Malta and Sri Lanka were the only economies with significant aid in which there was a strong positive association with investment.

Among the most rapidly growing economies in the 1990s were China and India, countries that still contained most of the world's poorest people. But total aid to China, the greatest success story, averaged only 0.4 percent of its GDP (less than 2 percent of national investment). As mentioned earlier, total assistance each year to China over the past decades has been tiny in relation even to the value of the *annual increase* in its GDP and it paid little attention to the policy reform prescriptions of the World Bank and the IMF. So external aid really had nothing to do with the Chinese economic miracle.[11] India received on average only 0.7 percent of its GDP in aid and started to grow successfully during the 1990s, also largely going its own way on economic policy. On the other hand there were several former socialist economies, like Moldova and Kyrgyzstan, which got more aid and their economies declined. Aid to African countries has accumulated the best part of a trillion dollars over 50 years and they generally followed the Bank and IMF prescriptions more closely. Yet a large proportion of their economies grew very slowly, or declined. Zambia received large inflows of aid and had −2 percent growth in the 1990s. Côte d'Ivoire received 26 adjustment loans and its economy declined steadily.

Thus, the countries that had the smallest amounts of outside assistance relative to the size of their economies were the ones that escaped poverty. This was perhaps because assistance was small and the recipient governments were able to use it selectively and advantageously. On the other hand, those countries that received very large doses of foreign assistance in relation to the size of their economies were the ones that did not move out of poverty. Some got worse.

Researchers revisiting the aid and economic growth found a positive association in countries with good institutions and good policies, including macroeconomic stability, fiscal discipline, trade openness, private property rights and the rule of law – that is, in relatively well organized economies, but a negative association in countries with poor institutions and policies.[12] Further research then showed that, within the good policy category, high-aid-to-GDP economies grew faster than low-aid-to-GDP economies, which would provide the justification for continuing to provide aid.[13] However, the high correlation between aid and growth in "good policy" countries was itself challenged and then resurrected by other researchers. There was found to be a correlation between certain types of short-term directed assistance and growth but this was also challenged and later resurrected.[14] A study in 2008 found no link between aid and growth and explained this in a follow-up paper in 2011 as possibly due to the impact of aid in appreciating the exchange rate (the resource curse effect).[15] Meanwhile another found a positive long-run (but no short-run) effect on growth.[16]

Even if we accept that the countries with good institutions and good policy did grow as a result of aid it is still difficult to draw conclusions for aid policy. This is because countries with strong institution and good policy do well as a result of exploiting *all* their resources more efficiently (capital, technology, skills and natural resources) whether local or foreign. Such countries are also more likely to have a culture and societal expectations that favor economic growth. Thus, many good-policy countries may not face a foreign resource constraint but can use foreign aid money in a beneficial way, even if they do not need it. On the other hand, economies that have poor institutions and organizations tend to use all their resources poorly, not just foreign aid. Thus, countries with good institutions and policies do well with or without aid and they do not really need help but they deserve it; countries with poor institutions and policies do poorly with or without aid and they do really need help, but do not deserve it.

Most recently, a study re-examined the main research findings and found them all inadequate.[17] This study allowed for greater time lag between aid flows and their impacts and looked only at the more measurable "early impact" assistance such as real investments in infrastructure and program aid. It concluded that "over the last three decades, substantial increases in aid receipts were followed on average by small increases in investment and growth." The study excluded less measurable areas such as technical cooperation, education and health. However, this selective approach seems open to a further challenge since by excluding capacity building and social service assistance it also excludes the more controversial areas of aid. If "hard aid" which actually flows through to additional real investment only earns a small return then when capacity building is factored in, the growth effects of aid will be even smaller.

During the 1990s, which is the period most studies have assessed, it was difficult to sustain the argument that aid caused growth since growth rates in Africa and elsewhere were all very weak. But the lack of a positive correlation did not prove that aid was ineffective. If causation was reversed and aid money was pouring into poor economies *because* they were doing badly then a negative correlation could arise even if aid was effective. Efforts to prove causality through "instrument variables" have been tried but without convincing results. However, as Easterly points out, if reverse causation were true then the poor economic performance in Africa in the 1990s would have implied that without aid growth could have been strongly negative.[18] Clemens's study suggests that if Africa had received an average level of aid rather than the high levels the continent actually received then its per capita GDP growth rate would have been approximately 0.5 percent lower annually over 1973 to 2001 (−0.8 percent, compared to the actual −0.23 percent).[19] If the act of getting rid of all the "excess" aid (often as much as 10 percent of GNI) would reduce growth by only one-half a percent then this again implies that the effect of aid on growth was very weak.

The other scenario is that of the first decade of the 2000s when there was relatively strong growth rates in poorer countries worldwide. Radelet identifies 17 "emerging economies" in Africa whose average per capita growth rate over 1996–2008 was 3.2 percent, not far below that of East Asia.[20] He attributed the increase in African growth to a) the rise of democratic governments; b) stronger economic policies and lower costs of doing business; c) the end of the debt crisis and IMF influence; d) new technologies such as mobile telephones and the Internet; and e) a new generation of leaders. Of these causal factors it is doubtful whether foreign aid contributed much and it is still no more possible to prove causation. There were many reasons for strong growth other than foreign aid and strong growth could occur despite ineffective aid just as weak growth could occur despite effective aid.

The debate on aid effectiveness has two camps and others sitting on the fence. The aid-optimist camp is represented by Jeffery Sachs. In 2005, he announced that "the time to end poverty has arrived, although the hard work lies ahead. ... I have shown that the costs of action are small and indeed a tiny fraction of the costs of inaction," arguing the world community should commit to specified goals and its leaders should adopt a global plan to meet them.[21] Nicholas Stern, the World Bank's former chief economist, is another aid-optimist who thinks that when we use what we have learned, aid works. He writes: "The time is right to create a framework for a deep and lasting partnership for development. There is indeed a very powerful case for aid."[22] Paul Collier, who also seems to be in this camp, adds, "Far from Africa needing to emerge from aid dependence the continent is entering on a phase during which 'big aid' will make its most vital contribution."[23] Summing up the long debate, he finds that, when all the evidence is taken into account, aid had over 30 years raised the annual economic growth rate by about 1 percent in the poorest countries,[24] a slightly better result than that suggested by Clemens.

Collier's proposals for assistance seem to amount to a kind of Hippocratic oath – that development aid should first *do no harm*. Roger Riddell, more in the aid-uncommitted camp, writes in the same vein:

> If it can be shown that it cannot – ever – make a difference, then it should not be provided. However, if it can be shown to be *doing some good*, then whether 20 per cent, 50 per cent or 80 per cent of development aid is judged to be "working," or whether we have insufficient evidence to judge how much aid is effective, becomes a secondary issue. The onus is always on trying to improve its impact and effectiveness whether most of it currently "works" or whether most of it does not.[25]

These assertions suggest that aid justifies itself if it simply delivers any positive result at any cost.

The failure to find the answers has led to much hand wringing. In the aid-pessimistic camp, Easterly, discussing World Bank assistance, states,

> [E]conomists are no closer than they were 50 years ago to figuring out how to accomplish the basic mission of making a poor economy grow. ... The genuine success stories, where poor countries have achieved long-term growth, have been pitifully few ... And in some of these it's far from clear that Bank aid was a major factor, or even any factor at all.[26]

Pritchett, another doubter, writes, "[I]t seems harder than ever to identify the keys to growth. For every example, there is a counter-example. The current nostrum of one size doesn't fit all is not itself a big idea, but a way of expressing the absence of any big ideas."[27] A 2005 Bank report came to the conclusion that "different policies can yield the same result and the same policy can yield different results, depending on country institutional contexts and underlying growth strategies."[28] Riddell states that the "honest answer" about whether aid works or not is that we still don't know: "Cross-country studies seeking to find the answer to the question 'does aid work?' do not provide a reliable guide on the overall and explicit contribution of aid to development and poverty reduction – they never will."[29]

Successful cases of development that clearly result from long-term large aid inflows have indeed not been identifiable and that surely is in itself significant. The star emerging economy of South Korea started to grow rapidly after aid ended and the Koreans also disregarded the advice of the aid donors.[30] In Africa, Botswana is held out by some as an aid success story but in fact aid also ended following an initial burst in the 1960s, after which enormous revenues from diamonds started to transform its economy. Botswana succeeded where other mineral-rich countries failed not because of aid but more likely because of good leadership and a well-organized civil service that successfully managed its diamond revenue bonanza. Today that civil service is worrying about a future without diamonds.

In the original model of economic development foreign aid was assumed to pass through into investment on a one-for-one basis and to have a similar impact on growth as private investment, filling a gap in savings at low levels of income. The more recent modified version holds that aid provides not just real investment but also human capital but in the long run it still performs largely the role of investment, focusing on public goods with a long-term payoff. Through institutions, infrastructure and education as well as funding of the productive sectors aid was supposed to lay the groundwork for long-term growth that would not be provided by private investment. This simple model linking aid and investment has not proven valid but it still serves as a consistency and reality-check in relation to long-run growth and we have nearly 50 years of experience in which to judge "the long run." As such, on fairly common assumptions about the rate of saving and the return on investment, a 10 percentage-point boost in the savings rate translates into investment expenditure should increase the long-run growth rate by 2 percent to 3 percent per annum and should certainly not be much below 2 percent.[31]

Overall, most assessments have put the growth payoff of foreign assistance at around 1 percentage point per annum, the aid-optimists claiming impacts at 1 percent or above and the aid-pessimists claiming impacts below 1 percent and as low as zero or below. Yet the 1 percent growth effect still implies that the investments yield very low returns compared to what might reasonably be expected. There are several possible reasons for this. Firstly, and obviously, the investments may simply have failed through poor concept and design, lack of local ownership, bad management or corruption. Secondly, some of the aid may have gone into consumption, both directly as in the case of (non-emergency) food aid and indirectly as in the case of investment goods that are effectively for consumption (the ubiquitous cross-country vehicles that adorn capacity-building projects and the foreign trips which provide opportunities for upscale consumption).[32] Indeed, one element of aid-funded foreign education that may be perceived as consumption rather than investment is social-science training. Thirdly, rates of return might be very low because of the macroeconomic, systemic factors outside the project such as the resource curse or an adverse business environment (for example, onerous regulations or poor access to finance), which weaken the link to investment.

Figure 3.1. Malawi ODA/GNI (%)

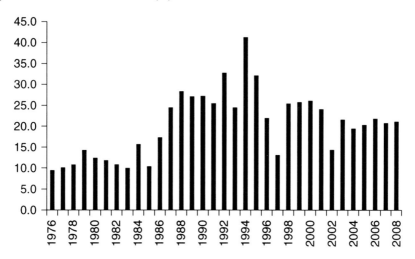

In this context let's think about my first country, Malawi. Is it really conceivable that nearly 50 years' worth of aid comprising as much as a quarter of the country's gross national income has been an essential input without which the rate of growth would have been strongly negative? Would the country have collapsed without all those foreign-aid workers? Or, alternatively, could the very large foreign resource presence have actually created its own problems (diseconomies) that diverted effort and discouraged growth and is that at least as important a reason why aid has done poorly?[33]

The figure above shows Malawi's reliance on aid over more than 30 years. The level of ODA to GNI in the most recent period 1998 to 2008 was about double that of the first 10 years shown (1976 to 1986), averaging around 23 percent compared to about 11 percent. The decade in between saw volatility as aid policy towards Malawi wavered, with major impacts on the government's budget. Bilateral donor annoyance over the autocratic rule of President Banda resulted in a slowing of aid over 1988 to 1993, with a recommitment in 1994; Banda's departure from office was "rewarded" with ODA/GNI of 40 percent for the year. The average level of aid dependence over 1998 to 2008 was, in fact, more than double that of the first years after the country became independent in 1964 when outside help really was needed.

Reverting back to the previous thought, if foreign aid to Malawi on the scale of the past 10 years was the equivalent of an investment in capital projects (physical capital) and capacity building (human capital) then on reasonable assumptions (even with leakage into consumption) it should have fuelled an increase in the Malawian long run growth rate of around 4 percent per annum. Yet the economy stagnated, suggesting very poor returns on aid investment as well as to the country's investments as a whole. Easterly cites a related, if extreme, case in Zambia. He argues that if Zambia had converted all the aid it received since 1960 to investment it could have had a per capita GDP of about US$20,000 by the early 1990s. Instead, Zambia's per capita GDP in the early 1990s was lower than it had been in 1960, hovering under US$500.[31] Reverting to Clemens's estimate, a 0.5 percent reduction in growth rate resulting from a removal of aid worth up to 10 percentage points of GNI might well be accurate and if so it would indeed mean a wholly inadequate rate of return to aid, nowhere near what is required for "take off" when it is considered that the average rate of growth of several East Asian economies has been nearer 10 percent per annum for many years.

In conclusion, Collier's "do no harm" rule and Riddell's "do any good" rule, simply stated, are both unacceptable. A 1 percentage-point increase in the growth rate is also unacceptable. These levels of achievement are wholly inadequate compared to what is needed if the majority of the populations of poor countries are to emerge from poverty. Whatever the reasons, such meager returns would strongly suggest that poor countries should be looking to other kinds of resource flows to fuel the kind of growth that is needed to escape from poverty.

Micro-level Evaluations of Development Projects: The World Bank's Performance

Leaving aside the well-intentioned but very problematic cross-country big picture approach to assessing effectiveness, we can look at the more usual method which has been at the project level. In the lead among donors in the application of micro-evaluation at project level has been, as usual, the World Bank and the evaluation data provided by the World Bank makes a convenient basis on which to consider development effectiveness at project level.

To assess effectiveness the World Bank has an evaluation infrastructure that has mushroomed over the past 20 years. Its first evaluation unit was created 30 years after its foundation, in 1973; the next entity, an inspection panel, was created in 1993 as a result of pressure from the environmental lobby. Since then, under donor pressure, there has been a proliferation of evaluation capacity to the point in 2012 where about 1 in every 5 professional staff of the institution is involved fully or part-time in formally evaluating projects before during and after execution, while the rest carry out continuous monitoring leading to evaluation.[35] The Bank's Independent Evaluation Group (the IEG) has been providing evaluation scores for several decades, as shown in Figure 3.2.[36]

This story depicted in the figure is that the performance of the Bank's completed projects declined for eight years from the end of Robert McNamara's agricultural reform era in 1980, hit bottom (56 percent satisfactory) in 1988, rose and then relapsed in 1994 (63 percent) possibly as a result of disruptive organizational reforms under President Barber Conable. Since 1993 it has trended upward for 16 years barring occasional small dips to reach and exceed 80 percent satisfactory, the level of 1980. Transport projects have recently been the highest-performing sector, almost 100 percent satisfactory; health and nutrition projects showed the worst performance with lower than 60 percent satisfactory and public sector governance projects came second from bottom with about two-thirds satisfactory. East Asia and the Pacific has been the highest-performing region, with over 90 percent satisfactory projects over 2006–2008. Operations in Sub-Saharan Africa showed the worst outcomes with about two-thirds satisfactory.

Figure 3.2. 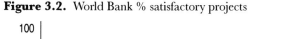 World Bank % satisfactory projects

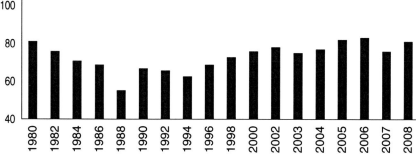

While performance has been variable, the World Bank's current overall 80 percent plus success rate for projects on the ground would seem to be a direct challenge to the critics of foreign aid. This is a seeming success story that would surprise a venture capitalist who expects high-risk projects to fail frequently. In fact, even a 60 percent satisfactory rating, which is the worst of the sector outcomes, would be considered quite reasonable in a high-risk environment.

There are, however, reasons for doubting these high numbers. First of all, what could explain the 14-year rising trend in quality even in countries that exhibited poor performance over a substantial part of this time period? Evidence from individual projects has suggested that complexity and implementation problems got worse, a sure indicator of deteriorating, not improving, results. In fact, the most rapid improvement in "project entry" quality was registered at the least likely time – in the middle of a disruptive reorganization over 1997 to 2001 when administrative budgets were severely cut.[37] An analysis by the Bank suggests that project results might have improved because of better economic policies in the recipient countries, but the growth recovery started at the end of the 1990s while the reported improvement in projects started at the end of the 1980s, leaving 10 years without a satisfactory explanation.[38] Another possibility is that the improvement was simply a form of grade inflation as the institution convinced itself that it was doing better.

Cost benefit analysis, a relatively rigorous if still imperfect technique, fell into disuse as the Bank moved its money into less measurable, non-tradable goods projects such as health, education, environment, public sector management and institution building.[39] The Bank has instead been in the lead in introducing more superficial assessment approaches using performance indicators based on partial outcomes often without reference to project costs and here the evaluators have also reported that performance evaluation is weak.[40] Among the small proportion of projects for which cost benefit analysis is performed, a rapid improvement has been claimed; but the evaluators have also judged half of these analyses as of poor quality.[41] Estimated rates of return to projects in the 1990s were very high, averaging around 20 percent, which would imply quite healthy economic growth rates of 4 percent or more per annum if they were duplicated across the economy. Yet the 1990s was a period of low growth. In Eastern Europe and the Former Soviet Union the average growth rate was minus 1.6 percent per annum while average project returns averaged no less than plus 26 percent. In Sub-Saharan Africa average growth was 1.6 percent in 1980 to 1990 rising to 2.4 percent in 1990 to 2000, yet the estimated rates of return were around 20 percent.[42] Such results were not because the World Bank's projects were beacons of light amid darkness. On the contrary they were complex and difficult to manage which was aggravated because they went to difficult places. The Bank's evaluators in 2000 stated that "many activities take place in countries characterized by scarce human resources, weak infrastructure and weak implementation capacities."[43] Thus, the World Bank's projects showed high returns on paper even where development assistance otherwise seems to have failed.

Another complication is the recent shift by the donor community in general, and the World Bank in particular, to what is called randomized impact evaluation (RIE). This technique usually demands a more detailed and costly approach using a counterfactual as a benchmark for the level of project achievement. That is, it asks what would have happened if there had been no project.[44] While this is a very reasonable question it is difficult to answer it. Impact evaluations in practice have significant methodological problems and up to 2005 this approach was only used for a very small number of projects.[45] The inconsistent approaches to evaluation have resulted in a comparability problem. It was only in 2004 that the Bank launched the Development Impact Evaluation Taskforce to strengthen its evaluations with RIEs. The 25 or so years of prior assessments are almost entirely based on partial evaluations. At the same time, the areas in which quantitative assessments are difficult such as capacity building are also ones where counterfactuals are particularly difficult to identify and easy to underestimate. The evaluators in 2005 said that there were serious deficiencies in diagnosis, design and evaluation of capacity building projects.[46] If the counterfactual has been underestimated in capacity-building projects and if these projects have comprised a large and increasing share of the Bank lending over the past 10 years, then the rate of improvement of overall project performance would have been exaggerated.

The tendency to exaggerate performance does not necessarily imply the failure of development assistance. But it does not provide much comfort about its effectiveness either. In a moment of candor Francois Bourguignon, the Bank's chief economist responsible for setting up the Development Impact Task Force, signaled his agreement:

> [M]uch (though not all) aid has been wasted on poorly conceived and executed projects and programs, often fettered by debatable conditionality. … [M]eta-analysis of ninety seven different studies on the impact of aid and growth, drawing on three different

approaches used in the literature, concluded that at best there appears to be a small positive, but insignificant, impact of aid on growth.[17]

Leaving aside the results from the World Bank of what should be but are not, a rigorous evidence base for measuring development effectiveness draws us back to the traditional approach, looking at actual projects on the ground.

Development Effectiveness on the Ground

One issue of aid policy has been termed the "macro–micro paradox,"[18] whereby aid is not well correlated with growth at the macro level yet many aid agencies claim that a large proportion of their assistance is successful through projects at the micro level. Most recently a study by Robert Picciotto, for many years the evaluation chief of the World Bank, agreed that the case study evidence pointed to this paradox in World Bank aid. In 16 of 55 country-level evaluations aid was rated a success at the project level but not at the country level and in three it was considered a success at the country level despite being unsatisfactory at the project level.[19]

In order to look more closely at projects we can use the classification suggested earlier: capital assistance projects ("hardware") and advisory or capacity building assistance ("software") and a middle category that has features of both. Since we are trying to find reasons for the lack of correlation, or weak correlation, between aid and growth the bias here is towards the things that have gone wrong rather than the successes. Once again we have to distinguish between the intrinsic quality of work performed and the development impact of that work.

Capital projects

Capital projects have included, in particular, infrastructure such as transport, power, water and telecommunications. A prime example is road building and repair. While road projects have often been successful (the World Bank recently rated transport as its most successful sector), many have not. Failures of capital projects are often "hardware" failures rather than failures of approach or concept. Sometimes failure occurs because of inappropriate materials, poor design or possibly corrupt procurement, which results in below-specification materials or finish. Other cases might be less about technical issues and more about inadequate planning or participation and effort by project partners.

Roads have deteriorated prematurely due to failure to maintain them. A 1988 report by the World Bank concluded that US$45 billion worth of road infrastructure had been lost in 85 countries, which would have been preventable with maintenance costing less than US$12 billion. Failure to maintain could be due to inadequate specification of materials and design, which then leads to rapid deterioration. But it could also be due to over-specification of materials or processes, requiring expensive technology such as automated surface laying machines that require sophisticated maintenance. For example, road projects in Afghanistan have faced these problems to an extreme degree. If the response of the donors is to fund the maintenance program themselves, however, this then aggravates longer-term "ownership" problems.

Because in many cases the original decisions have been partly externally driven, poor local ownership and accountability has raised its ugly head when the time comes to maintain the roads. Thus, a large number of externally aided road projects are unsustainable in the longer run because of failure of the local government to raise revenue to pay for their maintenance – possibly on the belief that external agencies would continue to do so. Projects have also come to grief because of poor decisions made by dysfunctional road authorities.

Sometimes failure has been caused by an inadequate project rationale or concept. An obvious example is a prestige project; a president might order a multi-lane highway from his home village to the capital. (President Moi of Kenya had an international airport built at his home in Eldoret, a relatively small upcountry farming town.) Easterly cites a road project in the mountains of Lesotho to provide access to markets for grain.[50] The project never took off because the farmers already knew (from their travels in South Africa) that grain production was not competitive in local conditions. The road simply increased imports into the region and drove the few existing local farmers out of business. US$45 million for a roads rehabilitation loan to Sierra Leone in the middle of a civil war was diverted to compensate for the sabotage of the civil works that had just been built. The same is currently taking place in Afghanistan where roads built by the US are being continuously mined.

Some capital projects fail for what seem to be cultural or behavioral reasons, which may otherwise appear as ownership issues. Reports have found widespread failure of South Asian water supply infrastructure and one half of boreholes in western Kenya due to lack of maintenance.[51] An egregious example is a series of village water projects in Indonesia.[52] Here a road built by one village to an outside design had no culverts for drainage leading to crop failure on both sides (one from flooding and the other from drought); irrigation gates supplied by the project were allowing salinization of the fields; water supply had ceased within weeks of completion; a newly repaired dam was threatening to burst; school buildings were falling down because all repairs had to be done by outside contractors.[53] Failure to maintain water wells and other types of projects may stem from failure to take into account the intricacies of village social organization. New projects can often require changes in a traditional village balance of power, for example where the operation of new types of equipment require changes in gender, age or caste roles.

Finally, an infrastructure success story should be considered, far removed from road rehabilitation. This was in the telecommunications sector. During the 2000s an electronic money transfer service called M-PESA was introduced in Kenya. The service received a US$1.5 million (£1 million) "challenge grant" from Britain's DFID. Andrew Mitchell, Britain's minister for development in a 2010 speech at the LSE made this statement:

> And let us consider the massive success of M-PESA, the result of a collaboration which saw DFID seed-funding some early product development by Vodafone. Thanks to this partnership a simple but game-changing product – a mobile-phone based

money transfer service – has succeeded in allowing millions of the country's very poorest people to engage in the economy in ways they've never done before.[54]

Without question the rise of M-PESA has brought major developmental benefits to Kenya and possibly it was indeed a donor success story. But there are two questions. The first is why funding would go to a British multinational telecommunications firm to expand its business rather than a Kenyan entrepreneur. The second is why this firm needed free money from the British taxpayer and whether it would have done the same thing without this contribution, either using its own money or perhaps private venture capital. In the jargon of evaluation, did the DFID funding create additionality? Here we are not looking at a donor project that did not deliver adequate economic benefits but rather an innovation that produced enormous economic benefits but where it is questionable whether donor aid can be credited with them.

The reason for doubt is that Vodafone had a worldwide turnover of over US$50 billion in 2005, the same year that the British taxpayer stumped up US$1.5 million of free money. It is now the world's largest mobile telecommunications company measured by revenue. Furthermore, the company later apparently reaped further billions of dollars by avoiding taxes, leading to demonstrations on the streets of 10 British cities.[55] Prior to the DFID involvement Vodafone had already been working on the M-PESA concept with two other private companies, Sagentia, a UK technology firm and Safaricom, its cellphone subsidiary in Kenya. It is not the case that Britain's aid officials somehow catalyzed a winning innovation at birth. The cellular electronics industry has expanded remarkably in Africa without subsidies. Indeed, this is one sector where subsidies are not needed, in which case the brilliant results cannot be attributed to the subsidy. It is understandable that an aid agency, casting about for ways to show success, would be tempted to hitch its wagon to a star, but the developmental impact of such an alliance is doubtful.

Agriculture, Education and Health

Agriculture, education and health projects are a hybrid category in the sense that they involve a combination of capital assistance (to fund research stations, grain stores, schools, clinics and equipment) and technical assistance or capacity building (to train farmers, nurses, teachers and to strengthen ministries and regulatory agencies).

There has been successful agricultural assistance. One of the most successful efforts was the series of agricultural innovations known as the "Green Revolution."[56] These evolved from work in Mexico on high yielding seed varieties by US agriculturist Norman Borlaug in 1943, prior to the era of formal development assistance. Similar trials on seed varieties at the International Rice Research Institute in the Philippines were transmitted to India in the 1950s. This work eventually raised yields and output among millions of Asian farmers, although there were later found to be some adverse effects on the environment and income distribution. Transfer of the new techniques to Africa has, however, been generally unsuccessful due to lack of infrastructure, irrigation and fertilizers, diversity of soils and lack of buy-in by governments. A renewed Green

Revolution initiative for Africa was launched by the Rockefeller Foundation in 1999 and boosted in 2006 with a contribution of US$150 million from the Gates Foundation to form the Alliance for a Green Revolution in Africa (AGRA). Its success is, however, still considered hostage to old questions regarding the effects of chemicals on unirrigated land, as well as other issues.

A government program in Malawi which provided vouchers to smallholder farmers to buy subsidized nitrogen fertilizer and maize seeds appears to have resulted in large productivity increases. Helped by good rains, the subsidies were credited with record-breaking maize harvests in 2006 and 2007, nearly trebling 2005 production. It is notable that this subsidy program was initiated by the government in the face of *opposition* from the donors such as the World Bank. The subsidies have proved expensive and have since been cut back but the initiative has probably yielded valuable lessons for the government about dealing with outsiders' conceptions of development strategy.[57]

Despite the apparent overall success, with qualifications, of the high-yield seed programs in Asia, African projects have often failed.[58] Efforts to improve soil fertility and stem erosion and deforestation have often been unsuccessful. The 2008 World Development Report on agriculture cited stagnant cereal yields. Fertilizer was underutilized in Kenya for obscure behavioral reasons. Agricultural extension has had disappointing results which one study explained in terms of the lack of motivation of extension workers.[59] Farmer training, a time honored assistance initiative, has also shown indifferent results.[60]

One important case of troubled agricultural assistance to Africa was the World Bank–conceived multi-sector Regional Integrated Development Projects in the 1970s, which focused on agricultural support. The assumption behind these projects was that small farmers would raise productivity in response to packages of improved inputs such as seeds, fertilizer and equipment, similarly to the Green Revolution approach. Unfortunately, the projects were labor intensive, complex and relied on buy-in from local elites, which was often not present.[61] Observation of these projects in Tanzania at the time suggested a confusion of approaches with different aid donors "taking charge" of each region. Despite the high expectations and a plausible developmental rationale these projects were judged by the World Bank's evaluators to be 60 percent unsatisfactory over 1978–85, accounting for half of the decline in the Bank's agricultural portfolio performance. Seemingly unable to make headway the donor agencies started to withdraw from agricultural support and as we have seen the World Bank now lends less than 5 percent of its money to this sector.

Many health projects in Africa have shown good results. Oral rehydration therapy provided by the US reduced by 82 percent infant deaths from diarrhea in Egypt in the 1970s.[62] The elimination of river blindness in Niger was a significant achievement of the WHO and other agencies, as was the success with eradication of smallpox. Nutrients, protein supplements and de-worming drugs have paid off in terms of human height, weight and productivity, even though mortality remains high from preventable and treatable diseases in Africa. A successful humanitarian program (and therefore outside our strictly developmental focus) has been the US PEPFAR program to fight the AIDS epidemic. However, there are also a large number of failures. Behavioral and incentive issues are thought to impede success. Studies in Guinea, Cameroon, Uganda and Tanzania have found that 30 to 70 percent of drugs disappear before reaching the patients. Nursing personnel are absent and programs suffer from bureaucratic inefficiency. Many projects show no better results than continuation of existing services. Even de-worming's effectiveness on school performance has been challenged.[63]

Many education projects have shown ostensibly good results. Australian aid doubled school enrolment in Papua New Guinea. A scholarship program worked successfully for Kenyan girls and spilled over to improved performance among boys. However, for the usual range of reasons including design, behavior and commitment results can also be poor. Enrolment achievements have often not been linked to improved educational performance because of lack of textbooks, teacher absenteeism, corruption, patronage and intervention of political events on school life.[64] Even where textbooks are available they have not necessarily increased the performance of students.[65] In 2010, Tanzanian education received a "Millennium" achievement award for raising enrolments but at the same time results showed that a large proportion of students were well behind goals in reading and math.

A seminal study by Pritchett finds a negative relationship between education and the key growth indicator of total factor productivity. He lists reasons for this.[66] Firstly, much educational aid might not be actually raising skills, but providing a certificate of respectability; secondly, stagnant labor markets either could not provide jobs or available jobs were in unproductive activities such as failing state enterprises. The paper also found a negative relationship between increases in school enrolment rates and the rate of growth of skills and knowhow. However, as customary, these findings were later challenged using supposedly better data showing a positive return.[67]

One way of improving buy-in in projects has been through increase of transparency. A widely cited World Bank study in Uganda finds that only 13 percent of government transfers to local schools actually reached the schools, but the percentage increased to 90 after the government began publicizing in the press how much money was supposed to go to each school.[68] However, another study suggests that press campaigns were likely to be effective only in communities "that were literate and assertive enough to act when abuse was revealed."[69]

In some cases school meals have improved performance. School vouchers have had some effect. Cash grants to stay in school have successfully extended enrolment. De-worming and iron supplements may have raised attendance (although not scores). The large number of educational evaluations has in fact tended to lead to numerous recommendations with uncertain generalizability. Easterly sums this up: "one is left with the feeling that aid could improve education, but the literature is not clear on when, why or how."[70]

In 2002, an attempt was made to renew a global education assistance effort known as the Education for All Fast-Track Initiative which had been an important call to action by the main donors. Predictably things have not gone according to plan. A blog reported that the board of the Fast-Track Initiative had met in Paris to agree urgent measures to get the initiative "back on track." "As readers of previous CGD education blogs will be aware," it went on, "the FTI has come under serious criticism over the past year for failing to deliver the scaled up support that had been promised."[71]

Finally, it seems important to re-emphasize that education aid provided by external donors may often have been treated as consumption, not investment. The bracketing of education with trips to foreign countries and expense accounts can render it an incentive payment rather than an investment. In the worst case a foreign education is little more than a certificate of social status, not an acquisition of the technical skills needed for the future of the country.

Aid Software – Advice, Capacity and Institution Building

Capacity-building projects tend to focus on improving skills in areas such as policy, management, analysis, valuation, regulation and enforcement. As discussed in Chapter 2, capacity building and institutional development have come center stage since the 1990s. Capacity building superseded a prior effort known as "technical assistance," which focused more on the transfer of skills (professional, technical, artisanal, etc.) to fill particular slots. Technical assistance was found in a series of evaluations to have achieved little because of failure to build at the institutional level. It was no good filling slots in organizations that were dysfunctional – what was needed was a more root-and-branch approach. Yet two decades later it turns out that good results in institution and capacity building seem to have been just as hard to achieve.

Many of these projects are carefully designed and diligently executed. Riddell cites a number of examples of successful capacity building projects.[72] He lists USAID's work on the judicial system in Costa Rica; SIDA's help to build up Tanzania's Central Bank statistical department; DFID's help to the Rwanda revenue authority; help to Mozambique's customs service; assistance to the South African treasury and to the Ghana planning commission. These were projects that he states had clear goals, commitment and interaction.

However, in the general case of institutional and capacity building, good approaches to design are often by no means clear-cut. Moises Naim writes, "What passes for knowledge about institutional reforms is often nothing more than a series of partial findings with little capacity to provide universal prescriptions to guide efforts aimed at improving institutional performance in reforming countries."[73] Similarly, Rodrik finds that that while institution building might be central to development that does not necessarily imply much in terms of operational guidance.[74] Riddell, despite his reference to a list of what he thought were successful capacity building efforts, writes, "donors do not agree on what is or how to improve governance or what constitutes good governance or what their roles should be."[75] Even the definition of governance varies from donor to donor. It can refer to process and institutions for decision making, the actual exercise of authority, the operation of institutions or the traditions and norms by which authority is exercised.

One illustration of the difficulties of building capacity is in the attempts to reform civil services. A project in Tanzania required the government to set up an office, which oversaw the firing of former colleagues. The resulting conflict of interest undermined the project. To avoid such problems, donors set up independent project management units, but these have often drawn away the best people from the departments that were to be strengthened, undermining capacity in a different way. The problem has not applied only in the poorest countries. After the breakup of the Soviet Union in 1991 when severe inflationary conditions had taken hold, young graduates hired into donor project offices and paid in dollars were earning more than cabinet ministers and disrupting the incentive systems within the Russian Federation and other former republics.

A 2006 World Bank report claimed that Ghana, Mali, Senegal and Tanzania all achieved substantial improvements in the critical area of public financial management capacity between 2001 and 2004 and could achieve reasonably strong capacity within a 5–10 year period.[76] However, a Bank evaluation report the previous year on 55 African countries had found something different, particular difficulties in implementing financial systems, stating, "there is little empirical evidence to clarify what part of the problem international capacity building support can best help to solve; in what order capacity needs should be addressed; what can be expected of different kinds of interventions and why." The report also concluded that a project management unit's short-term benefit in efficient management was offset by the long-term adverse effects on morale, and hence capacity, in government.[77]

In Malawi, the evaluators found that the Bank had financed training, advisors and equipment to build capacity in public agencies in nearly every project for 10 years with little significant impact.[78] In Mozambique, the public finance system is one of the highest rated in Africa, with updated laws, a state-of-the art information system and exemplary budget documents. But reporting requirements are not being met and officials say that the new system involves complex arrangements, that they were never asked about the kind of system they needed and that it may in the end fail to produce satisfactory results.[79] Easterly writes:

> The World Bank did seventy civil service reforms in Africa in 1987–97 and over a quarter of World Bank lending is currently devoted to "capacity building." Yet the political scientists specializing in analyzing African states see little sign of effect of these Herculean efforts at making civil servants perform better, even seeing some signs of decline.[80]

Moss finds that institutional capacity in many poor countries did not improve over 30 years.[81] Zambia's graduate population, he writes, increased from about 60 at the time of independence to tens of thousands today but the capacity of government did not improve proportionally. A project that trained 2000 staff up to 1999 for the Zambia Ministry of Finance was assessed as a failure. Van de Walle asks,

> What does this mean for donor programs? Foremost, it means that the contemporary capacity-building efforts are largely Sisyphean, doomed to fail. The problem is not technical – it is not equivalent to the problem of building the perfect irrigation pump. Instead, it is about changing the current incentives that are leading local institutions to under-invest in capacity.[82]

Creation of laws and regulations has been problematic for conceptual as well as ownership reasons and not just in the poorest countries. In the former Soviet Republics, early attempts to help rewrite laws came up against a lack of consensus on what made good law, an example being corporate law and accounting standards where it was not clear whether the common law or the civil code principles were more appropriate. It was unclear how urgent it was to formalize bankruptcy law when all the enterprises that needed to be closed were government owned. These arguments were often carried on by outsiders largely without meaningful input from the local legal profession or legislative bodies, something which would be neither tolerable nor effective in the US or Europe.

The assessment of capacity-building projects is frequently over-optimistic. This occurs because of a tendency to underestimate existing local capabilities.[83] Donor projects, for example, set up business centers which provide free advisory services, but these can actually undermine existing local small businesses such as accounting or training enterprises. The donor money might be better used to fund improvements in these local services. One business support project conducted by the World Bank in Mauritius funded foreign marketing services to assist local exporters and was rated highly satisfactory, but its additional impact was exaggerated because some firms were already buying services, both local and foreign and did not need a subsidy and furthermore the subsidy to imported services may have undermined existing local business service network. Another likely case of exaggeration was a project in Latvia to restructure the local banking system after the breakup of the Soviet Union. At that time, private banks were already entering the market and could very likely have done the job better. This project was nonetheless also assessed by the World Bank as "highly satisfactory." In another case free technical assistance from the IFC was provided to a rapidly expanding and profitable bank in Bangladesh that was already hiring consulting services commercially. The impact of IFC's input on corporate relations may have been excellent but the developmental impact was zero.[84]

Recent capacity-building initiatives have aimed at strengthening "public–private sector dialogue" in Africa and elsewhere. It is questionable why external donor agencies are required to stage such a dialogue which perforce has to be demanded of the government by local private business and the donor intervention risks distorting the process because, for example, multiple dialogue channels that should emerge spontaneously tend to get diverted into an aid-driven, formal channel associated with free money. Worse, the dialogue process can stall as it waits for the free money, for example to meet luxury hotel expenses for dialogue attendees. If a dialogue becomes captured by aid money, there is a likelihood that behavior will change such that aid-opportunists rather than productive entrepreneurs come forward. Governments meanwhile must arrive at their own understanding that the private sector must not be blocked from creating wealth and that vibrant entrepreneurship within a democratic system is essential to progress.

One of the most important priorities for "capacity building" is to build up private-sector entrepreneurship and risk-taking capacity. However, it is very difficult for this to be done via free public money channeled through fearsome bureaucratic processes paralyzed by fiduciary concerns. Private-sector development aid is recognized as difficult. The World Bank has often rated its PSD projects as relatively low performing. Many efforts have been made to "learn the lessons" but many of the solutions are as opaque as the problem. One 2005 study, replete with development assistance jargon, concluded mysteriously that "business clients need to be able to make the transition between instruments – more coherent mixing, sequencing, information sharing and alignment of entry and exit criteria across PSD instruments would help business clients as they grow and graduate."[85]

Microfinance

One area in which donor agencies have been heavily involved and which thus deserves a special, if summary, look is microfinance. The microfinance story is not just about foreign aid. The initial push into microfinance was indigenous while later initiatives were driven by the private or quasi-commercial financial sector. Indeed, lest we think that the problem of outside intervention is only about government or foreign public sector failure, it is notable that one of the ways in which microfinance has run into difficulties has been due to the crisis of private markets. It is also a story about how outside support ran into trouble when it was *not* a product of aid, although aid had a significant role.

Following the work in the 1970s of Mohammad Yunus and the Grameen Bank and others such as ACCION International, microfinance grew into a worldwide movement by the 1990s. It was seen as a high-impact social development initiative and received extensive funding from the donor community. Today there are around 150 million micro-loan borrowers worldwide. Most of the 122 MFIs with over 100,000 clients were very small 20 years ago or did not exist. In Bangladesh, Mongolia and Peru as many as 1 in 5 working age adults now have micro-bank accounts. Sub-Saharan Africa is the least intensively micro-banked, although Ethiopia, Kenya and South Africa have fast growing institutions. The 13 biggest MFIs today in terms of lending (led by Grameen and BRAC Bank of Bangladesh, SKS of India and Bank Rakyat Indonesia) have over 40 million clients in total and on average over 13,000 staff members each, making them very large organizations providing very small credits.[86]

Despite, or because of, its rapid growth, by the middle of the first decade of the 2000s the development impact of microfinance started to be questioned. One element of this was the realization that, while microcredit could liberate some from the daily struggle for survival and reliance on moneylenders, it could lock others into intrusive peer pressure while facing still high interest rates, especially women who were the majority of borrowers. At least with moneylenders there was a common "bête noire" for the villagers to blame, but when it was your erstwhile friends that wanted to sell off your cow to repay your loan there was nowhere to hide. This situation was aggravated in the early 2000s by an excess supply of microcredit to several countries resulting in competitive lending and multiple borrowing. A dramatic event resulting partly from these problems was the announcement in 2010 by the state government of Andhra Pradesh in India that borrowers could stop repaying MFIs, following a spate of newspaper reports of suicides among borrowers.[87]

Another question was whether donor (or government) subsidies were in the end a help or a hindrance to the growth of sound banking even for the poor. Today on average MFIs with less than 10,000 borrowers are unprofitable, while the potential profitability of some of the larger MFIs is also uncertain because in some cases it is obscured by subsidies.[88] As a general rule subsidies to banks do not work because they protect inefficient banking or inefficient borrowing, or both, misallocating resources and thereby discouraging entry by good banks.

A third issue has been that the key problem preventing the poor from investing may not be access to credit at all, but rather income instability and risk and therefore what is needed is insurance and savings security more than credit. Insurance and savings do not, in addition, impose burdensome social obligations. Older mechanisms such as rotating savings and credit associations have been in existence in the villages of the world for a long time but have been overtaken by microcredit and the vested interests of both donors and recipients.

MFIs have evolved. The Grameen Bank, which pioneered peer group credit, has switched away from it, partly to avoid "reverse peer pressure" created when many borrowers default. Savings requirements have been changed; interest rates have fallen with competition though some MFIs still charge high rates. Micro-insurance has been introduced in a number of countries. Many non-profit micro-banks have switched to a for-profit model so as to raise capital for expansion. Holding companies have started investing capital in retail MFIs and MFIs have issued securities backed by loan portfolios. Some have issued IPOs, earning early shareholders (including the IFC) very large profits from exiting.[89] According to CGAP, 30 international "microfinance investment vehicles" were created in just 2 years between 2007 and 2009, an increase of 50 percent.[90] The general trend has been towards commercialization.

Investment in microfinance has been partly based on grants from aid agencies and NGOs (such as CARE and OXFAM) and the corporate responsibility departments of private banks, but latterly it has been largely mediated through public international financial institutions (IFIs). Foreign capital in MFIs rose from US$2 billion to US$13 billion between 2005 and 2010 of which the IFIs increased their holdings from US$1.7 billion to US$7.5 billion. Five organizations, EBRD, IFC, KFW, AECID and OPIC, have supplied most of the IFI funding.[91] Private individual and institutional investors hold a quarter of the total and their share has been rapidly rising while the aid agencies share has fallen.

After 2008 returns to foreign investment in MFIs fell. Oversupply of credit looking for outlets not affected by the world financial crisis spread the same problems to the microfinance market. Principal examples were Bosnia and Nicaragua, two of the largest recipients of foreign microfinance investment. Other major recipients such as Morocco, India and Pakistan, also ran into trouble. Just as in the wider banking system, investment drove irresponsible micro-lending and inadequate due diligence and encouraged multiple borrowing, a major retreat from the original peer group, hand-holding ideal of the Grameen Bank. Even prior to the lending boom of the early 2000s, however, the World Bank had tried to "sell" a US$100 million loan several times to a major Indonesian microfinance bank, BRI, which the bank refused because of its own concern that its lending discipline would suffer.[92]

Foreign investors failed to ensure that sufficient controls were in place and regulatory institutions such as credit rating were lacking.[93] Many of the largest MFI recipients of foreign loans faced significant write-offs (partly because of reverse peer pressure). IFC and KFW set up a US$500 million crisis liquidity facility in 2009 to prop up MFI balance sheets but it only came fully on line in September 2010 when US$76 million was disbursed in four months, leading to an unintended saturation of the credit market.[94]

In the ten most affected MFIs foreign capital funded on average 63 percent of their loan portfolios in 2008. Aside from the lending excesses, large outside investment created a structural problem for the MFIs because it replaced deposits, leaving them over-leveraged and free from the business discipline they would face if they had to protect depositors' funds.

How far is microfinance a story about foreign aid? It is notable that the principal pioneers of micro-banking in Bangladesh did not launch their efforts as a result of foreign donor sponsorship. Further, the large part of the foreign capital invested later on was not strictly aid but development finance, which was expected to ultimately earn a profit. Nevertheless microfinance investment was linked to foreign aid inasmuch as it was part of a broad social investment movement and it included elements of free services such as technical assistance. In that sense the extent to which it fulfilled developmental objectives is relevant.

A number of evaluations of microfinance projects in Thailand, Bangladesh, South Africa, India, Kenya and the Philippines were reviewed by Roodman. He concludes, "there is no convincing evidence that microcredit raised incomes on average. While many have sought that Holy Grail it still eludes us."[95] This means that there was no clear link between microfinance and poverty reduction, even though the latter had been the original point of the whole effort. Roodman concludes that the developmental impact of microfinance has been in building banking capacity, not on poverty and growth, nor on liberation from moneylenders.

Has microfinance investment by IFIs built efficient capacity? The conclusion is ambiguous. The excesses of outside investment in the early 2000s may have weakened rather than strengthened an industry that was emerging throughout the 1980s and 1990s. Here again the problems were not simply traceable to foreign aid but to the financial products of international banks which had very little to do with the fledgling banking services needed by the poor. The handholding of village basket weavers by socially motivated lenders was forgotten as MFIs became an "asset class" re-financed courtesy of JP Morgan Chase.[96] The Andhra Pradesh event and the other crises were indicators of these bad effects.

It can be argued, as Roodman does, that outside donations helped to build valuable micro-banking infrastructure even if it did not directly reduce poverty. But historically financial sectors have emerged out of internal demand, not out of philanthropy or the profit appetites of international investment banks. The English country banks that helped fuel the first industrial revolution grew up outside London as a result of demand from local traders, expanding sevenfold in the 25 years between 1784 and 1809.[97] The indicators are that microfinance will merge into mainstream commercial banking and in the end will be one component of the general development of banking systems. All in all, development impact may have arisen from early donor support of such institutions, but it has to be seen in the context of the indigenous initiatives, especially in Bangladesh, that were already ongoing and the more recent excesses which may have set it back and it may well not have been transformative on its own.

Participation

Almost at the same time as the emergence of capacity building as an assistance concept in the 1990s, the aid donors identified a lack of ownership and participation by recipients in project identification and design as the major causal factor in low project success. For someone working in development projects on the ground over a long period of time the "ownership problem" had always been blatantly obvious. Recipients simply did not buy and/or did not buy into projects that they had not been meaningfully consulted on, let alone generated themselves and this always vitiated the chances of success. But as long as aid projects were part of a program put in place at the top level and devolved downwards, the aid workers on the ground had to suspend disbelief and keep working, or find another job.

The World Bank formally initiated efforts to strengthen local participation in 1991 with a "participatory development learning group." In 1994, it introduced a "participation action plan." Twenty projects were designated participation "flagships." In 1996, a "participation sourcebook" was published. The participation and ownership agenda was formalized in 1999 when Poverty Reduction Support Papers (PRSPs) were adopted by the major donors as the basis for a new program to replace the discredited Structural Adjustment Programs. The PRSPs were intended to be participatory, requiring a consensus of donors, government and civil society. They were also tied to a debt relief initiative (the second HPIC initiative), which effectively made them conditions of debt relief and tied them to a debt relief timetable.

Unfortunately the PRSPs went beyond the simple goal of ensuring that the recipients buy into projects. They set up a new, time-intensive planning procedure to which governments were expected to adhere if they wanted continued assistance. The PRSPs immediately faced challenges. Martin Wolf in the *Financial Times* wrote,

> The World Bank is apparently calling for the restructuring of the political and social order of its developing country members – there is no reason to suppose that countries can be readily reordered to meet the demands of today's progressive sensibility ... The term [PRSP] suggests the presence of a benefactor prepared to dole out power to the deserving – but no such benefactor exists.[98]

A research team from the IDS at the University of Sussex warned that the short PRSP time frame meant that the process would end up like the one-way communications of the past rather than the lengthy and unpredictable ones needed for genuine participation.[99] Nancy Birdsall later wrote similarly, "the misguided imposition of policy conditions morphed into the misguided imposition of 'participation.'"[100]

There was also a problem that the PRSP process of participant deliberations would compete with the work of legislatures elected by a country's voters. Larry Summers, former chief economist, said at a World Bank retreat in May 2001, "I am deeply troubled by the distance that the Bank has gone in democratic countries towards engagement with groups other than government in designing projects … there is a real possibility it seems to me of significantly weakening democratically elected governments." There was an issue also of who exactly selected the civil society representatives and it was not clear which types of civil society agents should be selected.

By 2005, the evaluators at the World Bank warned that client countries were viewing the PRSP process as a source of cash not an expression of commitment to development. The status report to the Bank's Development Committee in 2005 concluded that the PRSPs lacked operational details and showed a continuing tension between aid and government objectives. They could not eliminate the "parallel parliament" problem and they put further pressure on government planning capacity. By 2005, only one-third of PRSPs, which were clearly political documents, were being presented to parliaments, while the "poor" were not being adequately represented in discussions.

The surest way to failure through non-participation has been to invent development projects from outside and then impose them in a serious conflict setting. In 2011, the *Washington Post* cited a US government audit of projects in Afghanistan, which reported that of the US$2 billion worth of projects started over 6 years by the Commander's Emergency Response Program half were badly constructed and had quickly deteriorated.[101] Failing projects included police stations, the Kabul Power Station funded by the US for US$300 million, a major road (Highway 1), a canal and even a water park. The commander had announced that democracy finished where the roads ended so road building was essential. Up until December 2009 there was no requirement for a formal commitment by the intended beneficiaries, no resources for maintenance and no monitoring of projects after handover. A report in June 2012 stated that the assistance failures had highlighted the limitations of an aid system designed largely to serve donors' political goals.[102]

Irrational Behavior?

Supposedly irrational or perverse behavior has been identified in many project situations, such as rural health, education and roads, where projects fail because of lack of effort (nurses and teachers don't show up for work, roads are not maintained). Outsiders puzzle over a community's failure to adopt an "obvious" win–win innovation, but the reasons are often really not hard to fathom. Rural projects come up against an innately conservative culture that adopts innovations cautiously and fears an innovational "Trojan horse" that would impose sudden changes in behavior, even if the village population at first agrees to the project. For example, pedal-operated agricultural processing equipment was promoted in a number of countries by the intermediate technology movement in the 1970s but did not catch on partly because it created gender conflicts. (Women, the traditional maize grinders, would have to be replaced by men.) Women in an Indian village preferred to walk a mile to wash clothes in a river rather than use a village well provided by donor aid because the free, social time at the river was important to their daily lives. If medicated bed nets are diverted to bridal veils or fishing nets on Lake Victoria this is because, rightly or wrongly, the certainties of food and marriage are given higher priority than the more uncertain issues of children's health and changes to such attitudes require time and not the requirements of Western aid. Finally, hand washing with soap has been shown to greatly reduce potentially fatal diarrhea in young children. Yet the required behavior change has often not occurred, even in an improving economy such as the Philippines. Why? One explanation was because of insensitive treatment of the overburdened mothers participating in the project.[103] Anthropological studies have shown the key importance of the social relations behind projects.[104]

Strange ideas from outside have been introduced to promote behavioral fixes such as time-stamped photos of teachers and nurses to lower absenteeism, an authoritarian intervention substituting for the process of improving accountability.[105] Such experiments continued over several years at the behest of outside researchers. In Rajasthan, India, the photos happened to work for the teachers but not for the nurses whose absenteeism got worse, presumably because it increased the alienation of the nurses from their employers. Some supposed beneficiaries also failed to attend clinics because they do not want to be treated badly by the nurses.

In the case of microcredit, there was an idea that the availability of loans would convert people en masse into entrepreneurs. In another case the micro-borrower was not interested in reducing her interest payments because she did not want to make profits, which would be spent on drink by her spouse. In the case of failure to purchase fertilizer by poor Kenyan farmers the problem was one that appears to be common with the poor everywhere, including the US – a preference for spending money when you have it and belt tightening when it runs out, rather than stockpiling to take advantage of uncertain future opportunities. One suggested solution, which like the time-stamped photo requires authoritarian oversight, is to create savings accounts from which withdrawals cannot be made until a targeted savings amount has been reached. (Who would set up these accounts – social workers or aid donors!)

The Cost of Delivering Development Projects

Projects are in principle supposed to pay for themselves in the sense that their benefits, intangible or otherwise, should exceed their direct costs. As we have seen, this probably does not happen in many cases. But in addition to their direct costs there is also an overhead cost of delivering assistance and this is generally not covered in any systematic way.

As mentioned in Chapter 2, the costs of overhead aid administration are in the range 6–9 percent of total official aid allocation, around US$10 billion a year across some 23 principal DAC countries worldwide. An additional cost is incurred by the new donors. These costs include the running of the agency operations worldwide and exclude the management cost of the projects themselves. In addition, governments incur a complementary, unknown, but large overhead cost.

Project costs are usually taken into account through benefit–cost appraisals in the case of hardware projects such as roads and power, but in the case of software projects the appraisals are, as we have seen, rarely done; while in both types of projects the overhead costs are often not counted at all. Counting the overheads is not so important for large-scale infrastructure or budget support projects because they are a very small proportion of the total; but for capacity-building projects which tend to be a lot smaller and more labor intensive the overhead costs may comprise a significant percentage of project costs. Over its lifetime an average World Bank project may cost about US$1 to US$1.5 million, spent on identification, preparation, implementation, management and several years of supervision and evaluation, plus the overhead costs of running the institution. For a not untypical project for capacity building in a small country involving a loan of US$5 million, the overhead burden could therefore be 20–30 percent of the total before counting the costs incurred by the government of dealing with the Bank. The IDA, which handles projects in the poorest countries, takes an administration charge of just 1 percent of loan value per annum, which cannot cover more than a small part of such costs. So the capacity-building projects often have to be subsidized by the infrastructure, adjustment or budget support projects.

The study of donor agency performance by Easterly and Williamson shows bilaterals as having lower overhead cost ratios and higher disbursements per employee than multilaterals as a whole who in turn had lower costs than UN agencies.[106] Of the bilaterals, the United States has the highest administrative costs, partly reflecting the way that Congress has imposed earmarks and other mandates on USAID. On average about US$6 million is disbursed per aid agency employee, while at the low extreme only US$30,000 per employee for the World Food Program and US$40,000 per employee at UNHCR has been disbursed.

The World Bank has for years tried to streamline overheads but in practice procedures have become inexorably more complicated and expensive, while the cost is often disguised because operations are increasingly covered by outside trust funds. The 1997–2001 Wolfensohn reorganization made extravagant claims about efficiency increases through switching resources from the "back line" to the "front line." But these did not in fact occur. Instead genuine frontline operations fell as a proportion of costs while backline costs such as central advisory functions, quality and fiduciary oversight rose, as depicted in Figure 3.3.

Initially, expenses were held down as part of Wolfensohn's so-called "Strategic Compact" with the board, but at the cost of severely de-funded and degraded frontline operations. Instead of simplification the Bank's own evaluators' estimates for what they call "demandingness and riskiness" increased greatly in the late 1990s when costs were supposed to come down. "Complex" projects increased in number from 43 percent in the first part of the decade to 77 percent in 1999–2000.[107] An example of the iron law of complexity was the World Bank's quick "Learning and Innovation Loans" introduced in 1999. These loans were streamlined at first but processing time more than doubled within 3 years. Another example of the operation of the iron law are private sector development projects which have been chronically prone to unwieldy

Figure 3.3. World Bank: Front line and back line costs (US$ million)

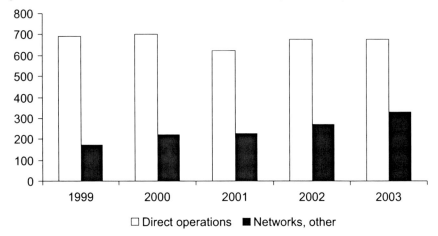

Source: *David Phillips, Reforming the World Bank (Cambridge University Press, 2009)*

design, lengthy delays, time extensions, lack of management continuity and failure of governments to contribute.

A phenomenon that is a likely counterpart of complexity is the intellectualization of assistance. One dimension of this is that the world's aid agencies seek top academic qualifications, apparently well in excess of those generally sought by the private sector. Judging individual abilities across cultures requires a universal currency and this has come to mean high-level academic qualifications. The World Bank usually has 2,000 or so PhD holders on its staff and such qualifications are also sought by other agencies. Whereas some work, such as medical research, macroeconomic or finance policy, may need top academic talent, the delivery of projects in poor rural and urban communities are not the province of top-level researchers, but rather those of technical specialists: small business developers, agronomists, water engineers, health workers and school administrators. The intellectualization of development aid is largely irrelevant to its objectives and more consistent with agency bureaucratic pressures. Through such pressures applied social-science jargon has spread to the farthest corners of the earth. In a Kenyan village in 2003 a notice pinned to the mud wall of a local artisan group's office bore the title: "empowering communities and stakeholders to participate in and increase value-added within product and service delivery chains." The imperatives of foreign assistance have required African blacksmiths to adopt terminology that would be considered idiotic by American or European blacksmiths.

In 2002, after the World Bank's 4-year Strategic Compact had been formally completed, top management was still launching appeals to reduce complexity. Later under President Zoellick the institution announced another simplification drive, this time with a fast-track procedure for so-called low-risk projects. But fast tracking has only invited closer attention and consequent delay by the quality inspectors. Other IFIs face similar if lesser problems. An IADB project to help microfinance banks in the Caribbean spent most of its life in arduous preparation and very little time in actual help. USAID takes more than 18 months to award its complex program contracts and its goal is to reduce this to around 300 days, but there is little chance of this being achieved.[108]

Coordination efforts have included, as we have seen, PRSPs and the so-called Sector-Wide Assistance Programs (SWAps) introduced in the 1990s, largely in health and education. However, again there is little evidence that they have lowered cost. Rather, more time is often needed to prepare, coordinate and monitor them. A lively debate greeted a negative report in 2010 on the use of SWAps (horizontal) as opposed to disease-focused (vertical) approaches in the health sector.[109]

As a general rule agencies do not factor in these seemingly unalterably large overhead (complexity) costs in estimating the net benefits of projects. Yet project assessments can only be meaningful as expressions of the net benefits of public assistance if they are related to the true costs of public assistance. Rates of return to capacity building projects, already suspect, are likely to be substantially reduced if assistance overhead costs are taken into account, inflated as they have been by the increasing complexity and intellectualization of development assistance. This therefore is another reason why, particularly for institutional and capacity building, we are not hearing the facts about effectiveness.[110]

Epilogue – Aid Effectiveness

Over many years much has been written and said about whether and how foreign aid fails or succeeds. Research has shown little or no correlation between aid and economic growth and the causal mechanisms that underlie this are still not generally understood. There has been much argument about methods and a tendency for old approaches to be recycled as new – most recently the debate has been, once more, about whether assistance is better provided bottom-up, on a case by case basis or top down through a "big push."

Whatever the level of achievement, the case has been amply made that aid has not performed adequately in raising the prospects for the poorest countries. Even in the rapid growth period of 2000–2007, Sub-Saharan Africa, a special focus of assistance, grew at a lower rate than East and South Asia, further widening the enormous gap. And even if it were in fact true that aid had achieved a little bit there is no systematic assessment of the cost of achieving this little bit.

And there is also the "absent presence," the issue that is never faced directly by the donor nations. This is the policy inconsistency in which whatever good an initiative might do, such as lowering trade barriers, might be more than offset by harmful actions elsewhere, a prime example being the subsidies to rich countries on the production of goods which could otherwise be made competitively in poor countries.

The key test of success is not whether an aid program makes "some difference" but whether the difference it makes approaches what would be required from the resources spent on it. The optimistic claims that aid has added a little more than 1 percentage point to the growth rates of the poorest economies do not, in fact, indicate success but failure. If savings of 10 percent or more of GNI has produced only 1 percentage point of growth then it would imply a very low rate of return to the investment in physical and human capital. On this basis aid inflows have, at best, been poor investments and, at worst, have created diseconomies that have led to negative rates of return to that investment.

There are, as has been stressed, many examples of small and some large successes, but small successes are not enough after so long. The probability is that in the end much of the assistance that has been provided, especially on the software side, has in aggregate been wasted. Anecdotes about appalling projects may be unrepresentative but they reflect a malaise that has been accepted as a norm by the donors, part of a structure of low expectations that cannot possibly be acceptable to the citizens of emerging economies who want to engage with the world. Such low expectations are inconsistent with the effort that is needed to bring the poorest nations on to a sustained and significant growth path that will end poverty.

Thus, the question whether aid has done "nothing" or "little" is really beside the point. Collier opines that, at a minimum, donors should abide by a quasi-Hippocratic oath: to do no harm.[111] But this conclusion is unacceptable even as a minimum if it means that resource expenditures need only earn a net return "above zero," regardless of cost. At the best aid's contribution is simply too insignificant to push growth rates to levels anywhere near the 5 percent or more real annual rate that is needed for the poorest countries to catch up with the rest of the world within the foreseeable future and is hardly a significant part of the economic development picture for the world's poor. It is more fruitful to look at broad developments in the world economy that might signal new possibilities. We turn to this later but first we look more deeply into why poor performance has occurred to see if this can help us to understand the importance of broader developments.

Chapter 4

WHY HAS DEVELOPMENT AID
DONE SO LITTLE?

It is a fallacy to think that overall poverty can be ended by a comprehensive package of "things" like malaria medicines and clean water. The complex poverty of low-income societies will slowly give way to prosperity the same way it happened in rich countries, through the gradual homegrown rise of political and economic freedom. [Democracy] cannot be imposed from the top by the IMF, World Bank, or U.S. Army…

William Easterly responding to Steve Radelet,
Council of Foreign Relations online debate, 1 December 2006[1]

The prime determinants of material progress are people's economic aptitudes, their social institutions and political arrangements.

Peter T. Bauer (1976)[2]

A recent study of 6,000 World Bank projects evaluated since the early 1980s found that: "even after accounting for a wide range of micro and macro variables, much of the variation in project performance remains unexplained."[3] The study was able to account for only about 12 percent of the variation in measured project outcomes, which largely reflected as-yet-unmeasured factors at both the country and project levels. The inability to successfully explain the variation in project outcomes is closely related to the inability to explain outcomes per se. This chapter considers the reasons for this inability.

Some aid commentators assert a phenomenon known as the "Samaritans dilemma"[4] and this may be a place to start looking for explanations. The Samaritans, that is "us the donors," have a psychic preference for "helping." So we feel better off when we help, no matter whether the recipient cooperates or does not. But once the recipient recognizes our Samaritan preference for helping regardless of response then it is motivated to reduce its own effort, thereby reducing the sustainability and impact of the assistance. Thus, according to this explanation the failure of aid has been due at least in part to some kind of game being played between well-intentioned and principled donors and calculating or feckless recipients. The recipients don't sustain the donors' projects because they think the donor will come to the project's rescue so they don't have to bother. Ergo the problem of aid ineffectiveness has something to do with moral hazard. The recipients might fail to act even in their own interests. But an alternative rather simple explanation is that often the recipients collectively do not want the help offered and are doubtful about the expertise or the good intentions of the aid donors, but they are divided amongst themselves about what to do about it and drawn into accepting the gifts reluctantly and by default. This is the "aid-recipient's dilemma" and the mutual misunderstanding involved is part of the story of the aid relationship.

Impact Evaluation: The Solution to Development Effectiveness?

In the last chapter, I mentioned the emergence of impact evaluation. To recapitulate, in about 2000 aid donors, wringing their hands at their inability to improve the success rate of foreign aid, revived the idea that expenditures of large amounts of public money should depend on evidence rather than on hunch, fashion or political influence. This was not exactly a path-breaking discovery but it was adopted with much fanfare by entities such as the World Bank's Development Impact Task Force, and the Evaluation Gap Working Group at the Center for Global Development, which urged a new approach and a new international body to oversee evaluations. Governments and agencies, it said, need to be encouraged to a) strengthen existing initiatives to conduct impact evaluations, b) build and share rigorous evidence, c) synthesize studies, d) build research capacity in developing countries, and e) link researchers, policymakers and project managers in an effective system for generating and using information.[5]

One might have been forgiven for wondering what another, large, development research program with close links to academia had to do with bringing a billion people out of poverty.[6] Nevertheless, a conference in Bellagio, Italy in 2006 agreed to create a new international agency with members from developing countries, bilateral and multilateral agencies, foundations, and NGOs, to finance impact evaluations and "build a strong body of evidence from which generalized conclusions can be drawn."[7] One result was the set-up of the International Initiative for Impact Evaluation (3ie).[8] 3ie has been funded to the tune of about US$30 million so far, for approximately 70 impact studies. The evaluation movement has since developed an impressive momentum. For example, in October 2010 the British government set up an Independent Commission for Aid Impact.

Despite the excitement surrounding the re-discovery of evidence, and its significant cost, the usefulness of sophisticated evaluations for assistance policy nevertheless remains seriously problematic.[9] There are several categories of problem. The first and most obvious and one that may rule out many of the results obtained, concerns their general applicability. Results obtained in one project and one place are not necessarily valid at wider scale; they are not necessarily reproducible either across the economy or between economies. We saw this in connection with the large number of education evaluations, which threw up many suggestive results but did not seem to be able to provide an overall sense of when and where assistance should be carried out.[10]

The second category of problem lies in methodology. In the case of randomized impact evaluations (RIEs), the validity of the results can be negated in many circumstances; for instance, a) if the chosen sample of assisted entities for assessment is causally related to the outcome then there may be an invalid relationship between the project and the outcome; b) if the assisted and non-assisted (control) samples are not randomly selected, or are self selected (e.g. if those included are the ones that showed more interest in the outcomes) or are endogenously selected (chosen because they seem more likely to benefit) then they may give incorrect results; c) if "spill over" occurs whereby members of the non-assisted (control) sample are affected by the intervention, or "contamination" occurs, whereby members of assisted and non-assisted samples receive assistance from elsewhere, then the outcome will be changed; or d) if "data mining" occurs, where results vary according to which data are selected such as the specific years in a time series, then the validity of the measured relationships is reduced. There is an understandable tendency to home in on data that produces results that support a hypothesis and thereby justify the time and cost of doing the research. Finally, there is the problem that impact studies are usually only looking at the impacts, not costs, of assistance programs.[11]

These are not obscure, hypothetical problems. In particular, problem c) is more likely to occur the longer the study takes and therefore longer-term studies which should in principle be more accurate may also be the most subject to bias. These various technical issues seriously affect the validity of results. Curiously, to a large extent spillover is often what development is about – as it refers to the transfer of skills and knowhow from assisted to non-assisted farms, enterprises, clinics and schools. So in order to avoid spillover, evaluators seemingly need to identify or construct artificial non-developmental scenarios for their research studies.

A third category of objection concerns the quality of the data collected. This may be a matter of the competence of collectors and memory of respondents and is often assumed away by researchers who consider it a rather boring and trivial problem of organization on the ground.[12] However, it is not trivial because the perennially poor motivations of those giving and receiving surveys (due to cultural reluctance to respond to personal questions, or desire to please, or simply to "survey fatigue") can distort much data in an unknown direction and render it meaningless.[13] And this can be a problem of the *aid relationship*, one of the main points of this book. Skepticism about the efficacy of assistance and antagonism towards repetitive surveys initiated by donors, which provide little or no benefit to the respondents, is a systemic issue of aid relations that frequently distorts or undermines responses.[14] Howard White addresses this issue with the admission that Ghanaian survey respondents were given as a reward the pencil used by the interviewer.[15] This pencil "seemed to make them happy" – thus presumably eager to participate in the next survey.

Pritchett writes that the successful provision of public services depends on a pattern of unique principal–agent relationships that make generalizations about success very difficult.[16] In some more complex areas like institution building, or democracy creation, qualitative evaluations may have to be undertaken, while only the more quantifiable cases (e.g. the effects of vaccination on children's health) are susceptible to RIEs. If the methods cannot be standardized and if there are inbuilt biases in some areas of evaluation, then the use of RIEs will not improve the allocation of aid, while with non-reproducibility it may not lead to conclusions about whether aid should be provided at all.

But the more that evaluation reaches into the groves of academia the more complicated and costly it becomes. Here indeed is an illustration of the intellectualization of development assistance. The World Bank seems to be part of the academic distraction. One Bank blog post states, ingenuously, "development economists are spending hundreds of thousands of dollars and many hours of their time designing, implementing, and analyzing the impact of various interventions. If all goes well, in many cases this leads to one really nice paper."[17] One such "nice new paper" was a meta-study reporting on randomized evaluations of 15 projects for business training, a simple intervention with clear aims. Despite the long experience with this assistance tool, the study concludes that "many of the key questions needed to justify large-scale policy interventions in this area remain unanswered."[18]

In the context of category three another World Bank blog reported that in one study members of a control group got annoyed at being "randomized out" and that this altered their responses to the surveys because they were not interested in talking to a survey team if they are not getting any of the assistance benefits.[19] The negative psychological effect offset the positive effect of receiving the benefit and invalidated the results of the study. However, it also turned out that if a non-assisted (control) individual lived in the same household as an assisted individual then the psychological disincentive was not so bad. This complicated response pattern suggested that there should be not one but two control groups – those who have heard of the program and those who have no idea about the program – and that a study should check whether there was some downward trend in the former, at additional cost and time.

On the other hand, some treatment groups responded favorably simply because the members were happy to have been selected. Thus, the program might be useless but the participants might get a confidence (and performance) boost just because they were picked. This effect would obviously bias upwards the results of an assistance input. This very same effect was discovered in the 1920s at the Hawthorne Works in a study well known to all beginning students of sociology.[20] One would expect research designers to be aware of the possibility that the research process could itself affect the behavior of the objects of the research. Some are, and there have thus ensued discussions about whether particular cases are really "Hawthorne" or some other type of effect.[21]

Another problem is the time required for accurate evaluation. An ongoing high profile assistance initiative known as the Millennium Villages Project (being conducted in Kenya, Ghana and Nigeria) has become a bone of contention between the planning enthusiasts and the impact evaluation hawks. The hawks dismissed a mid-way "before-and-after" report as likely to exaggerate the effects of the project because there was no counterfactual assessed.[22] They asserted that much more careful evaluation was needed and that it was better to wait and get the right answers rather than make hasty decisions. Many members of the evaluation industry indeed seem to regard a main objective of evaluations as being the provision of information about whether "pilots" should be "scaled up," and sufficient time is needed to find this out. Thus, after 50 years of development assistance, many argue that development assistance is still about experimentation, pilot projects and proofs of concept.

How far is proof of concept a justifiable reason to wait for the answers? Clearly it is disastrous to spend millions of dollars on projects that fail. But equally it is disastrous to cause several years of delay waiting for a clear answer (especially since it may not in the end be provided) as to whether a particular type of project for village development is satisfactory. This academically driven process does not seem to get even close to the type of momentum needed for bringing countries out of poverty. The proving exercise, sensible as it may seem in principle, will also very likely not lead to insights about fundamental causes nor lead to replicable projects in other locations and environments. There is indeed an absurdity in requiring development momentum to be calibrated to the timing of sophisticated and costly evaluations repeated to the satisfaction of outside researchers. It is questionable what relationship the laborious process of quasi-experimental evaluation bears to real-world processes of economic social and institutional development where a dialectical, trial-and-error procedure, democratic or not, flawed or not, leading to optimal interventions or not, has apparently been the norm since "Turnip" Townsend introduced crop rotation in eighteenth-century England!

More formally, the "unbalanced growth" concept of one of the classic thinkers, Albert Hirschman, might be enlisted to explain why the optimization instincts of the evaluation industry are unlikely to lead to the beautiful goal of ending poverty. Hirschman believed in a process of trial and error. Lack of balance would create pressures which would call forth "resources and abilities that are hidden, scattered or badly utilized" in a process of learning by doing that would otherwise not take place.[23] In other words, a dynamic process of error, learning and adaptation (by the government and people of the country) is critical to development. Just as impact evaluation cannot capture the systemic issues of the aid relationship, it is also unlikely to capture the effects of the broad societal learning process.[24]

The extensive evaluation effort ultimately responds to a demand from the donor community to satisfy its own political constituency's desire for evidence to justify its own expenditure, rather than the requirements of the recipient economy. Supporting this notion, Banerjee and Duflo regard the build-up of long-term associations between researchers and practitioners as beneficial in their own right, often apparently at the discretion of the researcher.[25] Yet there is also a reasonable question about how far it is justified for donor agencies to stage trials and pilot projects in other people's countries, including staging evaluations that set up treatment and control groups. On what developmental or ethical basis do donors unilaterally design research in other people's countries that is supposed to introduce behavior changes such as better teacher attendance in those countries?

While clearly there is a justification and a need for all governments and public sectors to evaluate their own expenditures, the process is usually through the equivalent of a general accounting office, public auditor or public accounts oversight entity answerable to the parliaments or executives of the affected country. It cannot be successfully executed through foreign research agendas nor by the demands and often quirky requirements of politicians in donor countries. Thus, the emergence of the evaluation industry as it is currently proceeding may be simply one more example of a process that is inconsistent with the building of useful domestic capacity and institutions in poor countries, even as it claims to assess capacity building projects.

Can the new evaluation process nevertheless provide, after all, a new insight into what goes wrong in development assistance and how aid strategy can be improved? Easterly provides some faint praise: "[T]he RE methodology has had a positive demonstration effect showing the scientific method can be applied with marginal interventions in an aid world that too often ignores any existing evidence (or any need to find such evidence)."[26] Nancy Birdsall of the CGD writes more forcefully that "the lack of emphasis on good evaluation has been immensely costly. In the absence of timely, credible and independent evaluation many aid dollars have been misdirected."[27] She cites the Structural Adjustment Loans and Credits (SALs) of the IMF and World Bank as an example of projects that could have been modified or killed if they had been properly evaluated. The CGD closely monitors the rate of establishment of new evaluation bureaucracies.[28] Duflo and Kremer are much more effusive: "Just as randomized trials revolutionized medicine in the twentieth century they have the possibility to revolutionize social policy in the twenty first."[29]

Regarding Nancy Birdsall's assertion, on what grounds would impact evaluation have killed the SALs? While RIE might have been able to find out whether a particular SAL worked or not it would not necessarily have been able to find out *why* it worked or did not work precisely because the causal explanations of success or failure in SALs as in other aid projects are often outside the explanatory confines of the project. Indeed, as mentioned in relation to education projects, the RIE impetus might end up simply delivering a laundry list of diverse actions that worked in diverse situations. The academic culture of the evaluation industry also encourages continuous and confusing challenges to research findings such as the positive effects of de-worming on school learning, which had been regarded as a sure thing and is now in question.

At best, project-level RIEs might tell us whether specific projects worked, and might be able to provide some generalizable lessons for other projects, but they cannot get to the bottom of exactly why they worked and so the generalized answers are unreliable. In the case of the SALs, their (partial) phase-out derived from a groundswell of political opposition which emerged probably before RIEs would have had a chance to produce conclusions.[30] From another perspective Andrew Natsios, former head of USAID, is also skeptical. He writes that the oversight function, or counter-bureaucracy, "has become infected with a very bad case of Obsessive Measurement Disorder (OMD), an intellectual dysfunction rooted in the notion that counting everything in government programs (or private industry and increasingly some foundations) will produce better policy choices and improved management."[31]

Howard White, head of 3ie, the impact evaluation center, seems to be sanguine about the possibilities of evaluation despite his award of pencils to interviewees. He writes that RIE studies "are well placed to address the question of which programs work or not. And, properly designed, they can be embedded in a broader evaluation design which also addresses questions of why an intervention works in a specific context or not, and at what cost."[32] This observation supports a relatively narrow view of what RIEs can achieve. However, in reality the RIE method has been elevated within development assistance discourse to the status not only of a superior assessment method but also a promising new aid strategy, shall we say, a "grassroots learning strategy" which could be contrasted with a "big-plan strategy" for development.[33]

The evaluation surge seems to be more an indicator of the weakening, and not the invigoration, of development assistance thinking after 50 years. The effort is turning in on itself and the latest initiative is to sort through past projects and approaches to identify ones that worked. No longer can a new grand direction for assistance be proposed, but rather the efforts of the donors are now directed at looking over their collective shoulder.

But let us leave aside now the thorny issues of the evaluation of evaluation and move on to look at why, in the end, evaluations of projects cannot explain the fundamental reasons why many projects fail, and search for a possible answer as to why the survey of 6,000 World Bank projects could not satisfactorily explain the differences in results of more than 12 percent of them.

Beyond Evaluation: The Aid Relationship and Its Origins

In the introduction, it was suggested that *quality is not necessarily the same thing as impact.* Rather in the end, the problems of foreign aid in the poorest countries are not to do with technical inadequacies or even poor project concept and design, but have to do with the "aid model," or the "aid relationship." This does not mean that aid is itself wholly responsible for the failure of an economy to grow because this would suggest a level of subordination, which only exists perhaps in some post-conflict countries (e.g. Somalia, Afghanistan or South Sudan). Therefore, it is not right to make an extreme claim as some have done, that aid is *the* problem setting back development.[34] Nevertheless, if it is likely that aid is making a negative contribution in some economies and a very weak contribution in others despite large resource inputs then this is prima facie a reason for accepting that it has had a deleterious role. What then is the background to the aid relationship?

One of the first places to look in trying to understand present relationships between rich and poor countries is their past relationships. This requires keeping in consideration the legacy of the social and cultural relations of the colonial era and their impact on factors such as incentives, motivation and accountability in the present day. Failures of aid might be explained by corrupted and distorted incentives resulting from the legacy of subordination in colonial times. The problems of the aid relationship might be thought of as depending on a) the extent of past social and cultural subordination, and b) the intensity of present aid dependence.

Looking at the major target of foreign aid, Sub-Saharan Africa, we find that several thinkers such as the anti-colonialist Samir Amin considered that the subcontinent was not on the whole more backward than the rest of the world in pre-colonial times and indeed had quite complex social formations, sometimes accompanied by the development of the state, customs, laws, conventions and ethics. Therefore, he thought the effects of colonialism had been to set these countries back.[35] In this context the historian Paul Bairoch cites evidence of relatively centralized societies in Africa with formal political systems and advanced legal institutions as long ago the fourteenth century in Mali. Major cities in the fifteenth century included Gao (population 60,000) and Kano (50,000). Benin with a population of 70,000 was a "well-ordered urban center with a system of water conduits and a sizable artisanry working at an advanced level."[36] Before the Portuguese conquest of Kilwa on the Tanganyika coast, its population had reached 30,000. The population of the ancient city of Zimbabwe had reached 40,000 by the end of the fifteenth century. Urbanization rates were higher than those of the Inca and Aztec empires, and of India and even Portugal.[37] Undeveloped societies were not the blank slates that the early colonizers imagined, a perception that affected the way the two sides were able to communicate from the beginning.

European colonization of Africa was formalized after Bismarck's Berlin Conference of 1884–85 left only Ethiopia and Liberia as independent nations. The effects of colonial occupation or "protection" on local economy and society varied according to the actions taken by the colonial rulers. For example, in some countries colonization took the form of active expropriation, taxation and forced labor, while in others the colonialist posture was more laissez faire.[38] Poll and hut taxes were used to raise revenue and to pressure the peasantry to work within a cash economy, often with adverse labor contracts. In the Belgian Congo, natives were required to gather rubber and in Uganda to maintain roads. Employment within the colonial administration, military or domestic service was often favored by the colonized population because it avoided the more punitive employment arrangements outside.[39] In any case, colonial rule involved the formal subordination of domestic society, culture and institutions to a more powerful external force; but it also conferred benefits through infrastructure, health and agricultural innovation (albeit to export commodities rather than produce food for the local population). Many current African leaders grew up under colonial rule or its immediate aftermath and absorbed these contradictory influences.

A number of studies looking at the effects of colonialism on African economies have found long-lasting effects on development through its effect on institutions.[40] The types of institutions that emerged under colonialism were influenced by the characteristics of the region being colonized. For example, the existence of cash crops and minerals affected the scale of agriculture and the extent to which laws affecting plantations and mining protected the elite while restricted the entry of the commercial strata. Forced mine labor has been associated with lower per capita income in the modern era. Institutions were also influenced by the inherited legal system (for example, common as opposed to civil law) as it affected investor rights.

Not all the institutions passed down by colonial rule were incompatible with national aspirations. The inheritance was complex. British colonial rule through local chiefs rather than from the center has been found to be associated with better modern-day institutions, allowing more local accountability and faster modernization.[41] Higher inequality during the colonial era has not been found to be necessarily associated with lower economic development in the more recent period, while larger colonial investments in areas like roads, health and education have had lasting positive effect. The use of local chiefdoms to implement projects (roads, agriculture, health, education, etc.) seems to have had a positive effect on the quality of governance post-colonization. Countries with stronger initial civil society or tribal infrastructure (e.g. Zulu, Swazi,

Sotho, Tswana) survived better, and that involved the existence of a recognized hierarchy of chiefdoms.

After independence some countries were able to take advantage to some degree of better pre-colonial institutions that had existed at the time the colonizers arrived. On the other hand, countries where there were fragmented tribes and relatively chaotic conditions continued to be chaotic. After independence in some cases the nationalist governments who had initially rejected the authority of the chiefs as tainted by colonial endorsement formed alliances with them in order to assist local development by mediating between powerful local groups. In sum, institutional development during colonial times has been partially maintained.

While the ultimate impact of the types of institutions that developed during the colonial era was ambiguous, in one dimension, geography, colonization seems to have been an unambiguously negative factor that impeded accountability and retarded development. The colonial power often interfered with landholding by awarding territory to one group even if another had already claimed the same land. It drew boundary lines that often split ethnic, religious or linguistic groups into different countries while it combined into single countries groups that did not want to be with each other. Where there were no major divisions some countries consisted of random collections of families, clans and villages. In all these cases allegiance to the nation was weakened or frustrated, and this reduced the ability of independent governments later to make collective decisions about public goods such as education and economic management.[42]

In Africa, after independence some weaker nations gained their legitimacy partly though the endorsement of international organizations such as the UN, IMF and World Bank, leaving them more vulnerable to international pressure. As Van der Veen put it, states sometimes consisted of little more than a few former independence agitators, the indigenous remnant of the colonial army and a foreign-aid budget. Nevertheless, the new rulers of African states who benefited from the system, workable or not, affirmed the decision of the Organization of African Unity in the 1960s to retain colonial boundaries even though they led to conflict.[43]

In a "natural" as opposed to an "artificial" (colonially formed) state there is more likely to be stronger collective national allegiance. The artificial state has a more localized group identification, such as the kin network or the local village or region. Where different ethnic groups are clustered together within an artificial state civil war has been more likely.[44] In some cases, third-country alien groups were permitted by colonial powers to settle, creating alternative sources of conflict, whether overt (as in the case of the Indians in Uganda) or covert (the Indians in Tanzania).

Ethnic fragmentation in artificial states created conditions for war and conflict after the departure of the colonial rulers. There was a larger civil war risk from fragmentation and also larger military expenditure overall due to the large number of sovereign states each wanting defense forces, relative to the total continental population. One study showed that civil war would decline if African unity was more pervasive.[45] The "optimal" size of a country was estimated at 13 times the average size of an African state.

Of course, geographical fragmentation did not apply only in Africa. There was the Sykes–Picot Agreement between Britain and France during World War I, whereby

Northern Palestine went to the French, Southern Palestine to the British, and Central Palestine including Jerusalem was ruled jointly. Then later the French swapped Palestine for control over Syria. Another key example involving a merger of disparate national groups was the lengthy and ultimately futile effort by the British to prevent the split of India and Pakistan at independence which left permanently disputed territory such as Kashmir within India. In Latin America, the Quechuas were split between Bolivia and Peru and combined with the Aymaras in Bolivia. At independence, the new South American states were controlled by European-origin elites who stuck to the colonial demarcations and were often little more than a collection of courts, customhouses and military units.[16] Latin American states still correspond closely to Spanish colonial divisions.

It also cannot be suggested that nations that did retain their "natural" independence were not prone to warfare, since the two most devastating wars in history were between nations that had not been recently colonized and were in fact trying to expand or protect their "natural" states. However, there is arguably a difference between nations going to war in their own perceived national interests (whether the interests of an elite or of the popular majority) and nations that fall into wars or corrosive internal ethnic conflicts because of unworkable political systems imposed on them by external powers.

Size of country is also important for quality of governance and the ability to decentralize. Economic reform has been more likely in larger countries; infrastructure has major scale economies, while individualized and duplicated national infrastructures such as airports and airlines, ports and power utilities create excess capacity and increase costs. Large cities in large countries can also reap scale economies, which apparently exceed the costs of congestion.

A key research finding has been that although colonial geographical fragmentation occurred in colonies across the world it was much worse in Africa than elsewhere.[17] Fourteen out of the 15 most ethnically heterogeneous countries in the world are in Africa; on the other hand 8 high-income countries are among the most ethnically homogeneous and none of the top-15 most ethnically diverse countries are in the high income group. Ethnic diversity is associated not only with conflict but relatively low schooling, political instability, underdeveloped financial systems, high government deficits and insufficient infrastructure. Forty percent of African countries are also landlocked, far more than the next highest, Europe and Central Asia (23 percent) and the numerous land borders impede trade.

Collier et al point out that polarized societies are more prone to competitive rent seeking and less likely to achieve consensus on the production of public goods like infrastructure, education, and good policies.[18] Lack of cooperation between ethnic groups can postpone needed economic policy changes because the first group to accept the changes may bear a disproportionate share of the cost. Ethnic diversity alone accounts for about 28 percent of the growth differential between the countries of Africa and East Asia.

Ethnically diverse societies are also more likely to be corrupt because each ethnic group that is allocated a role in the power structure is likely to look after its own interests rather than those of the nation. Two ethnic groups may gain from espousing conflicting economic policies. After President Moi took over in Kenya in 1978, the road investment share of the Kenyatta coalition home regions fell significantly while the share of the Moi coalition home regions rose significantly. Similar fights over the "common pool" of resources occurred in Ghana where the price of cocoa was used as a weapon against the Ashanti, resulting in a steady decline in production. The use of cocoa as an economic weapon was a classic example of "killing the goose that laid the golden egg."[49]

There is a relationship between country size, openness and growth. Larger economies are more likely to be able to finance their imports through mineral exports, whereas in a small, landlocked economy there are barriers to trade, a tendency for monopolistic structures and a more risky environment for new investors. It has been suggested that the African Union would do better if it was founded on infrastructure building agreements rather than trade agreements.[50]

Aid Dependence

If the distorted relationships enshrined in the colonial system were a deterrent to modernization, then the level of reliance on outside donor aid after independence might be expected to reflect those same distorted relationships and therefore be indirectly a deterrent to modernization for many former colonies.

Aid dependence needs firstly to be defined. There tends to be confusion between aid dependence and aid effectiveness. If aid is effective then dependence might in fact be a good idea, at least in the short to medium term, especially if that aid stimulates higher than average growth.[51] However, if aid is ineffective, reliance on it is counterproductive. But if it is ineffective then also by definition a country is not in fact dependent on it. Where dependency becomes problematic is when aid is ineffective but simultaneously creates conditions that lead to its perpetuation, so that countries that do not "need" it in fact continue to accept it. These conditions may be economic (inadequate savings), institutional (weak governance capacity) or social (dominance by outside cultures). Nevertheless, despite the problems of defining dependence, publications by the World Bank and the DAC continue to measure aid dependence in terms of the size of flows. They use measures such as ODA/GNI, ODA/exports, ODA/public expenditure and ODA/investment. For simplicity we will also stick to these definitions.

Although ODA remains a tiny fraction of the GNI's of the donor countries (0.32 percent in 2009 even after the increase towards the end of the first decade of the 2000s), it is often a large fraction of the GNI's of individual poor countries. Almost 400 million people live in countries where foreign assistance has comprised 10 percent or more of their gross national income since 2000.[52] A total of 29 countries in 2000 received more than 10 percent of their GNI in aid, falling and then rising again to 22 in 2009.[53] Nine of these countries are in Sub-Saharan Africa. They are Liberia, Rwanda, Guinea Bissau, Sierra Leone, Congo, Zambia, Malawi, Mozambique and Burundi and they have received aid worth over 20 percent of their GNI in some year during this period. Several additional countries such as Togo, Tanzania, Uganda and

Zimbabwe have received over 10 percent on a long-term basis. Many others, such as Ghana, Madagascar, Zambia, Guinea and Senegal are receiving up to or as much as 10 percent of GNI in aid.

Several countries outside Africa have experienced high aid dependence. The most extreme example has been to certain non-viable Pacific islands such as US aid to Micronesia (the Marshall, Gilbert and Mariana Islands, and Nauru). Very large amounts of aid have poured in on the basis of the islands' status as US-administered territories with little impact on economic activity beyond expanding the government and retail outlets selling goods to government officials, while viable fisheries and tourism interests were taken by Japanese investors. More typical dependency cases are Timor Leste, Tajikistan, Cambodia, Kyrgyzstan, Kosovo, Laos, Mongolia and Nicaragua who have experienced an aid share to GNI of more than 10 percent at some time during the past 10 years.

In Sub-Saharan Africa over time the share of external assistance to GDP has increased steadily. For 34 Sub-Saharan African countries the average ODA/GDP increased from 3 percent in the 1960s to 7.5 percent in the 1970s, 11.2 percent in the 1980s and 15.3 percent in the 1990s.[54] However, while ODA/GDP rose steadily in Africa it remained about stable overall in other developing countries. In the case of Latin America and East Asia over this period, the ratio was negligible (1–2 percent) and falling. Even in the Pacific Islands as a whole it was higher than in the African countries only during the 1970s and has since fallen. South Asia peaked in the 1980s at 8.5 percent and fell to 6.5 percent in the 1990s. In Latin America, the decline of aid was fuelled not only by rising incomes but by opposition to IMF programs and the payoff of obligations by Argentina, Brazil, Bolivia and others. India has introduced policies limiting aid from all except the largest donor programs.[55] Thus, ODA/GNI has continued to rise only in Sub-Saharan Africa. No other region has experienced this and only a few countries outside Africa. Thus, despite extreme cases like the Marshall Islands, the aid dependency problem is largely an African problem.

How large are the dependency ratios in the high, but not extreme, cases? If aid is overvalued then it does not in fact comprise such large shares of the recipient economy as first appears. This clearly applies to that proportion (around 8 percent) of aid flows that are nothing other than the donors' expenditure on their own administrations. Even so, the levels of dependence are very large and in the largest cases they must have major repercussions not only for the economy but also for the society and institutions of these countries. To get things in perspective a 15 percent share of GNI is about the same as the contribution of the entire industrial sector in many African countries.[56] If the flows from NGOs and charitable organizations are included, this adds significantly to the amount of free money and resources flowing into the poorest countries and a sizeable number must be receiving 15 percent of their economies in donations and charity.

Even Tanzania and Uganda, rich in minerals and agricultural resources, who achieved independence 50 years ago, are still receiving about 12 percent of their GNI in official donations (and counting donations from NGOs this could well rise to 15 percent). Ghana, the first African colony to gain independence from Britain in 1957 at a time of hope for the future, has up to now still been receiving over 8 percent in official donations plus more in NGO aid, despite the fact that it has a relatively skilled population and exports its doctors to Britain. Malawi, my first country, independent nearly half a century ago, has, as mentioned, received on average more than 20 percent of its GNI in official donations for many years but its per capita GNI is still ranked 204th in the world.[57] Recently, Malawi has received an average of about US$800 million a year in ODA, plus a further significant amount in NGO contributions.

Mozambique has been held up as an aid model, having grown steadily since the end of its internal wars, reaching 8 percent growth per annum between 2000 and 2009.[58] Despite its high potential for developing a robust tourism industry and some mineral wealth, it has received heavy injections of aid, with ODA/GNI of over 20 percent of GNI, far higher than the average for Sub-Saharan Africa. Mozambique's growth rate has been regarded by some as a vindication of the aid volume but the additional annual growth it has achieved compared to the average Sub-Saharan African growth rate 2000–2009 has in fact been very low in relation to the amount aid it has received above the average.

A country's economic dependence on aid is not a matter only of its proportion of the national income but also as a proportion of its national budget since the budget is the source of most public goods investment – including infrastructure, education and health. Any country that receives over 20 percent of its GNI in aid probably does not need to raise significant revenue through its budget. Any country that receives over 10 percent is likely to have as much as 50 percent of its budgetary expenditure covered by foreign aid. If a government's budget is 50 percent or more funded by donations, there are major repercussions on its need for and capacity to raise revenue, its decision making and its accountability to its people. These are excessive levels of assistance when maintained continuously for decades and are likely to have complex disincentive effects on local capacity.

In my first country, where aid has been running at nearly a quarter of GDP, ODA and non-official grants have been approximately equal to total government expenditure and have exceeded the value of gross capital formation for most years since 2000. Many other poorer countries in Africa have been recipients of aid inflows valued at more than 50 percent of their central government budget, as have a few countries outside Africa such as El Salvador, Tajikistan, Kyrgyzstan and Nicaragua, though not on a sustained basis.[59] In Uganda, Andrew Mwenda, a notable African critic of aid, wrote in 2006 that if 50 percent of the national budget is funded by foreign donations then the government's behavior changes: it can avoid accountability to its citizens, delay reforms, incur additional debt, expand the military, promote corruption and fund an oversize government (such as 68 cabinet ministers in Uganda). "To promote democracy the West should discontinue future aid flows."[60]

Some writers have suggested that aid dependence only creates harm after it passes a point of diminishing returns. Collier put this point at more than 16 percent of GDP, implying that dependence is not at a harmful level in most poor countries.[61] Others have proposed an "aid Laffer curve" where diminishing returns have been estimated to start (somewhat unhelpfully) within a range from as low as 10 percent to as high as

50 percent of GNI.[62] An aid Laffer curve could exist if aid reduces the average return on investment and the rate of growth, in which case the economy would improve its performance if aid was reduced.

Beyond the numbers on dependence there is a wider story about social/systemic effects, and it is these systemic effects that may provide the clues to how aid perpetuates itself. One explanation is that the increase in aid beyond the point of diminishing returns may be diverted into subsidies to consumption and government services, but a reduction in aid may not lead to a corresponding decline in consumption. So there is a "ratchet effect," whereby once consumption increases it tends to stay at higher than previous levels even when aid falls, due to changed expectations. This then lowers the long run savings rate and increases reliance on external resources, and is one of the causes of a "dependency culture."

A second explanation is in aid's potential for changing the structure of an economy through changing relative prices. This type of effect is the result of a large inflow of resources relative to the size of an economy, otherwise known as the "resource curse." The typical resource curse works like this: firstly, a large inflow of resources within a booming sector (for example oil or copper) causes the exchange rate to appreciate; secondly, the booming sector draws capital and labor away from other sectors such as manufacturing and agriculture, decreasing their efficiency; thirdly, the combination of the appreciated exchange rate and the high wages in the boom sector increases costs and export prices, reducing export potential. Rajan and Subramanian, two of the principal authors in the aid/growth debate who find no link between aid and growth suggest that aid acts like a major resource inflow.[63] If the growth of exports is thus reduced by aid, this counteracts the very economic policies that poorer countries are advised by donors to adopt.

Aid dependency may therefore perpetuate itself by reducing the economy's ability to export. Various writers have found that the employment-generating, labor-intensive sectors that are critical to development in poorer countries grow more slowly in countries that receive more aid, and that the performance of economies dependent on mineral exports such as oil has been worse than that of resource-poor countries.[64]

Explanation number three is that if one lucrative source of government income, such as aid, is dominant then this dominance can also undermine the incentives to build public financial management and can damage the process of dialogue between the government and the citizens of the country. This is because the government has less need to convince the citizenry that its expenditures are worthwhile. Large resource flows including aid lessen the need to raise revenue from the population or to exercise oversight over the allocation of resources, thus potentially fuelling corruption. Such governments have tended to be less democratic and care less about maintaining legitimacy.[65] This seems to have occurred in Nigeria as a result of oil revenue dominance and the same has been found for aid flows in Tanzania.[66] Very large flows of aid could be undermining the economic growth of Malawi for the same reason. Botswana, on the other hand, is one country that seems to have avoided the problem despite its enormous diamond revenues.

A study looking at 100 countries over 40 years found that at higher levels of foreign-aid dependence (per GDP) democratic institutions become weaker.[67] It found that if a country received the average amount of aid in relation to GDP over the entire period, its democratic score would fall from an average level in the initial year to one associated with a total absence of democratic institutions. Thus, the resource curse could potentially affect social, cultural and institutional development just as it affects the economy.

The same tendencies affect non-government organizations. Some local NGOs are established in the expectation of receiving development aid and only exist for that reason. Indigenous NGOs in low-income countries find themselves in an environment that is propitious for abuses. Their governance structures rarely provide for mechanisms of accountability for their managers, since as recipients of foreign cash they often do not have dues-paying members, an autonomous board of directors or an effective state agency to monitor them.

How do poor countries withdraw from, or avoid, such dependent situations? The example of the US Marshall Plan is often cited as a model. This is because the aid flows were temporary and self-liquidating, largely completed by the early 1950s.[68] Why therefore would a "responsible" government not follow this model? Superficially this might seem plausible, but the Marshall Plan is in fact not a good model for poorer developing countries, and particularly because the fundamental political relationship was completely different. Firstly, Marshall Plan aid was much smaller relative to the economies receiving it (between 2 and 3 percent of recipient GNP) than the flows received by low-income developing countries in the present day, and therefore less intrusive within economy and society. Secondly, even war-devastated European countries started with much better resources (skilled labor, managers and entrepreneurs) and institutions (financial and judicial systems and public administrations) to absorb outside assistance. Finally, the recipients had to deal only with a single donor, in contrast to the dozens of bilateral and multilateral agencies and hundreds of NGOs in the field today, so Marshall Plan aid was not disbursed in the form of hundreds of separate donor-managed parcels in each recipient nation.[69] In Taiwan and Korea relatively effective assistance might also have been partly attributable to the presence of a single or dominant donor.[70]

Aid Dependence and Local Ownership

The "foreign-aid resource curse" may weaken public accountability and the kind of collective reform action that is needed to promote development. The conception of dependence as "perpetuation of high aid inflows despite their ineffectiveness" implies an ongoing condition of weak governance and accountability. A lot of the discussion of these issues has been part of the sociological and anthropological discourse over the past 20 years. Social scientists concerned with development have long tried to explain why projects that are to be conducted within local communities have to be "owned" by local communities in order to empower them, or else the project is unlikely to succeed. I have already alluded to this in discussing rationality and participation. Empowerment of recipient communities, nations or governments requires clear incentives for local participation. However, the incentive systems that operate in large aid institutions such as reward for securing project approvals are antithetical to the slow, painstaking and uncertain path required to create genuine participation and genuine empowerment in the real world.

As we saw earlier the idea of local participation and buy-in was only taken up in a formal way in the World Bank from the early 1990s, culminating in the PRSPs. But the PSRPs still answered to assistance deadlines rather than the pace of change in local communities or civil society, and so to push the participatory process forward civil society participants tended to get selected by the donors.[71] As Van de Walle puts it,

> It is far from clear that government officials are more likely to feel committed to programs and policies that donors are pressing them to adopt because external agents have empowered a coalition of local actors to participate in decision-making processes. On the other hand, governments that are committed to a course of action they have negotiated with the donors are unlikely to look with favor on participatory processes that slow down or undermine policy implementation.[72]

Post-conflict situations are often thought to be ones where the role of outside donors is clear-cut because of the urgent need for outside help in reconstruction. In countries such as Somalia, the lack of infrastructure, failure of laws and regulations, and disruption of government may be such that rehabilitation requires outside intervention and control during a recovery period. But the value of outside assistance has not always been clear even in these situations. In post-conflict Bosnia, for example, the Office of the High Representative overseeing the Dayton peace accords intervened in the political process and as a result, it has been claimed, weakened the development of post-conflict institutions.[73] Intervention included encouragement to non-nationalist parties, appointing top officials of the central bank, human rights chamber and constitutional court, and decreeing constitutional changes. One of its methods was a so-called "Bulldozer Committee" which was established to force through changes in laws and regulations, sometimes creating other unintended problems. The NGO sector still remained weak after 7 years partly because the aid agencies hired away citizens who might otherwise have been active in civil society organizations.

The donors in Bosnia were accused of inconsistent aid policies, uncoordinated funding, lack of quality control or accountability, and misuse of local NGOs. "NGOs lack credibility, directing their attention more to international donors, power has been dispersed, decision making made more complex, while ethnicity has been "over-institutionalized.'"[74] As a middle-income country with a relatively highly educated population Bosnians were quicker to react to and felt less obligated to tolerate counterproductive outside assistance.

A blog reported on the sociological effects of aid dependence in Bangladesh. Even though aid constitutes a small part of the economy, dependence had built up its own class of beneficiaries who prospered from aid and had acquired a vested interest in its continuity. Aid dependence thus generated its own dynamics, which influenced the political behavior of successive regimes and the workings of the administrative as well as the business community. The process "impacted on the political economy of Bangladesh where new social forces were financially and politically empowered whilst large numbers of people, from de-subsidized poor farmers to disemployed factory workers, became its victims."[75]

Finally, as is implied in the Bosnia example, it is not the case that the aid relationship creates difficulties only in the poorest countries, only that in richer countries it is not pervasive. An account of assistance by the US to Poland stated this:

> The major way that Western donors assisted the former communist countries in their "transition" to a market economy was through "technical assistance" in the form of consultants sent to the region. Although the consultants were initially welcomed by their hosts, within a short time after their arrival, the Poles had coined a derisive term for them – the "Marriott Brigade," after their penchant for staying in Warsaw's Marriott and other luxury hotels. Whether in Poland, or farther south or east, within a matter of a year or so of its arrival, the Marriott Brigade had alienated many of the people it was trying to help.[76]

Aid Fragmentation

As mentioned, one of the reasons why the Marshall Plan is not a relevant model for poor countries is because present-day aid recipients are not transacting business with just one donor. Dependence on external aid is indeed made more damaging because of the disarray on the side of the donors. In particular there is the problem of fragmentation of assistance between multiple countries and agencies, which was discussed briefly in Chapter 2. While aid observers may differ about the existence or interpretation of aid dependence, there is unanimity on the problem of fragmentation, and the urgency of "harmonizing" programs, reiterated at every international donor conference since Monterrey in 2002, enshrined in declarations of intent at Rome, Paris, Accra and Busan. In 50 years of aid, no major aid agency has been closed or merged. Agencies considered to be outmoded or ineffective have been allowed to continue or grow in parallel with new ones. The fragmentation problem has increased relentlessly despite the many declarations of intent to stop it.[77]

This problem has been documented throughout the whole aid era. As long ago as 1962, the DAC Chairman's Report called for better coordination of aid programs.[78] In 1966, the DAC issued specific guidelines for the coordination of technical assistance. In 1983, the DAC focused the attention on the need to improve coordination at the country level and by 1984, a general agreement was reached to expand consultative groups to coordinate aid. The 1985 DAC Review of 25 years of ODA concluded that donor competition for attractive projects remained a problem due to "both administrative constraints and donor inhibitions resulting from political or commercial considerations." By 1986, the DAC High Level Meeting recognized that the "responsibility for aid co-ordination lies with each recipient government." Aid fragmentation is a well-recognized problem but the donors have a systemic inability to address it, which goes back to the fundamental motivations for giving aid that we discussed in Chapter 2.[79] According to the World Bank, between 1997 and 2004 there was a relentless upward trend in numbers of projects (from 25,000 to 60,000) and a downward trend in their average size (from US$2.5 million to US$1.5 million) as fragmentation increased.

The estimates of donor and project proliferation are confused by seemingly differing definitions of agencies and projects, and differing methods of counting them, but in any case they are impressively high and increasing. The World Bank stated that the number of bilateral donor nations grew from 5 in the mid-1940s to at least 56 today.[80] Knack et al. cite a finding that the median number of official donors in recipient countries in 2000 was 23.[81] There were 61 separate donors in Lesotho in 1981 financing 321 projects, in a country of only about 1.4 million people. In 2002, there were 25 official bilateral donors, 19 official multilateral donors, and about 350 international NGOS conducting 8,000 development projects in Vietnam – where aid's share of GDP is actually lower than in most of Africa.

One estimate is of over 90,000 active projects in 2008 directed at 3,400 recipients.[82] A Brookings Institution Study estimates 80,000 projects financed by at least 42 donor countries, through 197 bilateral agencies and 263 multilateral agencies.[83] The study found that if half of the smallest donor programs were terminated only 5 percent of country program aid would be affected.

Anecdotes about lack of coordination and duplication are commonplace. Several donor agencies might fly in to town to work on a project without any awareness of each other's program or presence and the duplication of school desks, hospital beds or training of civil servants. The OECD has estimated the efficiency losses associated with an average of 263 missions annually to aid-recipient countries at US$5 billion a year.[84] Governments deal with multiple demands by donors for access to high-level officials to discuss particular programs requiring particular policies and procedures. The situation is such that the governments of Mozambique, Kenya, Tanzania and Ghana, have declared a mission-free period every year so that civil servants can get on with their work.[85]

In 2006, according to the World Bank, more than 100 major organizations were involved in the health sector alone, leading to confused roles, piecemeal approaches and lack of sustainability.[86] In the 1990s, Mozambique had 400 health projects. Tanzania had over 2,000 donor projects in total. Ghana had 60 ministries and agencies receiving aid and 400 donor missions a year.[87] Each year Tanzania files 2,400 reports to aid donors and hosts 1,000 aid missions from donor countries. In 2006, half of the aid effort to Tanzania (through more than 700 projects managed by 56 parallel implementation units) was not coordinated with the government nor between the donors. Tanzania received 541 donor missions during 2005 of which only 17 percent involved more than one donor.[88]

Different donors usually insist on using their own unique processes for initiating, implementing, paying for, monitoring and reporting on projects. Recipients can be overwhelmed by requirements for audits, environmental assessments, procurement reports, financial statements, project updates and "mission reports," often requiring substantive commitments by governments as a condition for continuation. A retiring

World Bank executive director, otherwise a strong supporter of the institution and of aid in general, commented:

> it has been painful to watch the administrative burden placed on countries when dealing with all of us who want to help them in their quest to develop their economies … we simply do not understand the magnitude of the difficulties we bring to the table with costly reporting standards, numerous and large mission visits, and duplication of effort across the board that can diminish the good we are trying to accomplish.[89]

Each year tens of thousands of government officials also spend much time traveling the world from meeting to meeting, conference to conference and workshop to workshop, picking up expenses and shopping in foreign cities while they remain themselves skeptical of the value of each trip but unable to turn their back on the prestige value of foreign travel and the chance of additional cash that can be passed on to their extended families.

One study showed that donor fragmentation got steadily worse over the period 1975 to about 1990. There was then a brief improvement associated with the reduction in aid following the ending of the Cold War, and then a relapse. Since about 1993, proliferation has resumed its steady increase.[90] Easterly and Williamson find that the aid effort was splintered across agencies, countries and sectors for each single agency, many of which accounting for a tiny fraction of total net ODA. The ten biggest donors – the United States, Japan, IDA, EC, France, United Kingdom, Germany, Netherlands, Sweden and Canada – account for the large majority of the ODA and the 20 smallest agencies account for only 6.5 percent. They conclude, "Despite all the rhetoric about reducing fragmentation and improving coordination, there is no sign whatsoever in the data about any reversal of these counterproductive practices."[91]

The situation is made worse when there are multiple agencies operating out of a single-donor country. The US foreign assistance system is characterized by a proliferation of distinct structures. According to Unger, "with a swarm of objectives, shifting priorities and incessant organizational turf battles undermining productivity and unity of voice, the overall aid system has suffered from a self-perpetuating downward spiral even as bright spots have emerged."[92] One estimate is that the United States actually has more than 50 different offices giving foreign assistance, with overlapping responsibilities for an equally high number of objectives.[93] Easterly calculates that overall the probability of two randomly selected dollars in the international aid effort coming from the same donor to the same country for the same sector is less than 0.05 percent.[94]

In addition to the proliferation of aid agencies there are as we saw in Chapter 2, a very large number of non-government agencies operating in the aid field. There are hundreds of thousands of registered NGOs receiving funding in the donor and recipient countries. These range from large-scale organizations such as CARE with 12,000 employees to a vast number of micro-organizations. What is more, the numbers have increased exponentially during the same period that the donor community has been attempting to develop a common policy to deal with the proliferation problem. The estimates of the number of NGOs and private voluntary organizations based in rich countries operating in the development field range widely. The current UIA yearbook lists 64,000 civil society organizations worldwide while another study estimated that the number of active foundations in the US alone was 76,000, and the web-based Directory of Development Organizations publishes a list of 70,000 development organizations.[95]

The kind of confusion that can be caused by fragmentation was detailed in a background paper for the IDA15 Replenishment in 2007, which examined a health program in Rwanda. The program faced firstly problems of "policy incoherence" and fiscal disarray because only one-quarter of aid for health was channeled through the central or local government. while three-quarters went to NGOs or was directly managed by the donors through their own projects. Secondly, the mix of assistance was inconsistent with the governments own health strategy. US$46 million was earmarked for HIV/AIDS, US$18 million for malaria and only US$1million for general childhood preventive care, whereas the HIV/AIDS prevalence rate was relatively low (3 percent) and infant mortality was still high (118 per 1,000). Thirdly, assistance has been volatile, based on annual aid commitments, which has prevented long-term planning for the training of doctors and nurses, and anti-retroviral treatments.

One of the more important recent escalations of fragmentation has been the launching of the specialized global funds, many of which have been put under the management of the World Bank on the grounds that it was best equipped to manage. As mentioned in Chapter 2, these funds cut across more than one region and the partners contribute funds to a common pool. Very large funds include the Global Fund to Fight AIDS, Tuberculosis and Malaria (GFATM), which has committed US$18 billion, and the Global Alliance for Vaccines and Immunisation (GAVI), which has committed US$4 billion. In addition, there is the Catalytic Fund of the Education for All Fast-Track Initiative. PEPFAR of the US is a bilateral pooled fund that combats HIV/AIDS. These funds were expected to harmonize sectoral assistance, but in practice they have aggravated fragmentation by introducing a new dimension of "vertical funding,"[96] while crowding out more general assistance to health. PEPFAR funding in Mozambique, for example, has been greater than the entire Mozambique health budget and, like Rwanda, has diverted funds from basic needs to train health workers to buy medicines and bed nets. While PEPFAR has been key to suppressing HIV/AIDS with new laboratories and doctors this has often been at the expense of the next-door health center, which runs short of staff and medicines.

Another way that the fragmentation problem was supposed to be addressed was through the multi-donor coordination initiatives such as the PRSPs. We have already noted in Chapter 3 some of the PRSP's problems. There has been little or no evidence of changes in how donors conduct business.[97] One of the Ghana health sector PRSPs in 2002, touted as a highly successful sector program, only included a third of the donor resources going to the health sector such that PRSPs were turning into yet another parallel structure. Donors have also attempted to coordinate aid through pooling funds into budget support and sector programs (SWAps).[98] Not only has harmonization through pooling failed but the pooling comes up hard against the countervailing pressure for increased performance based funding, which is more difficult when funds are in large pools rather than tied to specific deliverables through projects.

The British aid agency DFID in March 2011 issued its Multilateral Aid Review in which it pronounced on the capabilities of 40 multilateral agencies.[99] It scored 9 agencies as very good, 13 as good, 9 as adequate and 9 as poor. In the top category was a mixture of agencies that included some global funds, the Red Cross and one UN agency. At the bottom were mainly UN agencies. The review found that

> the system is complex and fragmented, with overlapping mandates and co-ordination problems. … Too many organisations lack a clear strategic direction. … There is still much room for improvement for the multilaterals as a group on transparency and accountability. And poor partnership working between multilateral organizations is undermining the effectiveness of the system.

DFID minister Andrew Mitchell writes in the preface,

> I was extremely concerned that a small group of organisations have been assessed as having serious weaknesses. I will be taking a very tough approach to these organisations. We will not tolerate waste, inefficiency or a failure to focus on poverty reduction.[100]

The intractable problems of foreign aid such as dependence, fragmentation, broken accountability chains and other structural deficiencies are thus blamed on the nine luckless agencies that have incurred the displeasure of DFID when indeed the problem is system-wide and has no practical, piecemeal cure in terms of singling out culprits.

Principals, Agents and Accountability

Allied to the problem of fragmentation is the complex chain of decision making that characterizes development assistance, referred to in Chapter 2. The concept of principals (who are responsible for overseeing actions) and agents (who are responsible for carrying out actions) can be used to explain the complexities of the chain.[101] Principal–agent relationships work well when objectives are aligned but can become dysfunctional if the agents face inappropriate incentives and alignment breaks down.

In complex chains without close monitoring and constant adaptation problems emerge. For example, there is a tendency towards domination either by the agents (the managers) who may become self-policing (for example, through monopolizing information) or by the principals who become micro-managers (for example, through imposing excessively demanding standards), in both cases resulting in likely breakdown of effectiveness. The larger the number of principals and agents and the longer is the chain of decisions the more likely it is that alignments will be distorted, accountability will break down and effectiveness will be lost.[102] This is the more so if the chain extends across borders. Links are broken, leading to incomplete contracts and unobservable outputs, which result in misunderstanding of requirements, poor design, mis-targeting and misappropriation.[103] Mirroring the broken international link, domestic accountability is lost because expenditure decisions (good or bad) are made outside the domestic governmental process. Thus, (poor) decisions made externally crowd out decisions made locally. Bad strategy developed outside intrudes upon and degrades strategy developed inside.[104]

The cross-border assistance chain results in breaks in accountability worse than would occur within domestic public expenditure programs where the funders (taxpayers), executors and beneficiaries reside in the same country and negotiate with each other through a national legislative and executive authority. Even with delays, badly managed or ineffective federal programs in the US do face an accounting by the federal government, as they do in all other democratic systems. But the most stringent oversight of an aid agency cannot usually penetrate the complications of delivering projects to multiple recipients in foreign countries, and attempts to apply controls often aggravate the problems they are trying to fix, as may be discerned from the bureaucratization of the World Bank under relentless oversight pressure from the US Congress.

Even though it is a single large agent and thereby helps to reduce aid fragmentation complexity of the overall system, the World Bank itself turns out to be a microcosm of the principal and agent problem. Its governance, broadly defined, includes several categories of principals – country shareholders, debt holders, outside interest groups and some larger clients who are also de facto principals. The problem of multiple stakeholders and multiple clients is exacerbated by lack of consensus on the appropriate development product in many areas as we saw in Chapter 2. Governance is also fractured between the board of directors and the board of governors, the latter of which has delegated most of its powers back to the directors, while the top management can circumvent both and consult directly with shareholders representatives such as the US treasury.[105]

The principal–agent complexity of the World Bank's governance is aggravated by the imbalance of voting power, also known as the "voice" issue. After 7 years of opaque discussion of this issue by the OECD Governments, the voting representation of the non-OECD countries on the IBRD board was increased in 2010 by a total of just 3 percent. The complications and the snail's pace of reform led one director to lament:

> it really doesn't matter if you are a Pavarotti if you have to sing in Madison Square Garden during a Nick's match … because you will not be heard anyhow. … Our board's acoustics are so bad that … in reality, no one has a voice.[106]

Even after reform the European nations hold nearly 30 percent of votes while China and India together, which account for one-third of the world's population, hold 6 percent, and both these countries are now donors. The US retains its 16 percent share allowing it a veto over constitutional changes.[107] The large poorer nations, frustrated as voters, can instead exercise some power as borrowers. The borrower group is itself divisible into power groups with the ten or so largest borrowers (who account for about 60 percent of the Bank's loans) such as India or China having considerable influence on institutional policies.

Within this indeterminate system, the agent (i.e. Bank management) has established control and has become largely self-policing, regardless of the fact that the board

Figure 4.1. The World Bank: Principals and agents

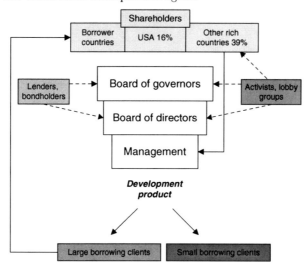

directors have offices in the same building and meet very frequently, twice a week. Management controls the agenda, is able to select the information it provides to the shareholders and other principals, and manages their continuous demands for more transparency. The internal accountability problems of this one agency clearly indicate how the whole system could be at risk. Reinikka sums up some of the ingredients of the agency problem as follows:[108]

1. Distance and ex-country location means a break in accountability. Recipients cannot get proper feedback to the donors and donor cannot evaluate success on the ground.
2. Donors affect the relationship between provider organizations and policy makers through interfering with spending patterns and budgetary process.
3. Donors use inconsistent approaches to government, providers and beneficiaries
4. Project-management units and parallel budgets undermine budgetary coherence and capacity.
5. Project-level objectives and expenditure breakdowns between donors are inconsistent.

Donors complicate the principal–agent structure by setting up their own project-management units because they are under pressure to deliver and need to circumvent processes that are likely to delay their efforts. With 30 or so agencies and many more NGOs running large numbers of individual projects in one country, this can result in special implementation offices running into the hundreds. These offices do two bad things. They circumvent government or agency capacity (even if they are supposed to be strengthening it) and they hire away some of the best talent often from the very agencies they are trying to help, creating a perverse incentive for local officials. Highly paid staff hired away by the agencies are also motivated to continue with projects regardless of success and to hide poor results.

Despite their relative good rating overall, the vertical funds GAVI and GFATM are criticized for using parallel implementation agencies. For their part, governments allow alien organizational units to be set up because of their own short-time horizons and the political pressures they face.[109]

This misallocation of capacity occurs despite the 2005 Paris Declaration on using a country's own implementation systems, provided that in the donors' opinion they were adequate for the task. (To those that were not considered adequate, the donors offered more assistance.) At the follow-up 2008 Accra High Level Forum in September 2008, the donors agreed the following:

- to use country systems as a first option for aid programs in the public sector;
- to be transparent when they decide not to use country systems;
- to support country-led reform programs;
- to develop corporate plans for using country systems; and
- to channel 50 percent or more of government-to-government aid through country financial management systems.

The set up of well-funded extra-budget and extra-government implementation facilities fosters rent seeking. Not only are officials encouraged to leave government but some moonlight to form NGOs to capture, semi-legitimately, available aid money,[110] while others might form shell companies to capture aid-funded procurement contracts, illegitimately.[111] These types of effects create an environment that links the inflated expectations and salaries of "poached" officials ultimately to more open forms of corruption, and they are fundamentally inconsistent with the aim of "building capacity."

It is no surprise that a 2008 survey found a weak correlation between the quality of a country system and its use by donors.[112] In Ghana, the proportion of aid using country public financial management systems fell from 61 percent to 51 percent even though the quality of the system was said to have improved. In Mali, despite strengthened local mechanisms in the health sector, some donors did not use them. The achievements of the 2008 Accra conference compared with their targets were rated poor in the documents for the follow-up Busan conference.

In summary, the "broken links" in the process of aid allocation seem to be important explanations for, on the one hand, the lack of success of assistance programs and, on the other, the lack of accountability, faulty oversight and continuation of unsuccessful programs.[113]

Aid, Accountability and Democracy

Accountability may be thought of as either the horizontal accountability of agencies of government (the president, parliament and judiciary) to each other, or the vertical accountability of the government and leadership to the citizens of the country. Vertical accountability is considered to be especially weak in low-income countries where there are weaker civil society agents such as community organizations, trade associations and unions. The undermining of accountability harms democratic processes. To the extent that development assistance undermines accountability, despite its aims to the contrary, it undermines democracy. In this respect research by Easterly and Knack found a nil or negative relationship between aid and democracy.[114]

As mentioned, an instructive example of the attempt by the donors to render their programs more democratic has been the PRSP. But the PRSP preparation has been a type of shadow legislative process, often treated by donors as more important than the national budget; because governments undertake a PRSP largely to get access to funding they treat it as to some extent mutually exclusive with the budget. Thus, even if the civil service understands and accepts the program, parliament may know little about it. In parallel, the NGOs that are expected to be participants in the PRSP negotiation are often the creatures of aid funding. As such they are often formed in order to access donations rather than as expressions of the emergence of civil society.

The World Bank's response to critics such as Summers who warned that the PRSP might undermine democratic institutions was to extend its reach into the parliaments themselves. A "Parliamentary Network" was formed in 2000. Training seminars in the PRSP process for parliamentarians were started in 2001 in six African countries. A review for the 2002 World Bank Governors Development Committee claimed that, while the participation of parliaments had been limited, there was some "good practice" where individual parliamentarians had been involved or where progress of aid programs was being reported to parliament.[115] The Development Committee professed itself pleased that countries had "seized ownership" of the interim stage of the PRSP negotiation process which, it declared, "served a useful purpose by encouraging countries to … launch a broader process of rethinking current strategies, and to produce a time-bound road map for the preparation of the first PRSP." Somehow the committee members thought that countries could not plan their future without time-bound roadmaps designed to the requirements of outside benefactors.

The World Bank's external relations department currently describes the parliamentary network as an "independent and non-partisan" network of 800 parliamentarians from 110 countries concerned about fighting poverty and promoting transparency and accountability in development, providing a platform for policy dialogue with officials from the World Bank and IMF. Apparently the World Bank has identified some "non-partisan" politicians, something that might well have defied the efforts of lesser agencies. A reasonable person might think that their non-partisanship was their agreement that trips around the world at World Bank expense are a nice idea. In 2010, the World Bank External Affairs Parliamentary Team announced on their website a training program for parliamentarians, their staff and their organizations, responding to "a growing demand for deeper knowledge of the World Bank from members of the Board of the Parliamentary Network on the World Bank and other partner parliamentary organizations as well as MPs engaged in development." The program's aim was to explain "why the World Bank is the world's premier development institution" and to "provide examples of how Parliamentarians can engage with the daily work of the [World Bank Group]." Clearly parliamentarians had time to spare. As the Bank's website explained it, "there are a lot of things that we do and will continue to do with parliamentarians, a vital constituency with a major role to play in contributing to sustainable development."[116] Thus, the Bank thinks that it is reasonable to co-opt not only the executive but also the legislature of recipient countries, seemingly regardless of the potentially distracting, if not corrupting, effects of cash for expenses that the aid donors were already handing to civil servants.

At the Busan forum in 2011, the international donor community endorsed parliamentary co-option. Clause 21 of the Busan declaration announces that the donors should "accelerate and deepen the implementation of existing commitments to strengthen the role of parliaments in the oversight of development processes, including by supporting capacity development backed by adequate resources and clear action plans." The time required for donors to finally "discover" the legislative process in their client countries is probably one of the keys to understanding the aid relationship problem.

The attempt by foreign aid agencies to strengthen democracy is not just a reaction to criticism of programs such as the PRSP. It has been a deliberate assistance initiative, which has among other things involved aid for constitutional and legal systems, activist groups and legislative institutions. The US created the National Endowment for Democracy in 1983 and later formalized democracy promotion as a counter-terrorism vehicle. For a long time, however, social anthropologists and institutional development experts have fought against the presumption of foreign aid agencies that they can simply import and transfer political, legal and other systems from rich countries,[117] and especially that they can engineer democratic change. In 2010, Nobel laureate Douglass North attempted to bring together the argument in an all-embracing theory of social change.[118] As he and his coauthors put it,

> [T]here is a complex evolutionary economic social and institutional process at work in all societies which cannot be simply telescoped in time or jumpstarted through outside efforts. This process depends upon indigenous shared knowledge, beliefs, and expectations, and the stability of emerging institutions (norms, rules, laws) and organizations, including civil society organizations, that arise along with those beliefs. External efforts to bring about institutional change cannot succeed unless they can somehow be channeled through, or reinforce the natural indigenous processes at work. This is at the heart of the problem for outside agencies in accelerating development, especially in institutional and organizational capacity terms.

While aid has tried to strengthen democracy by direct assistance to parliament itself, its support is mainly focused on the executive branch of government. This is understandable since it is the executive arm that is needed in order to implement aid programs. Yet the focus on the executive branch also carries unintended anti-democratic consequences. For example, it has tended to accentuate presidential authority, resulting in different kinds of effects on the political system and accountability. Presidentialism in Africa has been associated with strong-man rule which still characterizes some post-independence regimes, and as such aid has become enmeshed in a patrimonial system and the politics of patronage.

Patronage is very important in peasant societies where it maintains stability within a recognized hierarchical system. In the societies that emerged in Africa after independence, state institutions such as law enforcement agencies had yet to achieve legitimacy and could not be relied on especially by the poorest whose access to legal and executive institutions was particularly limited. In weaker states, politics still revolves around patronage. Political parties tend to be patronage providers rather than policy makers (the more so because of ethnic fragmentation).

Aid donors become "patrons" through selection of individuals, communities, organizations and government agencies for assistance, awarding of fellowships abroad, and even through handouts for attendance at meetings. The provision of expensive conspicuous consumption goods such as SUV vehicles is entirely consistent with the traditional system based on bribery and gifts to leaders.[119] Widespread patronage, "patrimonialism" or "clientelism"[120] tend to weaken the institutions required for democracy by reducing respect for government.[121]

To the extent that foreign aid more easily supports presidential and patronage systems rather than legislative power then the attempt to support democratic institutions could be self-defeating. But this failure does not justify the co-option of the legislature in order to provide it with technical assistance. The appropriate assistance to democracy is non-assistance, or extremely cautious, light-touch assistance leaving democracy to evolve according to the dialectical process of development, in the manner suggested by Douglas North. In the end, aid to the legislative branch and the executive branch both carry risks of undermining democracy and this is in the very nature of foreign aid that has been the focus of this book. Aid to the judiciary may also carry such risks.

While aid's deliberate strategy of assistance may have interfered with the evolution and style of leadership and democracy, the "foreign aid resource curse" which we have discussed provides the macroeconomic conditions that strengthen this tendency because a large flow of aid over a sustained period can undermine vertical accountability. The opinion of the voters is less important to governments that are substantially funded externally. They need to spend less time negotiating for voters' support or developing popular participation, while spending more time negotiating with external agencies. At the same time the citizenry, for a lack of transparent access to the leadership, may fall back on buying favors, accentuating the patronage system of presidential rule. This is still more likely with substantial ethnic fragmentation and weak cross-cutting civil society groups.

The systemic interference with domestic decision processes and undermining of accountability could be a further explanation for the diseconomies of foreign aid and the diminishing returns to aid that we have been discussing. Aid funds to rulers entrench their position and democratic infrastructure set up by external donors are almost a contradiction in terms.

Taxation and Institution Building

A seminal study by Acemoglu, Johnson and Robinson find that differences in the quality of institutions explains more than 50 percent of income variation between poor and rich countries.[122] If free aid money undermines such institutions and associated capacities, then it is impeding development. A key area where institutional capacity can be undermined is in the budgetary processes of poor countries, i.e. the process of taxation and expenditure. As mentioned earlier, significant dependence of the national budget on foreign aid can damage capacity because public programs are not paid for through taxation and important decisions on development expenditure are taken as a result of agreements between governments and external agencies. As discussed earlier, dependence of the budget on foreign assistance has been high in many poor countries. In 2005, 22 of the poorest countries (including 16 in Sub-Saharan Africa) received ODA inflows equivalent to at least half of their total government expenditure. In 12 of these the ratio of ODA to government expenditure was 75 percent or more and it may be inferred that such levels of budgetary dependence interfere significantly with domestic strategies and decisions.[123]

Institutional development specialists have in recent years stressed the importance of the process, whereby the rulers of a country have to go to the voters or to parliament to convince them that incomes should be taxed to pay for public goods, an exercise in vertical accountability. This process is not only essential to "ownership" of the political process by the people of a country but is also essential to building experience in securing expenditure commitments in the teeth of political opposition. Taxation is thus important in the development process for several reasons. Firstly, countries need to raise tax revenue to pay for public expenditure. Secondly, tax administration is an important part of the capacity of government. Thirdly, and most importantly, taxation is a key channel for political negotiation between a government and its citizenry.[124] The most important elements of tax capacity are the ability to draft laws, develop budgets, collect revenue, design accounting systems, manage expenditure and conduct audits.

The history of taxation is an important subplot in the history of many countries. This is because levying and paying taxes has been an expression of the state of relations between the leaders and the led. The English Revolution of 1642 and the American Revolution of 1776 can both be put down to opposition to the taxes levied by a sovereign authority (Charles I and George III). The process of negotiation between kings and taxpayers helped to develop private property rights and the rule of law. The Bolshevik revolution of 1917 was triggered by opposition to paying for the programs of the rich (the First World War). The US political process is chronically bogged down in questions about taxation and the size of government. The "Tea Party" groups organized during 2009 were modeled on the anti-tax revolt of the Boston Tea Party when colonists protested British tea taxes by throwing a cargo of tea into Boston Harbor on 16 December 1773. If taxes have triggered revolutions then this is indicative of their key role in the development of the process of government. Nicholas Kaldor, the eminent British Economist, asked as long ago as 1963, right at the cusp of independence for many countries, "will developing countries learn how to tax?"[125]

If donors are providing the majority of public finance and governments are primarily accountable to them, then it may simply not be possible to also expect a credible social contract to develop between the state and its citizens. Aid may then be counterproductive in terms of local ownership and accountability. In this respect, Moss et al. state, "although governments typically complain about conditions, it is still easier to manage donor demands than the slow and politically difficult task of building or improving domestic revenue collection."[126]

There are two sides to the budget – raising revenue and spending it. Sidestepping both sides through foreign-aid cash that enters the country outside the governmental process therefore commits two sins, not just one. Donors claim that to avoid corrupt practices and quickly reach their target population they need to be able to channel aid outside of government. While small pieces of targeted assistance from an NGO charity might justifiably go via a privatized process, the cumulative effect of large ex-budgetary inflows is that the very systems that are needed for good governance in the longer run fall into disuse. The World Bank's evaluators have found that channeling funds through the budget plays a significant role in making government agencies take the budget process seriously. Previously, donor money was "invisible" to those making decisions in ministries responsible for the budget.

How far does aid in fact displace domestic revenue? Grants (the major part of ODA) have been found to be particularly culpable, having a significant, negative effect on revenue, while loans are less so probably because they require a funding commitment for debt service.[127] While research is not conclusive on the negative aid–revenue relationship, it is clear that in many cases of high aid-dependence taxes are displaced by aid.[128] In Ghana, it was found that the gap between budget and actual expenditure tended to increase as donor financing increased, suggesting both fiscal indiscipline associated with aid and a tendency to plan expenditure to satisfy external donors rather than domestic needs. It is also likely that large volumes of aid result in increased levels of government consumption, with aid being diverted away from investment.[129] Volatility of aid flows creates an additional problem because even when it does pass though the budget if it cannot be planned ahead it will be treated as a supplementary inflow. In such cases the marginal rather than the average budgetary dependence is important, and at the margin the percentage of foreign financing for government expenditures may be 100.

Collier makes a contrarian point that if aid reduces the tax burden on firms by displacing taxes it could have a positive incentive effect on private businesses, which would be beneficial even if it reduces government capacity.[130] However, this seems implausible. The atrophy of key civil service capacity and potential for lower standards of accountability may invite misallocation of public resources and corruption. A weak and unaccountable public service is likely to do much more damage to private business than can be compensated by lower taxes.

How much aid does in fact pass through government budgets? From 2001 to 2003 gross bilateral aid to Africa rose by 25 percent, but the amount available to governments actually fell by US$400 million. In 2002–2003 only 28 percent of aid reached recipient government budgets.[131] Things have started to improve since the early 2000s but some scores remain very low. In 2007, the average share of DAC donor aid recorded on partner budgets increased to 48 percent, leaving more than half of aid funds from DAC donors still outside the budget.

The Paris Declaration initiated a monitoring system for aid performance which included as "indicator 3" the share of aid captured in government budgets. The CGD's QUODA aid performance index found that on this dimension two agencies scored reasonably well.[132] These were the Asian Development Fund (80 percent), and the World

Bank (66 percent).[133] Closer to the 50 percent mark were the European Commission, the UK and Denmark each of which had a 57 percent score, while the Netherlands was at 56 percent. At the other end of the scale were Portugal (11 percent), Spain (24 percent) and the United States (28 percent), multilateral donors with the smallest share were the global fund (GFATM, 33 percent), and the UN agencies (35 percent).

What is one to make of these numbers? Harking back to the aid motivation issue, it is clear that some aid donors have little interest in the terms of the Paris, Accra or the Busan declarations because in the end their incentive is strategic, diplomatic and/ or commercial, not developmental. Secondly, one might well ask how it is that in the "model" case, that of the World Bank, one-third of funding was still not recorded in the budget of recipient countries, while for donors for which well under 50 percent of aid funds flows through budgets (such as USAID) the issue is more urgent. A third problem is that if the legislature is weak or co-opted then even where funds are going through the budget politicians may be cowed by administrations that present faits accomplis based on large injections of aid money some of which might directly or indirectly pay for parliamentary salaries or foreign visits. What is at stake here is the importance of independent parliaments unencumbered by donor cash.

Expenditure is of course only the one side of the story. While a number of budgetized aid mechanisms such as budget support funds (BSF) were introduced they can only go part of the way.[134] Even this partial way is limited by the fact that before a budget support loan appears in the budget various conditions have usually been agreed on by the executive with or without legislative consent. Far more important than this limitation, however, is the fact that BSF fails the main test – it is not part of the bargaining process between the government and the people mediated through taxation. The money is a gift. The negotiation is irrelevant. Democracy is not tested. Thus, again, assistance programs to fund democracy can be a contradiction in terms.

The Fruits of the Democracy–Accountability Gap – Corruption

For a long time, donors ignored or glossed over the problem of corruption. The reasoning was that it was complex, politically fraught and neutral in its (implicit) behavioral effects; it probably oiled the wheels of development even if it supported a socially unjust system. There was also a sense that people from rich places had little justification for condemning the behavior of poor people, including poorly paid government officials with large extended families depending on them.

The exposure of corruption as not only unjust but also as a negative force in economic development changed this thinking. This new perception was signaled by James Wolfensohn at the World Bank Annual Meetings in 1996, following which a research program started that showed the likely damage caused and led to an extensive anti-corruption drive.

However, whereas most observers now agree that economic and social damage results from corruption there is as yet little evidence that donors overall are moving beyond rhetoric and reducing assistance to corrupt governments, while at the same time, as this chapter attempts to demonstrate, there is a lot of reason to believe that the aid process itself fuels corruption.[135] Indeed, the donors, having set up a system which is easily, and almost rationally, corruptible, are pursuing the culprits with zealotry and setting up additional costly and delay-inducing oversight systems to try to track it and stamp it out.

Sometime after Wolfensohn's address to the world the World Bank moved to institutionalize the corruption fight. Paul Wolfowitz in 2006 introduced formal anti-corruption mechanisms and expanded a watchdog organ known as the Department of Institutional Integrity, later put under the command of the former boss of the "Scorpions," a South African corruption and crime fighting agency more experienced in the pursuit of dissident politicians such as Jacob Zuma than officials setting up shell companies or inflating invoices. The World Bank's indignant reaction to the possibility that people in poor countries were misappropriating its money meant that at its re-launch in 2008 the Integrity Department had significantly larger staff than the equivalent oversight functions of all the other international financial institutions combined despite a lower case load,[136] yet it was about to expand further to meet the challenge of blacklisting firms. Its power to blacklist has since been strengthened by a "cross-debarment" agreement with other international institutions whereby a firm excluded by one is shut out of a large market apparently without legal due process, a potentially crippling anti-business measure that could itself invite arbitrary behavior, even corruption!

Wolfowitz's concern with corruption in the World Bank's projects may have stemmed from the Iraq war reconstruction effort, which had been part of his own responsibility at the Pentagon. Transparency International has said that failing urgent steps Iraq would become "the biggest corruption scandal in history."[137] Yet it was taking place under military rule and unusual enforcement powers. Supplying large amounts of free money to a country without an effective government is an inescapable environment for corruption, as is evident also from US assistance in efforts in Afghanistan.[138]

Among the extensive writings on the general issue of corruption, Svensson finds that there has, not surprisingly, been a relationship between large windfalls from mineral exports or aid inflows and the growth of corruption.[139] Numerous other researchers have found the same.[140] More surprising is that large inflows from foreign or other sources may increase corruption on such a scale that the provision of public services can actually be reduced. This is because corruption becomes systemic and reduces the incentives across society to act in the public interest. In Nigeria, for example, during the 1990s despite huge taxable oil revenue inflows, education funding was reduced and school enrolments actually fell. In Zaire, large aid flows apparently created a corrupt system that perpetuated itself long after the fall of Mobutu. With more than half of the government budgets in Africa being funded by foreign aid, corruption increased systemically as a result of both actual and expected aid money. It has been particularly problematic in situations of conflict between powerful groups who compete for access to government, because they fear that refraining from illegitimate access will simply allow others to obtain it.

Corruption can be classified into "grand" and "petty." Leaving aside the disruptive and criminal "grand corruption" of former leaders such as Suharto, Marcos, Mobutu or Abacha, and "meso-corruption" by top officials, it is not surprising that a relatively low-paid civil servant with expectations raised by continual contact with well-paid outsiders and obligations to an extended family in a country with inadequate safety-nets faces a strong pull into petty corruption such as inflating suppliers invoices within poorly controlled aid budgets. The painful story about the poor village woman with a child on her back who wanders from ministry to ministry paying bribes to obtain a simple public service is, rightly or wrongly, offset by the fact that much of the proceeds of her bribes might eventually find their way back to other equally poor people in the next village.

Corruption is bad in any situation. But it is almost inevitable that very large flows of poorly monitored free money (which are not often in any case expected to achieve useful results) get diverted into the pockets of individuals who do not have the right to them. Such behavior is of course also commonplace in rich countries where there is presumably less excuse.[141] Given the environment of poverty it is in many ways a rational response by those with access to the funds. Equally, the zealous pursuit of corruption by the aid community, which has led to an extensive swelling of the already swollen aid bureaucracy, is misdirected, hypocritical and largely futile. As a senior World Bank official once said about something else: "we have met the enemy and he is us."[142]

Fuelling corruption undermines the rationale for development assistance, especially for capacity building, and provides another key explanation of the aid-growth failure. Aid money entrenches a corruptible patrimonial or clientelist system and encourages unsustainable consumption, which reduces the long-term rate of savings and in turn necessitates more aid. In other words, the patrimonial system and associated corruption are strengthened by foreign aid. The ethnic fragmentation of many poor countries aggravates corrupt behavior because public goods are fought over by different ethnic groups. Finally, under any system corruption is almost bound to emerge simply through the effects on incentives and behavior of very large flows of free money and goods into a society of very poor people.

As a rule the simple transfer of a rich country moral code to a poor country may be as inappropriate as the transfer of a rich country technology.[143] The corrupt behavior that stems from severe economic hardship cannot be extinguished according to the requirement or through the social engineering of an alien power. It needs a long period of increasing prosperity and societal learning, no doubt familiar to students of the political history of New York and Chicago.

Alienation and the Social and Political Determinants of Aid Ineffectiveness

The aid donor–recipient relationship in many of the poorest countries has been alienative. Those countries that have emerged to middle-income status have generally not undergone this experience, or have done so with much less severity, because aid inflows have had much smaller impacts on their economy and society. In the poorest countries by contrast even those public officials whose careers are bound up in the aid business and who support its continuation for this reason often do so with considerable misgivings because they feel alienated from a system that provides so little gain for the high cost in terms of their commitment of time and intellect and which is a distraction from the work of building their own communities. The "aid fatigue" often described in relation to donors applies as much, if not more, on the other side. Low expectations mean that commitment to programs is reluctant; the lack of ownership, which so puzzles and frustrates aid donors, is very easily and rationally explained by these low expectations. Whereas there are, unsurprisingly, cynical or corrupt individuals who are prepared to play the system and extract from it whatever they can get, there are far more genuinely concerned individuals who are simply not prepared to be accountable for a system about which they have serious reservations.

An otherwise thoughtful recent work on foreign aid asserts that aid has two tasks.[144] First, it should increase the accountability of those in power; second, it should expand the capacity of state institutions to promote development. This is difficult to achieve because low capacity facilitates rent seeking in patronage-based, poor economies and so governments in such places are uninterested in strengthening their own capacity. As we have seen, there is a fundamental contradiction in the statement that foreign aid must increase local accountability. If aid assists clientelism and patronage, then it cannot also increase the accountability of those in power. There seems indeed to be a contradiction between high levels of foreign aid and accountability whether the society is clientelist or not.[145]

The "two tasks of aid" story seems to epitomize the confusion that we saw in the ambiguous statements cited in Chapter 3. Stated as simply as possible, a prime reason for the failure of foreign aid is that the recipients, to a large extent, are not interested in it. Does this mean that they are uninterested in their own national development? No. It means that the terms on which much foreign aid, particularly the software component, is supplied are simply inconsistent with what they believe will work; and by distracting attention in many ways from the critical needs of their societies, they sense that it may be delaying their own efforts.

To reiterate, the presence of aid in many countries can weaken the fragile social and democratic institutions that it claims to nurture. The responsibility of governments to their people is eroded. Decisions on the future of countries are removed from public debate and confined within a narrow circle of civil servants and foreigners, retarding the growth of democracy. Ministers cannot justify or seriously question their government's expenditure when most of it is funded by outside donations, while a good part of the civil service is dedicated to processing the donations rather than developing the capacity to govern. What is the benefit to a country of a top-heavy donor-imposed monitoring and evaluation system when the government's own public accounts oversight body is not functioning? Donors want "ownership" by governments but in the poorest economies their presence can undermine it. If, finally, corruption itself is fuelled by aid, then that essentially seals the argument. Corruption is a major negative incentive to national efforts. If it is fuelled by aid, the donor community's mission to rein it in will be lost in futile and costly measures which themselves require additional aid flows.

The poor performance of aid programs thus has little or nothing to do with the specifics of individual projects. There are certainly bad projects and projects that were never required to perform well. There is no doubt some benefit to be gained from ensuring – through more sophisticated evaluation methods – that bad projects are prevented from going ahead. But bad projects are not the problem. Project impact studies are not relevant to identifying the cause of ineffective foreign aid.

Could Chinese Aid Be Different?

China, India and Brazil were formally recognized as donors at the Conference in Busan. Could there be a difference in the approach of these new donors that would avoid the power relationship problems and lead to an increase in aid effectiveness?

Of the three countries, none has been more controversial than China whose activities in Africa and elsewhere have become a matter of intense interest to Western donors. With its distinct worldview and caution about Western political strategy China only agreed reluctantly to join in a watered down Busan Declaration after strenuous efforts by the Western donors (notably the UK) to convince it to participate.

While China has provided aid in the past such as the construction of the Tanzania–Zambia railway in the 1970s, its current initiative can be traced to 1993 when it set up a foreign aid fund. In 1995, the Export-Import Bank of China began to provide low-interest loans to developing countries. In 2000, the Forum on China–Africa Cooperation was initiated; and in 2006, China announced its arrival in Africa by stating that it would commit US$20 billion over 3 years to support Chinese exports and business in Africa, a sum larger than that of any other donor to Africa, including the World Bank.

In 2009, China announced an eight-point plan to help Africa in areas such as climate change, clean energy, agriculture, health and education. It would provide a further US$10 billion in concessional loans and open its market to African countries by allowing zero-tariff treatment on 95 percent of exports from the LDCs in Africa having diplomatic relations with China (putting it on a par with the DAC countries, as discussed in Chapter 1). In July 2012, President Hu Jintao said in Beijing that China would lend a further US$20 billion to African governments for infrastructure and agriculture over 3 years.

Chinese aid to Africa and other poor countries has attracted criticism.[146] The main charges levelled have been as follows: that China's interest is to gain access to oil and other natural resources; that its aid is often not truly aid but investment; that China makes corruption worse through lack of conditions and a willingness to deal with whoever holds power, undermining DAC donors' efforts to promote good governance; that Chinese enterprises ignore environmental and social standards; that Chinese state enterprises investing in Africa use government subsidies that undercut African business; that its aid projects abroad rely on imported Chinese labor; that it is free riding on debt relief provided by the OECD donors.[147]

The skeptical view was reflected in a study from New York University in 2008.[148] The study reported that Chinese aid and investment grew extremely rapidly from a negligible level in 2000 to US$25 billion in 2007, largely through concessional loans and state-sponsored investment, allocated to Africa (44 percent), Latin America (36 percent) and Southeast Asia (20 percent). The total aid and investment flows to Sub-Saharan Africa are larger than US development assistance, while annual Chinese investment flows to Africa have been nearly as much as US direct investment.[149]

Aid and investment were primarily directed at raw materials and, secondly, at infrastructure. Oil comprises the large majority of Chinese imports from Africa and infrastructure financing is largely concentrated in Angola, Nigeria, Ethiopia and Sudan, all of which have oilfields. Thus, China is providing finance for resource extraction in the same manner as colonial era investments. Secondly, Chinese aid was motivated by political objectives such as the isolation of Taiwan. Only four Sub-Saharan African countries (Burkina Faso, Sao Tome, Gambia and Swaziland) still maintain official relations with Taiwan. (Malawi switched allegiance to China in 2007 in return for aid and investment.) Thirdly, Chinese aid and investment is used to open up foreign markets for Chinese goods and help Chinese companies invest in foreign markets.

A more favorable study implies the need to wait and see.[150] Much of Chinese lending has, it says, been in the form of business transactions between African and Chinese enterprises or purchases of stocks or bonds in African companies. But China has been open about this (referring to it as concessional loans). Furthermore, while Chinese investment and aid has gone to mineral industries, it has also moved across sectors. China's willingness to deal with corrupt leaders (e.g. Mugabe in Zimbabwe) is changing and it has also played constructive roles such as mediator in the Sudan. China's own labor market is tightening and its pollution problems are worsening, so that its labor and environmental laws are being modernized. Finally, with regard to free riding on OECD debt relief the majority of China's projects are in resource-rich countries where debt relief has been insignificant, and China claims to have itself offered debt relief of about US$3 billion, or equal to about a sixth of the value of its concessional and interest-free loans in 2009.

Perhaps partly to counter the widespread speculation about its intentions the Chinese government finally produced in April 2011 a policy paper ("white paper") on foreign aid.[151] In this it reported that the majority of its "concessional loans" have gone towards infrastructure and only 9 percent for the development of energy and resources such as oil and minerals. In response to the criticisms concerning the use of Chinese labor, the report cited technical-training programs and the employment of local workers. In response to charges of lack of transparency it provided a list of previous aid policy statements made at major UN conferences. In August 2010, the government held a national conference on foreign aid to define aid strategy. As the white paper put it, China's foreign aid thus entered a new stage.

China's resources are provided as grants, interest-free loans and concessional loans. Each category has a degree of subsidy with concessional loans having the smallest subsidy (2 to 3 percent), equivalent to IBRD loans with long repayment and grace periods. The first two offerings come from China's state finances, while concessional loans are provided by the Export-Import Bank are used mainly for infrastructure. By the end of 2009, according to the white paper, with total funding increasing by nearly

30 percent per annum, China had provided approximately US$32 billion in aid and investment to foreign countries.[152] The ODA component (grants and interest free loans) amounted to US$22.5 billion of which more than a half went to Africa.[153]

The white paper also sets out principles for China's assistance, which are as follows. It wishes to help countries build up their self-help capacity; to foster local personnel and technical forces; and to build infrastructure and domestic resources. It will impose no political conditions, and will respect recipient countries' right to independently select their own path of development. It will never use foreign aid as a means to interfere in a countries' internal affairs nor gain political advantage; it will adhere to equality, mutual benefit and common development; it will foster mutual help between developing countries; it will keep pace with the times and pay attention to reform and innovation; it will be adaptive; and it will pay attention to lessons of experience. Additionally, China has announced flexibility on loan repayment; a promise to replace deficient materials; and, finally, Chinese experts will have the same standard of living as the experts of the recipient country.

The undertakings are, of course, no more than intentions. It is unknown whether China is any better at living up to its principles than the OECD donors. Some of these principles, such as the intent to avoid making other countries dependent on China, are untenable since many African countries are increasingly dependent on China as their trade balances with China remain in deficit. With regard to their undertaking to use and train local labor there is also ambiguity since the white paper itself states that over 2,000 "complete projects" have been delivered in which the Chinese have been responsible for the process from study to completion, bringing in Chinese labor as well as all or part of the equipment and materials.[154] It is, however, not clear what proportion of total assistance the "complete projects" comprise so it is difficult to gauge their importance. It is also difficult to gauge the amount of funding going to minerals and energy because the white paper reports fully only in the case of concessional loans, of which only a small proportion have gone to minerals. It may well be that a large proportion of the grants and interest-free loans went to energy and minerals.

The Chinese government's own policy paper therefore leaves room for doubt about how it will live up to its principles. But leaving that aside, China's aid policy has characteristics that mark it out. It is explicit on self-determination, lack of conditions, and respect for sovereignty, which is a more promising start than that which enshrined the earlier Western assistance programs. The promise that Chinese workers will live in the same conditions as local workers is an important gesture towards the gap between expatriate and local lifestyles that helps to fuel excessive consumption and corruption, although offsetting this is the potential for miscommunication due to a lack of interaction between Chinese and local workers. Finally, and most importantly, if lighter conditionality makes it easier to do business, albeit that it carries other risks, then Chinese assistance may significantly reduce the large transaction costs of OECD aid.

The attitude of Africans to the Chinese presence is mixed, with generally favorable elite opinion but skeptical popular views waiting to see whether China lives up to its ideals after some initial missteps.[155] The favorable opinions may reflect the fact that it is easier to understand simple business motives that may be superficially similar to those of nineteenth-century colonialism, but which have critical differences such as the lack of a colonial or military presence and a more level playing field for negotiation than existed when the markets were controlled by a few European multinationals.[156] If Chinese assistance has mineral or agricultural resource-extraction objectives, then commercial motives are possibly more transparent and understandable to the counterpart country. It is neither surprising nor problematic in principle that a rapidly industrializing economy with one-sixth of the world's population needs to procure resources. Much more important are the terms of the procurement.

The Chinese tend to come to do business armed with checkbooks and contracts (the "CC" approach) whereas the OECD donors look for participation, deliver papers and set conditions (the "PPC" approach). The first looks more like an arms-length trade, while the second is more a complicated embrace with opaque transaction costs that we have discussed at length and which undermine the donors' proclaimed goals of transparency such as, for example, the World Bank's Open Data Initiative.[157]

If "real" as opposed to "faux" transparency is an indicator of better aid, the Chinese may be making a good start. That, however, does not, of course, address the fundamental issue of whether foreigners, Chinese or Western, can create economic progress in other people's countries by making donations. On that score there may be reason to question the value of the substantial aid component of China's programs (especially the turnkey projects). If, in the end, even with a better, more equal, relationship, foreign donations are an unsustainable approach to the social and economic development of a country, then it does not matter whether they come from China or the US. Thus, while the power relationships between donor and recipient are a fundamental issue for aid effectiveness, they are not the only one.

Chapter 5

CHANGING THE DYNAMICS OF DEVELOPMENT

Donors and African governments together have in effect undermined capacity in Africa: they are undermining it faster than they are building it.

Edward V. K. Jaycox (1993)[1]

Ultimately it is Africans, wherever we reside, who will effect the transformation that we all seek for our continent. … Africa's diaspora is finding new and sustainable ways of returning its skills and training to Africa.

Francis Williams (2009)[2]

A Prospect for Change?

In Chapter 1, I suggested that what was needed to bring the one billion poorest of the poor on to a growth path was radical change. This statement was not a call for revolution but rather to draw a stark contrast with the incrementalism and low expectations associated with the aid industry over 50 years, so low in some cases that one might well think that there was a hidden agenda, to do nothing but appear to be doing something. In the case of some donor nations that see aid simply as an exercise in political influence this surely applies.

In the last chapter, it was suggested that the failures of development aid in the hardcore poor countries cannot be explained by a host of factors that are currently deployed to explain them. These include: the lack of good impact evaluation techniques; the corrupt practices of local civil servants and politicians; the lack of buy-in by government and business to the assistance approach of aid donors; the lack of ownership of these same programs by the recipient "beneficiaries"; the weakness of capacity within government. While all these may be of some explanatory value they are not however the fundamental causes of the problem, but more the symptoms. There is an underlying explanation for at least a part of this slew of problems and that is the system of power relationships underlying donations of aid. This is an explanation that is familiar to development anthropologists but seems to be little understood, or set aside, elsewhere.

Observation suggests that aid recipients throughout the societies of the poorest countries of the world are often reluctant partners. Many public officials in poor countries sense that the aid system is an essentially political process involving the maintenance of rich nation influence in their countries. Even those who do not perceive such a systemic explanation seem often wary of the dependence of their governments on donor assistance, uninterested in the details, skeptical of donor motives and expertise, and altogether doubtful about its benefits. Yet in aid dependent economies a large proportion of the top government decision makers see no choice but to buy into this system. This is presumably not the buy-in that donor nations want.

How can the social dynamics of foreign aid change? If the foreign aid model has failed for many countries then the question is whether there is a feasible alternative, functional, way in which the outside assistance, which will still be required in many poor countries in the foreseeable future, can be provided. The experience of the last several decades provides little or no realistic expectation of improvement.[3]

As it happens however over the past 10 years or so a new dynamic has emerged in international development that might go some way towards dealing with the problem, and which responds to Peter Bauer's assertion that "[t]he prime determinants of material progress are people's economic aptitudes, their social institutions and political arrangements." Attention has increasingly been attracted by the world's diasporas. The key importance of a diaspora in relation to our whole argument is that it can act as a "local resource" in terms of motivation, expertise and funds. Members of a diaspora to a greater or lesser extent see their home country as an important place in which to apply their skills and their money, and this differentiates them from both general market investors and aid donors.

The Emergence of the Diasporas

Belonging to a diaspora entails a consciousness of or emotional attachment to, commonly claimed origins and cultural attributes.[4] It is a population group that retains a material allegiance to another country from where it originated at some point in the past. To a greater or lesser extent, it remains an indigenous resource of the home country. This could refer to first-, second- and later generation immigrants, as well as temporary workers, provided that they perceive their country of origin as one where they owe a certain allegiance and perceive certain obligations. Thus, the Jewish or the Armenian diasporas are active well beyond the first generation, while the Ethiopian and Ghanaian diasporas are as yet a first generation phenomenon. As one study put it, "diasporas constitute invisible nations that reside outside their origin countries."[5]

The basis of the diaspora is migration.[6] The number of international migrants in the world has increased steadily, and at a more rapid rate than both the overall world population and that of the low- and middle-income countries.[7] Much of the research on migration concerns barriers to labor mobility into rich countries which have a far greater negative effect on development in poor countries even than barriers to trade. Thus, the elimination of such barriers would provide a major boost to world income.[8] The issue that we are considering here however is reverse migration and its possible impact on countries of origin.

Based on World Bank estimates there were about 220 million first generation migrants worldwide in 2011, excluding seasonal workers, over double the number of international migrants in 1980. This excludes a likely significant proportion of unrecorded migrants. The total recorded number represents about 3 percent of the world's population and is growing at about 3 percent per annum. The "low-income" countries according to the World Bank have seen emigration of 44 million people or 2 percent of their populations. Migration has accelerated to include all regions of the world. The total flows of new migrants to rich countries increased steadily from 2.4 percent per annum in the period 1970 to 1980 to 2.9 percent per annum in 1981 to 1990, to 3.1 percent over 1990 to 2000.[9]

The largest diasporas in the United States are from China, Cuba, El Salvador, India and Mexico. In Germany the largest diaspora is from Turkey; in France from the Balkans, Morocco and Algeria; and in Japan and Canada it is the Chinese. The countries with the largest proportion of their citizen population away from home are Mexico, Afghanistan and Morocco where 10 percent of the total population (that is, first generation migrants) of their home country lives outside. Other countries with significant proportions of their population living outside are Algeria, Bangladesh, the Philippines and Turkey.[10] Africa's recorded migration includes about 21 million first generation migrants to overseas countries (2.6 percent of the Sub-Saharan African population).

The motives for migration are varied. They depend on economic circumstances in the origin and destination countries, the expectation of higher income, rising skill levels, and the prevalence of economic crises and cycles. Migration is also influenced by political conditions (such as restrictions on freedom), and educational and research opportunities. On the demand side, one reason for accelerating migration to rich countries is the older average age of the destination country population compared to that of the origin country, which creates a need for personal services in destination countries that can be supplied by migrants.

Migration feeds on itself. The rate of migration is accelerated by the existence of stable migrant communities, which lower risks for new migrants. The costs fall and the attraction of migration increases as the stock of migrants expands. As migrant networks spread, private institutions and voluntary associations emerge to provide a range of services, including lodging, social services, legal advice, credit, job searching and the means to reduce the cost of undocumented migration.[11]

The Emergence of Skilled Migration

A key factor in migration since the 1970s is that the rate of skilled workers migrating has accelerated more quickly than that of unskilled workers thanks to rising education. The highest number of skilled emigrants as a proportion of total emigrants from their home countries has been from Africa and the Caribbean. In 2000, more than half of the university-educated population of Caribbean countries were living abroad, and close to 20 percent of skilled workers have left Sub-Saharan Africa.

A diaspora-oriented web journal reports that an estimated 20,000 professionals have been leaving Africa each year, with the numbers of Africa's technical and managerial talent living outside the continent more than doubling in a generation.[12] Nigeria and Ghana have exported thousands of professionals particularly in health and education.

In the UK a recent census report reveals that black Africans are now the most highly educated group in British society, with over 26 percent holding academic qualifications higher than A-levels, or college, in comparison with 13.4 percent for white adults.

This migrant profile is paralleled in the United States. A study by the *Journal of Blacks in Higher Education* reveals that African immigrants to the United States are also more highly educated than white and Asian Americans and are more likely than any other immigrant group, including those from Europe, to have a college education.[13]

According to the 2010 American Community Survey, the proportion of immigrants of over 25 years of age holding college degrees rose steadily between 1990 and 2010, from 20 percent to 27 percent. Under a category of immigrants that includes those of African origin the proportion holding a university degree in 2010 was 35 percent, significantly higher than for the native-born Americans (28 percent), while for Asians and Indo-Europeans the proportion was higher still at over 40 percent. In contrast, for Spanish-speaking immigrants, largely from Latin America, the proportion was only 13.5 percent. There has thus been a growing polarization in skill levels between "new immigrants" from developing countries who have come to the US to take degrees or skilled jobs, and "traditional" unskilled immigrants. This can also be deduced from regional statistics. In 2010, in "new immigrant" areas such as the District of Columbia and Virginia the proportion of immigrants over 25 with a degree was 50 percent and 38 percent respectively. In traditional migrant areas such as New Mexico, only 16 percent of immigrants had college degrees. Africans comprise largely the "new immigrant" category.

Table 5.1 shows that in 2000 41 percent of the tertiary-educated individuals born in the Caribbean region were living in an OECD country, 27 percent of West Africans, 18 percent of East Africans, 16 percent from Central America, and 13 percent of those from Central Africa. In four of these five regions, the tertiary emigration rate rose significantly between 1990 and 2000.

Individual countries show widely varying rates of tertiary educated migration. In Africa Gambia has lost 68 percent, Ghana 45 percent, Kenya 39 percent, and Uganda 36 percent. Malawi reportedly lost 21 percent.[14] In the Pacific island of Tonga 83 percent and in Papua New Guinea 37 percent of top students had worked or studied abroad. In comparison, Australia has less than 5 percent of its tertiary-educated natives abroad, and the United States has less than 1 percent.[15]

An estimated total of 35,000 trained doctors have left Sub-Saharan Africa, ranging from 12 percent of the total in Togo to 34 percent in Liberia. Sub-Saharan Africa and the Caribbean remain the regions with by far the largest share of their educated populations working in OECD countries. In the Caribbean the numbers are remarkable – Haiti has 83 percent and Jamaica 85 percent of its tertiary-educated population outside the country. Nearly all the doctors trained in the Dominican Republic and Grenada had left their respective countries in 2006.

The particularly high proportion of highly educated emigrants carries implications for the role of migrants in economic development. Up until recently this outflow was characterized simply as a "brain drain." More recently it has been argued that such emigration per se has not been the major problem. For example, the emigration of health professionals from Africa has been less of an issue than the lack of drugs and

Table 5.1. Tertiary-educated emigration rates by sub-region (%)

	1990	2000
Caribbean	41.4	40.9
West Africa	20.7	26.7
East Africa	15.5	18.4
Central America	12.9	16.1
Central Africa	9.8	13.3
South East Asia	10.3	9.8
North Africa	6.8	6.2
West Asia	6.9	5.8
South America	4.7	5.7
Southern Africa	6.9	5.3
South-Central Asia	4.0	5.1
Eastern Europe	2.3	4.5
East Asia	4.1	4.3

Source: Based on Frédéric Docquierac and Abdeslam Marfoukb, Measuring the International Mobility of Skilled Workers (1990–2000), World Bank Policy Research Working Paper no. 3,381 (2004)

other disincentives to stay. Emigration is thus to some extent a symptom rather than a cause of the problems in the health sector, and even if such losses are serious in the short to medium term they are also a potential long-term resource for the home country.[16]

The drain or gain effect is difficult to sort out. On the one hand, emigration might reduce growth in the origin country because of the reduction in the stock of already scarce skills of individuals trained at public expense.[17] On the other hand, to the extent that individuals have been overqualified in relation to their home country's needs or capacities their departure has limited impact and may be a positive gain at a later date if a well-educated diaspora can improve access to capital, technology, skills and business contacts for local firms in the home country.

The prospect of higher incomes in foreign countries has been shown to increase the demand for education in the home country, hence a "brain gain" to the home economy if a majority of this educated group does not, in fact, emigrate. Thus, one study found that high rates of emigration by tertiary-educated Fiji Islanders raised investment in tertiary education in Fiji as well as the stock of tertiary-educated people, even taking account of departures.[18] Other studies have had mixed results, some confirming this phenomenon and others not, with both positive and negative relationships found between the stock of skilled people in the home country and the level of emigration. The World Bank reports that there have been positive experiences of brain gain in the health and information technology (IT) sectors.[19] The expectation of emigrating may have increased the incentive to invest in higher education and specialized training such as IT (in India and Taiwan, China) and nursing (in Ghana and the Philippines).

Against the positive impacts of migrating are possible negative impacts of families missing a parent, but the effects here are also ambiguous. Children with absent parents in the Philippines performed worse in school and tended to be less socially adjusted,[20] while an alternative scenario was that remittances from family members helped to improve children's health and schooling when coupled with a strong extended family.[21] Some countries (such as China, Cuba and India) have programs to facilitate training for migration, suggesting that policymakers see the benefits of skilled migration.[22]

Different Migrants Have Different Impacts

Just as development aid is not a homogeneous commodity, migration is not either. Different categories of migrants achieve different results. The general rule is that migrants achieve what would be expected of them considering their economic and social home backgrounds. Typically, unskilled workers from poor families migrate to unskilled jobs and send back small amounts of money largely to boost their unskilled families' consumption. This applies to mine workers in South Africa, laborers in the Gulf States, fruit pickers in California and service workers from Haiti or Jamaica. Highly skilled workers from wealthier families, on the other hand, migrate to professional and skilled jobs and send back larger amounts of money both for consumption and for investment in real estate or business.

Young graduates from India (usually from wealthier families) have migrated to the US for advanced studies often with a view to staying on as a scientist, engineer or manager in a technology-intensive business.[23] Younger migrants also have a higher tendency to leave with plans to return after acquiring skills and wealth. Irish émigrés in the 1990s had life plans involving return home.[24] These are perhaps the ideal migrants in terms of the impact on the development of their home country, and also possibly that of the country of destination – for different reasons. They acquire technology while sending funds back home; then after a finite period they bring their acquired technology back with them along with their newly acquired wealth and invest in productive technology-intensive businesses which they own and manage. At the same time, their limited stay in the host country reduces social tensions while contributing to the economy.

It is likely that the more time migrants spend abroad the more they lose ties with their home countries and reduce their support. But there is also evidence that remittances increase over the first 10 years of migration, and beyond that the total amount may still increase due to increases in earnings over time. A study of 12,000 African migrants also found that males remit more than females and the more educated and those earning higher incomes remit more as a percent of earnings than the poorer.[25]

Unskilled migrants tend to have the least developmental impact on their home country. Firstly, unlike the relatively skilled migrants, unskilled workers may fail to make much headway in the job market for more than one generation. Secondly, remittances in these circumstances have in some cases funded substitution of leisure for work, making the recipients increasingly dependent on outside help.

How many Migrants Return?

The contribution of migrants to the economic development in their home countries is partly contingent on how many return. Returning migrants are now a more frequent occurrence, in South and East Asia, the Caribbean and increasingly in Africa. Economic crises increase both migration and return because the migration is seen as a temporary way to avoid economic losses as much as to gain income.[26] This "round-tripping" exercise occurred with Irish emigrants during the boom years of the later 1990s when a net 16,000 a year of highly educated Irish got relatively well-paid jobs back home, especially in the computer industry.[27]

Returns are a function of push factors (lack of success in the destination country) or pull factors (family, social and political goals and responsibilities, and changing economic circumstances at home). The decision to return has up to now been mainly due to family and lifestyle concerns.[28] There is a point where income benefits in the host country become less important than absence-related losses.[29] The second reason is where migrants have achieved their intended wealth targets. Thirdly, the push factor operates if they have not achieved adequate success abroad.[30] However, increasingly Indians who left for the US are being attracted back by rising prosperity at home. The lesser importance of income compared with lifestyle, combined with incentives such as improved research facilities and a good business climate, may mean that those countries losing skilled citizens could draw them back.[31]

Overall migrant return rates were measured at about 21 percent in a 1970–74 US immigrant cohort by 1980.[32] Of Indian PhD recipients in 1990, 64 percent planned to stay in the US, increasing to 68 percent in 1999.[33] The bursting of the 1999 technology bubble probably increased return rates and anecdotal evidence suggests that the expanding high-tech centers such as Chennai are pulling individuals back home, and that returnees are now more entrepreneurial and backed by capital.

In Africa a World Bank study for Burkina Faso, Nigeria and Senegal reported that returnees were relatively high in the former country at 25 percent, though low in the other two (3 percent and 9 percent).[34] While migration rates are extremely high among doctors there are also significant returns with 43 percent of those who migrated returning to Ghana by age 45. A blogger from the website *ReConnect Africa* writes, "From my experience of working with African professionals in the Diaspora, it is clear that returning home is increasingly on their agenda."[35] A survey by the same online magazine claimed that 89 percent of diaspora respondents indicated that they intended to return to work in Africa.

Return may be temporary and circular. Migrants can provide benefits through interacting with home on a regular basis without returning permanently. A key example of circular migration is India where about half of the migrant population travel back once a year or more on business. About a quarter are in regular contact on technology and jobs, or have invested money in startups or venture funds in India, and nearly half consider that they were likely to return to India in the future. Information-intensive, smaller firms plus social networks have become an excellent channel for technology transfer.

Indian émigrés in the US had a large impact on the development of Silicon Valley in California where they were running 9 percent of startup enterprises between 1995 and 1998, largely in the software sector.[36] Such people can return with knowledge of foreign technology, processes, governance, markets, the legal/contractual environment and methods of doing business, while at the same time their presence in the US or Europe helps to reduce the perception that poorer countries are risky as a source of supplies, markets or investment opportunities. Yahoo, HP and GE opened operations in India because their confidence was increased by the presence of Indian employees in the US.

The Emergence of Diaspora Money Flows

While skills, knowhow and experience are critical developmental resources, a principal benefit of migration is the money sent back to the home country. Migration is not a new phenomenon, nor are migrant remittances. Mine labor in South Africa has migrated from the neighboring countries for over 100 years. Farm labor from Central America in the US has existed for decades, as has Nepalese labor in India. But none has apparently had significant impact on the economic development of their home countries. So what is new?

There have been important changes in the nature of remittances. Firstly, there has been a rapid growth in their level; secondly, the skill and income levels of the migrants have been increasing, which result in higher flows per migrant; thirdly, the pattern of expenditure of remittances seems to have been shifting towards investment rather than consumption (as a result of the higher level of income per migrant); fourthly, other sources of diaspora money complement remittances as the home economy strengthens; fifthly, the emergence of high-speed communications has changed the nature of migration such that migrants can keep in regular touch with those they left behind and can conduct business more easily across borders; finally, the revolution in communications has affected the longer-term relationship of migrants to their home countries. The increase in flows has also been assisted by a steady reduction in remittance costs.

Since 2002 the value of worldwide remittance flows to developing countries has risen significantly faster than the rate of increase in migrant populations, which, as we have seen, has itself exceeded the rate of growth of the world population. The average annual rate of growth of officially recorded remittances has been about 12 percent per annum compared to 3 percent for the migrant population. A small dip in remittance flows in 2008–2009 as a result of the world financial crisis was quickly reversed despite a weak European economy, as the next figure shows. Recorded remittances to developing countries were estimated at US$406 billion in 2012 and are expected to reach half a trillion dollars by 2014.

In Sub-Saharan Africa recorded remittances in 2011 reached US$23 billion, rising from US$13 billion in 2006. The Sub-Saharan African share, while still small, climbed from 4 percent of the total in 2002 to over 6 percent in 2011. Current World Bank projections are for flows to Sub-Saharan Africa to reach US$27 billion by 2014.[37]

While India and China receive the largest totals of about $70 billion per annum each, some other countries receive larger inflows as a proportion of GNI. Former Soviet

Figure 5.1. World remittances ($ billion)

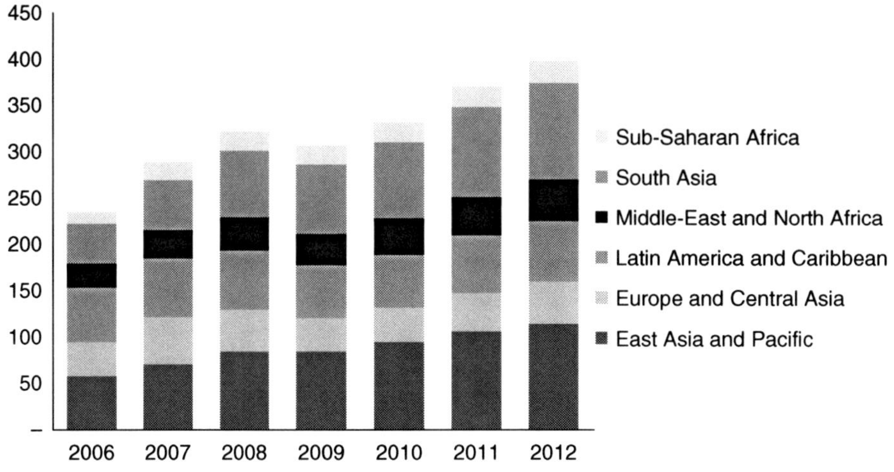

Source: Migration and Development Brief no. 18 (World Bank, April 2012)

Republics with large migrant populations have included Tajikistan which received 47 percent and Kyrgyzstan 29 percent in 2011, while in Africa, Liberia received 31 percent and Lesotho 27 percent of its national income from outside. Tajikistan is the extreme case of a "remittance economy" in which on average one individual in every family left the country in the 1990s to seek work in Russia and elsewhere. Remittances to that country are ten times as high as foreign direct investment and other private inflows.[38]

Elsewhere, Nepal, Moldova, Haiti, Honduras and El Salvador have all at some time received some 20 percent of their GNI in remittances. Bangladesh receives over 11 percent. Up to 25 other countries have been reported to receive remittances worth 10 percent or more of their GDP including very poor countries such as Tonga, Senegal, Gambia, Kiribati, Togo and Uganda. In several Latin America countries (notably Guatemala, and Nicaragua), remittances also account for a large proportion of GNI. Table 5.2 provides data for Sub-Saharan Africa in 2008, just before the financial crisis.

The first column shows in descending order the total estimated income from remittances and employee compensation sent back to Sub-Saharan African countries in 2008. In terms of total income Nigeria dominates the list with almost US$10 billion, although as a percent of its GNI this flow is not the highest. Nigeria is followed by Sudan, Kenya and Senegal. Malawi is at the bottom of the list with just about zero recorded dollars. As for the numbers of migrants, South Africa, Côte d'Ivoire and Ghana lead with around 2 million. In the case of Togo, Lesotho, Gambia and Senegal income flows exceeded 10 percent of GNI. The average remitted income per migrant for Sub-Saharan Africa was US$1,172.

Average recorded remittance as a percent of GNI for Sub-Saharan Africa (2.5 percent) has been relatively low by world standards. But the reported data are highly inaccurate. This can be deduced from the official data on income per migrant,

Table 5.2. Migration and remittance data for selected African countries (2008)

	Income, incl. remittances US$ million	Migrant numbes 000s	Income received US$ per migrant	Income received % GNI	Migrants % of home population
Nigeria	9,585.0	1,128	8,497.3	5.5	0.7
Sudan	2,993.0	753	3,974.8	5.5	1.7
Kenya	1,686.0	818	2,061.1	5.7	2.0
Senegal	1,365.0	210	6,500.0	10.6	1.6
South Africa	902.0	1,863	484.2	0.3	3.7
Uganda	750.0	647	1,159.2	4.7	1.9
Lesotho	414.0	6	69,000.0	26.2	0.3
Mali	405.0	163	2,484.7	4.5	1.2
Togo	307.0	185	1,659.5	10.7	2.7
Ethiopia	262.0	548	478.1	0.9	0.6
Côte d'Ivoire	185.0	2,407	76.9	0.8	11.2
Ghana	114.0	1,852	61.6	0.4	7.6
Burkina Faso	99.0	1,043	94.9	1.2	6.4
Niger	89.0	202	440.6	1.7	1.3
Gambia	80.0	290	275.9	10.9	16.6
Sierra Leone	47.0	107	439.3	2.4	1.8
Zambia	41.0	233	176.0	0.3	1.8
Burundi	28.0	61	459.0	2.1	0.7
Tanzania	23.0	659	34.9	0.1	1.5
Gabon	10.0	284	35.2	0.1	18.9
Malawi	1.0	276	3.6	0.0	1.8
Zimbabwe	N.a.	372	N.a.	N.a.	2.0
Sub-Saharan Africa	**20,749.0**	**17710**	**1,171.6**	**2.5**	**2.1**

Source: Global Development Finance (2011); OECD Development Cooperation Report (2011)

which are far too high for Lesotho ($69,000) and for Ghana far too low ($62).[39] Tanzanians apparently only send home US$35 a year, while next door Kenyans send over US$2,000 each, and Malawians only manage US$4 per head.[40] The flows per migrant in many African countries are thus significantly underestimated. According to one study, 73 percent of the total income flow was unrecorded in 2004.[41] By way of illustration, in the case of Ghana remittances reported by the Central Bank in 2007 were US$105 million, whereas those estimated from actual surveys amounted to US$1.8 billion.[42] In Madagascar, survey findings showed actuals of about 15 times the reported amount.[43] For Ethiopia, the survey estimate was about six times the level reported, at US$3.2 billion, a number that was a surprise to the Central Bank itself.[44]

Many of the unrecorded flows go through channels like Western Union, Moneygram or the Hawallah system, or arrive through informal channels or in the form of cash.[45] In the case of Hawallah, payments are made through setting off obligations in different countries without any cash actually crossing borders. While some Central Banks try to track the value of the overall flow through the money transfer agencies a large amount is still not recorded.[46]

To try to get closer to accuracy micro-studies on migrant behavior are being conducted. The above-mentioned study of 12,000 African migrants in nine OECD destination countries shows that three-quarters of income remitted is from the US and Europe, while 37 percent of migrants (slightly higher than the world average) remitted an average of US$2,638 each per annum, which is nearly three times Sub-Saharan Africa's GNI per capita. The weighted average annual amount remitted per migrant was US$1,263 which is close to the US$1,172 Sub-Saharan average shown in the World Development Indicators, but somewhat less than the apparent global average of about US$1,800.[47] The study also found that African immigrants in the OECD were probably remitting relatively high amounts, and educated migrants, especially Africans, send home a higher share of their income, especially if married and with a tertiary education.

The total income flows are also underestimated because of the narrow definition of migrants and remittances. To get round this, surveys by the World Bank's FAR program looked at recipients.[48] It found that 14 percent of the Kenyan adult population regularly receives payments averaging US$735 per year per recipient, which would amount to a total nationally of over US$2 billion a year. In Ethiopia, it was also found that 14 percent of Ethiopian adults receive remittances, averaging US$600 a year, which would amount in total to about US$3 billion. Both estimates are close to or above the highest estimates made elsewhere.

On the basis of these findings, if we assume an average of US$1,500 per formal migrant for the group of under-recorded countries and combine these with the countries that have fuller records then for all Sub-Saharan Africa total remittance flows would be closer to US$40 billion a year, of which Nigeria would account for a quarter. If we expand the migrant numbers to include the other components of the diaspora, including a) the seasonal and short-term workers, b) the second and later generation migrants, and c) undocumented migrants, then on the basis of an average income per head total income could easily amount to US$50 billion per annum or above. To try to confirm this we look later at balance of payments flows.

Aid and Remittances in International Finance

What is significant about the private inflows from the developmental point of view is not just their increase but the fact that they have started to look very large in comparison with the other traditional financing sources for developing countries, that is to say official aid, direct and portfolio investment. Remarkably, the 2008 value of officially recorded global remittances was also about equal to the imputed value of trade barriers that was discussed in Chapter 1. Figure 5.2 shows the main sources of worldwide funding including ODA and remittances up to the year 2010.[49]

Figure 5.2. World Flows: Finance and ODA ($ billion)

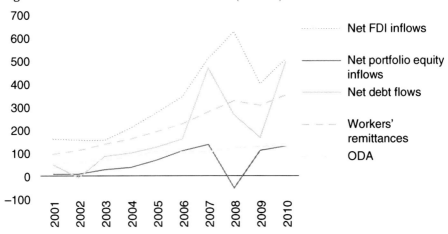

Source: OECD Development Cooperation Report (2011); Global Development Finance (2011)

In the recession of 2009, officially recorded workers' remittances worldwide almost caught up with world FDI for the first time, and easily surpassed total debt flows and portfolio equity combined. If non-recorded remittances were factored in the total may well have exceeded FDI. In 2010, partly as a result of record-high official lending by the World Bank and IMF to offset the crisis, debt flow recovered. FDI also partially recovered while net portfolio equity which was extremely volatile, fell below zero before a partial recovery. Worldwide recorded remittances exceeded ODA by a wide and increasing margin over the whole period and their rate of growth has remained robust while that of other components is uncertain or, in the case of ODA, subject to budget cutbacks in 2011.

Remittance flows have shown stability in the face of economic cycles in recipient countries. They have usually tended to rise when the recipient economy suffers a downturn or a natural disaster because migrants send more funds during hard times. Remittances come from both new migrants and the longer-term diaspora population, which makes them more stable over time, and they are a small proportion of migrants' incomes and therefore cushioned against fluctuations. The increase in public expenditure during the 2008–2009 crisis also increased demand for migrant workers. Yang shows that remittances to Filipino households increased following the 1997 financial crisis, as they did in Mexico in 1995, Thailand in 1998 or in Indonesia in 1998.[50] Kapur finds that the cash flow from the remitters contrasts with the "herd-like behavior" of foreign investors, and cushions the blow to the economy of foreign funds withdrawal.[51]

For our purposes the size of remittances within total capital and income flows to the poorest countries, and in particular Sub-Saharan Africa, is what is of particular interest. The numbers confirm what was discussed in Chapter 2, namely that the official aid is becoming more marginalized. ODA according to Table 5.3 has declined since 2002 from over 50 percent of the total recorded resources going to Sub-Saharan Africa dipping in 2007 to below 33 percent mainly as a result of strong growth of private capital before recovering somewhat as a result of the crisis.[52]

Table 5.3. Net resource flows to Sub-Saharan Africa US$ billions

	2003	2004	2005	2006	2007	2008	2009	2010
Total net inflows, excl. ODA	14.6	24.0	33.0	42.4	53.2	38.9	46.4	53.4
Net equity inflows	14.0	17.7	26.1	37.0	38.7	31.8	43.0	36.8
Net FDI	13.3	11.0	18.0	20.2	28.5	37.5	32.8	28.8
Net portfolio equity	0.7	6.7	8.1	16.8	10.1	−5.7	10.2	8.0
Net debt flows	0.6	6.4	6.9	5.4	14.6	10.9	3.4	16.6
Official creditors	1.4	2.3	−0.9	−1.9	2.5	4.9	9.8	13.0
Net long-term debt flow	0.9	2.7	4.8	−2.0	8.0	1.5	3.5	2.1
Net short-term debt flows	−1.7	1.4	3.0	9.4	4.0	4.5	−9.9	1.5
Workers' remittances	6.0	8.0	9.4	12.7	18.6	21.3	20.2	21.1
Net disbursements of ODA	26.8	29.4	32.4	40.4	35.6	38.5	42.5	43.7
Total inflows + remittances + ODA	47.4	61.4	74.8	95.5	107.4	98.7	109.1	118.2
ODA percent of total flows	56.5%	47.9%	43.3%	42.3%	33.1%	39.0%	39.0%	37.0%

Source: Global Development Finance (2011); OECD Development Cooperation Report (2011)

While the ODA share has declined in Sub-Saharan Africa it remains somewhat higher than in other regions of the world.[53] Similarly, recorded remittances still hold a relatively low share of total inflows, about 20 percent in 2009 according to official figures. However, if we include the unrecorded flows the picture changes. Figure 5.3 shows what would happen if we adjust the rate of remittances (shown by the dotted line) to a probable total of US$50 billion leveling out in 2009. With this adjustment private income flows would become the largest component, exceeding both ODA and foreign direct investment.

If this is an accurate adjustment then the importance of ODA in total "capital-like" inflows to Sub-Saharan Africa would be significantly reduced. This becomes more so if we focus on specifically development aid whose share was well below that of past decades, even including the surge in 2006.

Funds Transfer Mechanisms

One impediment to the growth of recorded income flows has been the cost of funds transfer. Almost 70 percent of central banks in Sub-Saharan Africa have cited high costs as the most important factor inhibiting the use of formal remittance channels.[54] In 2002, the IADB estimated the total cost of sending remittances to Latin America and the Caribbean at approximately 12.5 percent of their value. The Pew Hispanic Center estimated that the cost of the average remittance transfer ranged between 15 and 20 percent of the total.[55]

However, costs have fallen rapidly due to technological advance (notably the combination of cell phones and the Internet), competition between remittance agencies

Figure 5.3. Resource flows in Sub-Saharan Africa ($ billion)

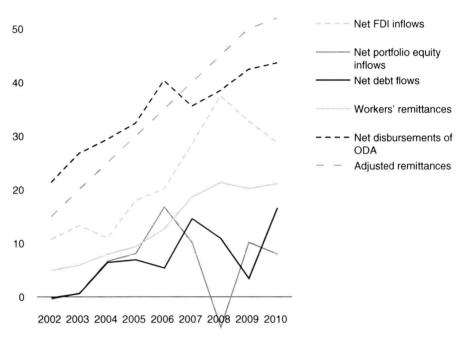

such as Western Union, and Moneygram and government action such as agreements between the Mexican government and the remittances agencies.[56] The rapid adoption of money transfer technologies in developing countries is greatly facilitating flows.[57] The availability of the M-PESA mobile money service in Kenya has revolutionized domestic transfers, reduced the share of remittances sent by hand and allowed smaller amounts to be sent electronically. There is some likelihood that an international electronic transfer process will be introduced.

A G8 summit in Georgia, Atlanta in 2004, agreed to support lowering of transfer costs and the World Bank proceeded to develop international standards for remittance services. In 2009, at a further summit in L'Aquila, Italy, the G8 countries agreed to act to reduce costs further. By 2010, the Multilateral Investment Fund of the IADB reports that it succeeded in promoting a reduction in costs of transfer from the US to the Caribbean from an average 15 percent of value to about 5.6 percent. The aid donor community has recognized the significance of the remittance phenomenon even if it has not entirely absorbed the implications.

The Total Picture of Diaspora Cash

In addition to formal remittance flows there are large inflows reflected in many countries' balance of payments statistics under the heading "private current transfers" which may include a part of the missing, non-reported remittances, second- and later generation remittances and the seasonal/temporary worker incomes. There is also a category known as "migrant transfers" within the balance of payments capital account. The numbers also include private charitable donations (e.g. NGO grants) and might have partially misclassified other flows like bank loans. Total private current transfers are typically double the value of remittances alone and have been increasing rapidly.

Both the definition and the measurement of these flows are, as usual, inadequate.[58] Central banks have different procedures for counting, and sometimes double counting. NGO grants are not identifiable from the overall numbers. Nevertheless, leaving aside the counting problem, private current flows have surged in Africa, India and other South and East Asian low-income countries, both mineral and non-mineral based, in broadly similar proportions. In low-income African countries migrant transfers on capital account combined with private current transfers, rose from about net zero in 1981–85 to 5.8 percent of GDP in 2006.[59] The next table shows IMF data for four African countries, which have relatively large diasporas.

Table 5.4. Total private current transfers compared to workers' remittances

US$ million		2005	2006	2007	2008	2009
Kenya	Recorded net remittances	368.6	545.1	628.8	602.8	570.7
	Total net private current transfers	2,325.0	3,367.1	3,824.6	4,269.0	3,961.4
Ghana	Recorded net remittances	99.2	105.3	117.4	126.1	114.4
	Total net private current transfers	3,099.5	3,289.2	3,667.6	3,940.8	3,576.7
Ethiopia	Recorded net remittances	157.1	155.1	341.4	365.5	n/a
	Total net private current transfers	1,690.4	1,802.6	4,121.1	5,367.4	n/a
Uganda	Recorded net remittances	177.0	226.1	248.4	399.8	372.0
	Total net private current transfers	876.3	1,116.6	1,569.9	1,815.0	1,554.3

Source: IMF Balance of Payments Database

Comparable to the earlier cited FAR survey findings on Kenya and Ethiopia, the four countries in 2008 showed total recorded total private current transfers of US$15.4 billion, whereas recorded remittances were only US$1.5 billion. Total private current transfers in these four countries are a significant element of GDP, averaging over 10 percent. The following shows the differences in the two types of flow as a proportion of GDP in 2008, just before the financial crisis.

Table 5.5.

	Remittances/GDP	Total private current transfers/GDP
Uganda	2.3%	10.3%
Ethiopia	4%	11.9%
Kenya	3.2%	6.2%
Ghana	0.4%	12.5%

Source: IMF Balance of Payments Database

For several other Sub-Saharan African countries, such as Tanzania, Burundi, Gabon, Congo, Madagascar, Zambia and Zimbabwe, the discrepancy may also be large since recorded remittances are tiny.[60] For Malawi, the recorded remittances are about zero but total private transfers exceed 3 percent of GDP.

Nigeria can be singled out because of its particularly large private current flows. According to IMF data a very large amount of private current income is coming into, or returning to, Nigeria on a regular basis, as shown in the table.

Table 5.6. Private transfers to Nigeria (US$ billion)

	2005	2006	2007	2008	2009
Recorded net remittances	14.47	16.71	17.77	19.06	18.20
Total net private current transfers	30.19	33.65	35.54	37.34	35.78

Source: IMF Balance of Payments Database

In 2008–2009 Nigerian remittance flows amounted to about 5.5 percent of GDP while total private transfers amounted to 11 percent. These numbers, which are significantly higher than those reported by the World Bank, may include some capital flows that have been misclassified as current flows. Nevertheless, in either case, transfers of US$36 billion per annum over 2007–2009 are a significant proportion of the total estimated capital accumulated externally by Nigeria over the past decades, which we discuss further below.

On the basis of the above estimates taking into account all the various types of private current transfers (but excluding the NGO grants) total current flows would be well above our previous estimate of US$50 billion per annum for all remittances. With a conservative estimate the amended profile could turn out as shown in Figure 5.4.

In this fuller picture transfers exceeded ODA from 2006. As much as or more than US$60 billion of private individual cash is flowing into Sub-Saharan Africa each year (excluding NGO grants). This would make private contributions by far the largest single item, well above the level of foreign aid and FDI, and a serious resource for development. With the rise of private foreign investment and portfolio investment above its pre-crisis levels the ODA would now be averaging no more than about 20 percent of total foreign flows in Sub-Saharan Africa.

In the longer-term, as the effects of the 2009 crisis fade, there is every likelihood that foreign direct investment in Africa will recover and strengthen, especially in the energy sector. With long-term energy prices rising, and new oil and gas finds in East and West Africa, the probability is that Africa's historically low share of global FDI will increase significantly in the medium term, further reducing the importance

Figure 5.4. Resource flows including total current private transfers Sub-Saharan Africa ($ billion)

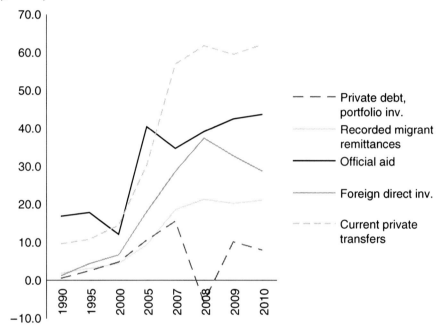

of aid flows. However, the impact on economic development of FDI flows and the resulting revenues will depend significantly on how African governments manage and control the likely very large resource inflows from energy exports. Even with good management, large-scale energy and mineral investment will not in any case induce the entrepreneurship, human capital and capacity improvements that come with diaspora investment, and investment out of resource flows from the diaspora will maintain a special role.

The Reversal of Flight Capital?

While total private current transfers are a significant proportion of GNI, this is still by no means the end of the story. Another even more important resource which is connected directly or indirectly with the diaspora may turn out to be returning capital. Like private transfers the statistics on capital flight are poor.[61] However, it is clear that for decades significant amounts of capital have been exported from countries in

Africa as well as other regions, and have been held abroad in bank deposits, property, financial asset portfolios, savings and pension funds, and that capital is potentially returnable.

The main determinants of capital flight in Sub-Saharan Africa, apart from simple criminality, have been macroeconomic and political instability, accumulating indebtedness and inadequate financial sector development. Aid does not seem to have directly caused capital flight overall despite some high profile cases but if it has added to debt it will have increased instability.[62] Capital flight reflected to some extent the poor returns and high risk associated with investment in Africa especially in the 1970s and 1980s when in many countries an adverse business climate was created by state controls on private business.[63] The vicious circle of external debt and the increase in capital flight occurred because indebtedness was aggravated by capital flight and then itself also induced capital flight, resulting in the need for further borrowing to fill the gap. Once capital flight is under way the capital exporters also tend to perceive a lower risk in continuing it.

While capital flight out of Africa may have been illicit, it may also have reflected a rational portfolio choice reflecting superior returns abroad.[64] With the recent higher economic growth the wealthier Africans who were able to invest abroad may now be prepared to seek investments in their home countries, which could therefore, ironically, gain more than they would have if the cash had stayed at home. One of the challenges for developing countries is to channel diaspora cash, and considerable work is under way to establish financial outlets for this.

Numerous attempts to estimate capital flight have been made. One report called "Global Financial Integrity" finds that between 2000 and 2008 illicit outflows worldwide increased by 13 percent per annum adjusted for inflation and reached US$1.3 trillion per annum by 2008.[65] Sub-Saharan Africa, despite having a small share, was one of the fastest-growing regions for capital outflow. According to this source, there was about US$60 billion per annum in capital flight from Africa over 2007 to 2009, equal to our estimate of private current inflows.

The countries with the largest cumulative transfer of illicit capital during 2000–2008, according to this report, were first and foremost China with over US$2 billion followed by Russia, Mexico, and Saudi Arabia. In Africa, Nigeria had the largest estimated drain of capital, at US$130 billion.

Numerous other estimates exist. Collier estimates that 38 percent of the private wealth of Africans is held abroad, the highest ratio in the developing world,[66] and that Africa's GDP per capita is 16 percent lower than it would be if flight capital had remained at home.

Another study puts total capital flight at a lower, but still significant, level.[67] Flows from 46 Sub-Saharan African countries for which data exist were US$184 billion over 1991–2004, averaging about US$13 billion per annum. Alternatively, capital flight from Sub-Saharan Africa rose from around US$15 billion in 1991 to just under US$30 billion in the year 2003 and then in 2004 declined to just US$1.1 billion due to capital return in the oil and mineral rich countries of Nigeria, Congo and Angola. The World Bank also has a lower estimate, that capital outflows from Sub-Saharan

African countries averaged US$8.1 billion annually from 1990 to 2005 with a cumulative stock of outflows from Sub-Saharan African countries of US$178 billion in 2006, or about 30 percent of GDP.[68]

A relatively authoritative research effort over several years puts capital flight for the 40 Sub-Saharan African countries over 1970–2004 in the middle of the range of estimates, at about US$420 billion (in 2004 dollars), or about US$13 billion a year.[69] If imputed interest earnings are included, it is estimated that the accumulated stock in 2008 was about US$607 billion. As such, the group of countries holding the capital would have been a net creditor to the rest of the world since their private assets held abroad exceeded their total liabilities. The amount of this credit would be about equal to ODA and net private capital inflows and well in excess of FDI. This net credit position is particularly high in the case of Côte d'Ivoire, Zimbabwe, Angola and Nigeria. "The gains from repatriation are large and dominate the expected benefits from other sources such as debt relief," states the report.[70]

In comparison with the annual flows of capital out of Africa ODA inflows to Sub-Saharan Africa over the 1980s were relatively low, averaging only US$6.3 billion per annum. During the 1990s, they averaged US$10 billion rising initially to over US$11 billion and then falling back to US$7.9 billion by 1999. Only from 2005 did aid flows jump significantly, and it is likely that the fiscal crisis in OECD countries will reduce the levels from 2011. Prior to the first decade of the 2000s all estimates suggest that annual capital flight was easily exceeding the annual total of foreign aid to Sub-Saharan Africa.

If we add the private current transfers to the potentially large inflows from returning capital, there is scope for a major boost to African investment from indigenous sources, either through the diaspora proper or through assets held by African nationals outside Africa, provided that economic conditions in potential recipient countries improve in terms of stability, security and governance. This is clearly a significant prospect.

Diaspora Flows and Development Impact

Like the aid-growth research, studies on whether remittances affect the growth rate of the economy have been ambiguous. Indeed one study finds a somewhat implausible negative association.[71] The assessment of the impact of remittances faces complicated two-way causality.[72] No clear remittance success story has been found just as no aid success story has been found, although far less research on remittances and growth has been carried out. In a nutshell, the principal ways in which remittances could increase economic growth are through raising the rate of investment, and secondly, increasing productivity through higher efficiency of labor and capital or better institutions. Remittances could directly finance an increase in investment in assets and human capital as they generate increased saving or improve the creditworthiness of domestic investors, ease access to credit or reduce the interest rates.[73] They could also increase investment if they reduce overall business risk by stabilizing the economy. All of these mechanisms are possible, though not necessarily achieved.

The effect of remittance income on the overall productivity of the economy may be relatively complicated. In the case of labor, remittances may encourage education and skill development in the longer run but in the short run they might reduce work effort. Regarding the efficiency of investment inflows they can provide a boost if the investor, remitter or recipient has some special insight into profitable opportunities (an informational advantage). If remittances increase the funds flowing through the banking system they might also increase bank productivity.

It is important to consider also the possibility that remittances could harm development. The first reason is the so-called "resource curse," which I have discussed in relation to foreign aid.[74] As mentioned, this problem occurs if cash inflows cause an appreciation of the real exchange rate and real wages, increasing the prices of exportable products and reducing their competitiveness. The impact would be larger in economies with high ratios of remittances to GDP. Most studies however seem to have found that remittance flows have not caused this problem. Their relative stability and countercyclical nature prevents the worst effects that occur from a sudden windfall, giving governments more of a chance to mitigate the effects of appreciation. Remittances are also often spent on domestic products and services using plentiful, low-cost labor such as construction workers so wages are not bid up. Perhaps more importantly migrants have tended to reduce their remittances when exchange rates are overvalued, and this offsets appreciation.[75] Thus, remittances are attracted by good macroeconomic policies and this is a kind of safety valve. Finally, it has been found that if remittance flows bring with them increased direct investment then productivity increases may limit cost increases. The role of migrant networks is enhanced if they promote investment as well as sending cash.[76]

Another potential drawback of remittances has been the possibility that they encourage less work and more leisure, thus increasing dependence on outside help rather than empowering local investment and capacity.[77] Remittances that go to consumption may plausibly have this effect. This has been noted, for example, in some Caribbean communities, and in Kashmir, India, where it has been attributed to the fact the cash is used to buy land for prestige and speculation rather than for productive activity. However, others argue that reduced effort is a legitimate welfare benefit, and still other studies have not in fact found a reduction in effort. One study determined that remittances reduce the supply of child labor but increase that of adult labor.[78] In another study, a rise in remittances reduced labor force participation in Nicaragua but increased self-employment.[79]

A final issue is targeting. Some critics argue that remittances, unlike aid, are not poverty focused but instead tend to assist those who are already outside the poverty trap because it is largely this category of families who migrate. However, remittances for consumption do in fact end up in the hands of poor mine workers, fruit pickers and laborers families, and even if this was a legitimate criticism it is by no means clear that conscious poverty targeting through aid has been successful, as we have extensively considered.

Diaspora Flows: Consumption or Investment?

A key question is the extent to which remittances and other flows including return of capital have been channeled to investment. To answer this question requires evidence on how diaspora funds are spent, the vehicles through which the funds are transmitted and saved, and finally the emergence of institutional structures that might be able to channel both funds and skills into productive outlets. There have been numerous descriptive studies about the potential for investment and the types of investment that are being made, but little firm evidence of the actual spending pattern.

In the case of returning capital, a large proportion would return in the form of investments, in education, real estate, small business and investible portfolios. Where remittances in general are concerned, the large majority of the flow, even to middle income recipients, is likely to be to consumption. The extent to which they are going increasingly into investment is not certain. One study from Ghana found that households receiving remittances spend their remittance income just like any other source of income.[80] That is, remittances do not have a statistically significant impact on the rate of household savings. Smaller remittances (under US$1,000 a year) tend to be spent mostly on consumption and medical care. Remittances of US$1,000–5,000 tended to finance durables, often furniture and cars, and home improvements. Those exceeding US$5,000 were mainly used to invest in rural house construction, while those exceeding US$10,000 were invested in the remodeling of city apartments and imported goods.

Outside Africa, the EIU found that families use remittances firstly to meet their basic consumption needs and then for land, home construction and repair.[81] Of the countries studied only in Brazil were migrant remittances being used significantly for business investment. The small proportion otherwise might be typically invested in a sewing machine to make clothes for sale, or possibly as collateral for a micro-loan. The evidence in other contexts (for example, Afghanistan, Democratic Republic of the Congo and Somalia) was also not compelling.[82]

More optimistically, other researchers have found that remittances do find their way into savings and investment, and spur entrepreneurial activity.[83] The propensity to save out of remittance income has been found to be higher for migrant families. Some find that remittances overcome capital market imperfections and allow migrant households to accumulate positive assets. One study found that found that a 1 percentage-point increase in remittance inflows in 13 Caribbean countries increased private investment by 0.6 percentage points compared to GDP.[84]

More optimistic results also came from research conducted in 2001 on 6,000 small firms in urban areas of Mexico, which found that remittances are responsible for almost 20 percent of the capital invested in micro-enterprises. In the ten states with the highest rate of migration to the US, it was estimated that almost one-third of the capital invested in micro-enterprises is associated with remittances.[85] Other studies of Sri Lanka and El Salvador show a relatively high propensity to invest remittance income in assets such as education and working capital for small businesses.[86] One recent cross-country study finds that enhanced information available to migrant networks about local conditions leads to increased cross-national investment.[87] At least part was being directed toward investment, strengthening the banking system and enhancing competition. In the FAR survey for Ethiopia, 14 percent of households reported that they used remittances for small business, savings and housing, while in

Kenya the survey reported that a third of regular remittance receivers say they use the money to invest in small business.[88] Nearly two-thirds of remittance receivers say they are able to save at least some of the money they receive.

In Africa remitters, as we have seen, tend to be of relatively high skill and income levels and these demographics point to higher rates of saving.[89] Households receiving transfers from other African countries are investing small amounts in business activities, housing, and other investments. But households receiving international remittances from OECD countries have been more likely to make investments, such as land purchases, construction, new businesses and farm improvement. This applied to 36 percent of remittance receiving households in Burkina Faso, 55 percent in Kenya, 57 percent in Nigeria, 15 percent in Senegal and 20 percent in Uganda.[90] In Egyptian households, remittances have increased the propensity to invest, mainly in residences and land. An increasing number of village associations and other social development initiatives in many African countries are channeling remittances to investment in agriculture (to finance irrigation and other agricultural inputs), equipment and small-scale businesses.

The IMF reported that households with access to remittances invested more in education, assets and small business, and that the impact was greater among poorer households without access to credit.[91] The report concludes that remittances may play an important role in fostering growth, although it also cites contrary findings. The World Bank concluded that, contrary to previous skepticism, remittances can encourage entrepreneurship, citing remittances from the United States in Mexico and the Philippines.[92] In 2008, Yang showed that increases in remittances in the Philippines are not fuelling consumption but paying for children's education and entrepreneurial activity. Remittances also have a social insurance function especially for conflict and post-disaster states (e.g. Haiti and Somalia), which increases long-term investment-type expenditure such as on girls' education.

The allocation of remittances to investment has taken place both directly through projects and indirectly through financial intermediation. Channeling through intermediaries may be expected to result both in more efficient allocation of investible funds and increased capacity of the financial intermediaries themselves.[93] This increased capacity has in some countries involved banks pledging remittance deposits as collateral for foreign borrowing helped by complementary improvements in country credit rating.[94] Table 5.7, from a World Bank report, shows some examples of how expected remittance flows have improved country ratings, favorably impacting formal investment.

In all these cases except Lebanon the credit rating rose as a result of the inclusion of expected remittance income.

Diaspora direct investment (DDI) may be able to compensate for market based FDI which has been historically disappointing in Africa, averaging, as we have seen, about US$30 billion a year over 2007–2009, a tiny share of the worldwide FDI, while market-based portfolio equity investment has not only been insignificant but also highly volatile. A recent study argues that because of the failure of FDI in Africa there remains skepticism toward foreign investment that deters investors and provides an opportunity for the less

Table 5.7. Impact of remittances on country credit rating and sovereign spread

	Remittances as percent of GDP 2004	Rating excluding remittances	Rating including remittances	Spread (basis points) saving
Serbia and Montenegro	7	B−	BB−	150
Lebanon	14	B−	B−	130
Haiti	28	CCC	B−	334
Nicaragua	11	CCC−	B−	209
Uganda	5	B−	B	161

Source: Global Economic Prospects (World Bank, 2006), 100ff.

risk-averse diaspora to step in.[95] The study reports that many diaspora investors return to their home countries to settle and establish a base, and with initial success they venture into upstream or downstream industries. One example of this has been Somaliland, a country that has had no formal donor recognition since it declared independence from Somalia in 1991 but is attracting significant diaspora investor interest.[96] Rather than the expensive financing deals required to attract FDI, diaspora entrepreneurs may simply need brokering assistance and introductions to people with whom they can work, such as are provided by the South African "Network of Skills Abroad."[97]

One avenue of investment, particularly in Latin America, which has expanded rapidly has been the collective vehicles known as hometown associations (HTAs), societies or trusts which pool money for community projects. In some cases these are matched by home governments. In Mexico, under the "3-to-1 program" HTA funds are matched by federal, state and local authorities and now number in the thousands. Similar associations have started up among immigrants from Asia, Indonesia, Malaysia, the Philippines, Guyana and Jamaica. HTAs collect funds from their members to support small-scale infrastructure in their hometowns.[98] For example, the Asociación San Mateo Cajonos in Mexico has supplied funds for paving of streets, a water pump, a dump truck and a school. Such programs do exactly the same things as community based aid projects, but their response to specific needs and the risk capital commitment by diaspora individuals suggest they will be better targeted and more effective.

Local government officials in Asia have sometimes spearheaded these initiatives by collecting funds from migrants for projects they have chosen. Philipino migrant communities have financed parks, libraries, hospital equipment and schools.[99] The EIU cites the case of one rural town in the Philippines with 56,000 residents which in 2001 boasted Internet cafés, car-rental services for returning migrants, video rental shops and a rural bank with over US$2m in deposits, 12 public and private irrigation facilities, 50 manufacturing establishments, six big private housing subdivisions and 32 day-care centers. The town's tax collection was one of the highest in the region.

State promotional centers attract diaspora investment by finding local partners and providing incentives such as tax exemptions. Special local, professionally managed, government bonds have been issued to finance improvements in urban infrastructure such as public markets, wharves and convention centers. Outside government an organization called Unlad Kabyan offers investment services to migrants, identification of investment opportunities and special startup funds for new businesses. Business networks such as Chambers of Commerce also promote investment through raising funds.

Efforts have not always succeeded. In Mexico, HTA investments have not prevented people leaving the rural areas to find urban employment. This suggests that even the diaspora does not always have the right idea. After all, it is unlikely that a new store or an upgraded road will stem the tide if the economy of a region as a whole is declining. The HTA initiatives are directed investments rather than investments through the open market and, as stated, sometimes investment through banking systems which go to the best opportunities regardless of geographical location might provide better results. This is especially the case where projects are hostage to the social constraints of small communities. In the latter context, one study quotes the member of a Mexican HTA: "because it's a small town and we're always jealous of each other … [if] we launch a productive project it has to be well organized, with discipline, with rules which enable us to succeed."[100] To get round such community rivalries one Mexican organization in the state of Guanajuato started the Mi Communidad program to attract migrants' savings for collective investment in small- and medium-sized enterprise projects.

How Much Investment?

As we have seen the non-aid private current flows to Sub-Saharan Africa could be running at US$60 billion per annum or more, which comes to 6 percent or more of the total subcontinental GNI in 2010, albeit varying widely from country to country. However, it would only be partly in the form of investible funds, at the most 25 percent, or US$15 billion, judging by the evidence, which amounts to 1.5 percent of Sub-Saharan GNI. Even assuming this relatively high propensity to invest out of these resources and a return on that investment substantially higher than that accruing to the average foreign-aid project, the contribution to economic growth from this source is likely to be no more than one half of one percent per annum averaged over the subcontinent. If we factor in to this amount the value of the accumulated investment in skills, knowhow and experience gained abroad by migrants to complement the investments, then the potential diaspora growth impact would be substantially higher, but would still perhaps not a transformative amount. This is then an important reality check on the potential role of remittance-like flows per se.

If we add to current private flows the potential value of returning capital, however, the potential diaspora contribution to growth would start to become more interesting. If the value in 2008 of the stock of African capital held overseas was US$607 billion, as referred to above, this is the equivalent of about 60 percent of Sub-Saharan Africa current GNI.[101] In principle, release of one-tenth of this stock, US$60 billion, back to Africa in the form of investments, combined with investment out of current flows and the complementary value of the skills and knowhow applied, could increase the worth of diaspora private investment overall to well over US$75 billion in a year over a limited period. If this could be realized, it could add something over 8 percentage points per annum to Africa's overall investment rate to GNI, fuelling a major increase in "indigenous" investment in Africa over a takeoff period, dwarfing both ODA and new FDI. One study of this issue estimates an even larger hypothetical increase in Sub-Saharan Africa's rate of domestic investment to GDP as a result of returning capital, from 18.5 percent to 29.6 percent, comparable to the proportions reached in some Asian economies.[102]

With respect to the recovery of illicit capital there have been some small beginnings. Nigeria, for example, recovered half a billion dollars from Swiss banks in 2005.[103] Though marginal compared to the cumulative stock of flight capital from Nigeria, it set a precedent. If this proves to have been the beginnings of a trend, it has the potential to be of greater importance than the increase in current remittances because returned capital is both larger and more directed to investment.

A further possible funding source for a resurging African economy is the substantial accumulated savings out of incomes earned outside Africa and held within host country financial institutions. Such savings are particularly high in the case of Zimbabwe, Liberia and the Congo where they are estimated to exceed 10 percent of national GDP. While hard data is not available, the World Bank estimates savings to be worth US$30 to US$50 billon per annum, 5 percent or more of Sub-Saharan Africa's GDI. If a part of this amount could be attracted into African financial institutions or investments each year, through diaspora bonds and mutual funds, then this could be a significant additional resource.[104] Such a reallocation, along with the other capital flows, would of course require that business conditions and incentives were appropriate.[105]

Taking all these sources together the overall value of diaspora resources for investment could approach US$100 billion a year, 10 percent of Sub-Saharan Africa GNI, more consistent with the requirements for the growth rates achieved in Sub-Saharan Africa over 2000–2007.

Of course, these are speculative estimates and they would require continuing improvements in the business environment in African countries in all its dimensions. An increase of this magnitude would be similar to the inflow of capital that occurred in Chile in the 1990s once it had cleared its debt problem, improved its macroeconomic management and reduced its country risk premium, which attracted a large proportion of the foreign direct investment flowing into the Latin American region in the late 1980s and 1990s. As a result of this program, Chile achieved investment and growth rates on an unprecedented scale.

A further supportive factor is the complementarity between professional migrant populations and direct foreign investment, whereby the presence of migrants on corporate payrolls in host countries can reduce perceived foreign investment risk. This has worked in the case of Indian migrant professionals, as discussed previously. In the US, according to one study, a one percent increase in the migrant stock is associated with a 0.3 percent increase in the FDI stock.[106] A similar increase in the number of migrants with tertiary education increases FDI by 0.4 percent. Furthermore, a 10 percent rise in the share of tertiary-educated migrants alone increases the FDI stock in their country of origin by an additional 0.5 percent. Migrant diasporas serve as a channel of investment information which integrates their home country with the global economy.

The various sources of expatriate "indigenous" capital to Sub-Saharan Africa could add up to a substantial resource for growth. But still another reality check is called for. The potential may not be realized, or may only be partly realized, and if it is distributed evenly over the subcontinent it might not be the major boost that it might at first appear. However, if these resources are concentrated within a group of more dynamic economies, then within those countries investment rates would be very significantly boosted with important potential effects on economic growth in specific parts of the African subcontinent, with potential spillover into the rest of Africa. This we will look at further.

Stories of the Diasporas

Very many diaspora organizations have emerged in the last few years to mobilize assistance. Their emergence is perhaps nowhere more noticeable than on the Internet. Websites have been set up to advertise jobs back home for emigrants and otherwise coordinate cultural, political and business initiatives such as collective investment promotion in many countries. Diaspora investor conferences and business plan contests have been organized and staged for many African countries through the Internet. The Ethiopian diaspora alone upwards of 12 news and media websites directed at its activities, located in various countries outside and within Ethiopia.[107]

Among the Internet-based organizations is AFFORD – the African Foundation for Development which was founded by Africans living in the UK as early as 1994. It supports entrepreneurs and SMEs, so far in the Congo, Ghana, Nigeria, Sierra Leone and Uganda, in business, marketing, and banking. AFFORD has helped create two business development centers in Sierra Leone and the "Hello Africa" Project to maintain networks of Ghanaian, Nigerians and Sierra Leonean communities in Britain. Another organization is IntEnt which was established in the Netherlands in 1996 by Social-Economical Entrepreneurship in the Netherlands (SEON), FACET BV and Triodos Bank, to stimulate entrepreneurship among immigrants. It offers fee-based support to entrepreneurs in Morocco, Turkey, Surinam, Ghana, Ethiopia, Afghanistan and the Antilles. AfricaRecruit visits university campuses in Europe and the United States to encourage African diaspora youth to seek employment back home.

There are also numerous aid-sponsored programs. The International Organization for Migration's MIDA program, launched in 2001 connects diaspora professionals online, and supports visits, investment and permanent return. MIDA has supported projects in Ghana and Senegal and selected entrepreneurs to receive training in business startup and management in donor countries such as Italy. Another program aimed at supporting diaspora assistance is the UNDP program for Transfer of Knowledge through Expatriate Nationals (TOKTEN), which began in Turkey in the 1970s and now covers some 50 countries, funding emigrant nationals with professional expertise to return to their countries of origin.

Electronic (virtual) diaspora activity is in a sense easy, since the barriers to entry are low and the effort correspondingly small. Thus, there may be a tendency to exaggerate the amount of productive effort that is under way. But on the other hand virtual activities lead to real, physical activities through the wide spread of information not previously accessible. The Middle East uprising of 2011 was a powerful indication of the real power generated by virtual power.

Many governments have held conventions to listen to ideas and maintain the diaspora relationship. One of the first actions of the new government of Kenya under Mwai Kibaki in 2003 was to reach out to the diaspora. Vincente Fox in Mexico appealed directly to nationals abroad when he came to office. When officials from the Dominica export and investment center visit the United States, they regularly visit diaspora organizations.[108] Even in post-conflict countries governments are trying to get closer to their diasporas to secure foreign investment. In Somaliland several individuals, all fluent in different languages, have returned since 1991 to serve in the Cabinet, while private investors have returned to look for opportunities, funding roads healthcare, education, electricity and manufacturing, and starting business-related journals.[109] Somaliland has attracted attention as a rare example of reconstruction and institution building without aid because it has not been formally eligible for assistance for the past 20 years.[110]

Diaspora members are less averse to investing in high-risk or emerging markets because of their detailed local knowledge and personal contacts. A World Bank report summarizes six mechanisms for professional diaspora networks to serve as catalysts in their home countries.[111] These are a) the "top executives model," whereby members of the diaspora who are top executives persuade their companies to invest in or outsource to their home countries; b) the "mentoring/venture capital model," whereby diaspora members who are managers or owners of firms work with startups in their home countries; c) the "diaspora members as investors model," whereby diaspora members use their knowledge to mitigate risks and reduce transaction costs in investing back home; d) the "setting new strategic direction/identifying new opportunities model," whereby diaspora members identify niche markets back home and develop business projects; e) the "return of talent model," whereby home country governments establish policies to encourage return; and f) the "basic outsourcing model," whereby successful diaspora members who own companies abroad outsource activities such as R&D or programming in their home countries.

India

The Indian diaspora is perhaps a model for other poor countries.[112] In the modern era it emerged initially in Britain. After 1947 there was an acceleration of migration by industrial workers, and later in 1972 an influx from East Africa following the expulsion from Uganda by Idi Amin. Indian immigrants have been increasingly highly skilled, particularly in the IT and medical professions. They total over 2 percent of the UK population, owning a relatively high proportion of businesses. There are over 1,000 organizations representing Indian regions or states, languages, religions and professions including academic and alumni organizations, and Indian political parties in Britain. The Indo-British Forum deals with non-resident Indian (NRI) policy in India. The NRIs have pressed for representation in the Indian parliament. In 2004, a dual-citizenship bill was adopted in the Indian parliament for the UK, US and a number of other countries and fiscal measures were taken to encourage inward investment.

In the US, the 1.7 million-strong Indian diaspora (based on the US Census of 2000) has a median annual income more than 50 percent higher than the US median income. Further, 67 percent of foreign-born Indian-Americans at work have college degrees, three times the US average, and out of these approximately 44 percent hold managerial or professional positions. About 300,000 workers of Indian origin were engaged in the IT sector in the early years of the 2000s at professional and management level with several hundred Silicon Valley startups having at least one founder of Indian origin. Out of a total of 13,000 Indian science and engineering doctorate recipients at US universities between 1985 and 2000, approximately 58 percent accepted job offers in the US. Out of these, a quarter was engaged in post-doctoral work and a third employed in industry.[113]

A study for the MPI citing the American Community Survey found similar results. Three-quarters of Indian-born adults age 25 and older had a bachelor's degree or higher, far higher than the US average.[114] In 2000, the Indian government formed a Committee on the Diaspora and in 2003 declared 9 January as Non-resident Indian Day. Interest in temporary or permanent return was found to be increasing among émigrés, some of whom were establishing their own companies. A high proportion held Overseas Citizenship of India (OCI) cards that encouraged interest by the diaspora in returning. Many returnees were the children of professionals who had left for the United States, now attracted back by high-level job opportunities.[115]

The launch of economic reforms in India in 1991 opened up new business opportunities for the diaspora particularly in high technology development through outsourcing ICT work to the huge pool of computer and software professionals in India, and providing technical and managerial knowledge for new businesses back home.[116] Many Indian engineers in the US in top-management positions were able to outsource back to IT companies in India at low cost, thereby boosting skills in India; and some Indians returned to India to manage outsourced investments and to train Indian professionals. Thus, the US Indian diaspora has helped build India's reputation for US and European companies seeking to outsource, as a source of exported goods and services, including R&D, and as a destination for investment.

The attitude of young Indians towards returning remains ambivalent because they have to face considerable difficulties at home in terms of factors like infrastructure availability, labor attitudes and the general living environment compared to what they would face in Europe or the US. However, the tendency to return is growing.

The Indus Entrepreneurs (TiE) and Venture Capital

In 1992, a group called The Indus Entrepreneurs (TiE) was established by Silicon Valley entrepreneurs from the Indian subcontinent to act as a network for mentoring of early stage companies. It now has reportedly 13,000 members in 13 countries.[117] Its membership is open, but its board and staff are of South Asian origin. Out of 53 local chapters, 25 are in the US and 22 in India. Its membership has been growing at about 20 percent per year, making it one of the world's largest formal entrepreneurial networks.

TiE focuses on promoting entrepreneurship in the Indus region (India and Pakistan). It has partnered with Microsoft Corporation to provide startup companies with technical support along with its own networking and mentoring services. It assisted the growing Indian IT industry in the mid- and late 1990s, some members investing in or starting their own companies or going back to manage US subsidiary companies. An estimated 200 IT-based companies have been started by returning professionals. Indian senior executives at US corporations supported outsourcing which drove the IT industry in India forward. TiE helped to start an International School of Business at which Indian professors teaching in the US, UK and Canada take sabbaticals. The TiE and the Silicon Valley Bank mounted familiarization trips for US venture capitalists, and some venture capital funds in the US now require their startup companies to have a back end in India so that they can save on research and development costs.

In the early 1980s, the early-stage venture capital model was transferred to countries like Taiwan and Israel by returning investors, bringing with them technical and operating experience and networks of contacts from the United States.[118] The more recent wave of migrants started from the 1970s as a result of changes in US immigration policy. By 2000 over half of Silicon Valley's scientists and engineers were foreign. Indian and Chinese alone accounted for over 25 percent of the region's scientists and engineers, approximately 20,000 from each country.

Transfer of the venture-capital model has required prior preparation. To compensate for lack of infrastructure returning entrepreneurs have had to set up private telecommunications facilities and power supplies, and in some cases circumvent still burdensome local regulations by incorporating their businesses in the US. The initial Indian venture-capital industry that emerged in the 1990s had been based on public sector funds and public banks, supported by relatively risk-averse multilateral institutions with little knowledge of technology-related industries, focusing on later-stage investments. By 1998 only 21 companies were registered with the Indian Venture Capital Association compared to Israel's 100 funds and Taiwan's 110 funds. However, with the opening up of the financial sector in the 1990s the situation changed markedly and momentum has built up. A group of new US$50 million to US$100 million funds, from major investors such as such as Walden International and E-Ventures (Softbank), have started to target early-stage investments.

While I have suggested that the Indian diaspora is a model for other countries, this is, however, subject to some important qualifiers. In this respect two factors are critical. Firstly, India has invested very heavily in college-level science and math education and it produces approximately 2.5 million graduates a year out of which nearly 300,000 are engineers and IT professionals and 40,000 are MBAs. (The US produces an overall total of 1.25 million graduates.) Secondly, India's access to the US and other rich-country labor markets may have carried a first-mover advantage, which allowed building of extensive networks of professionals such as the TiE.

The Overseas Chinese

There are an estimated 55 million Chinese in the diaspora.[119] Although there was considerable migration from the early nineteenth century until 1949 from coastal provinces to neighboring countries or regions, it accelerated following the open-door policy of 1978 when more Chinese went abroad to study or work.[120] The economic reforms since 1978 provided an opportunity, and the government appealed to the overseas Chinese for both capital and technology as part of the country's new development campaign. A government Department of Overseas Chinese Affairs was established. When many non-Chinese foreign firms divested after the Tiananmen Square crackdown in 1989, special regulations for encouraging investment were promulgated by the government. Regulations included the 1990 Law on the Protection of the Rights and Interests of Returned Overseas, which permitted remittances to be received and ordered local governments to support their efforts to establish commercial, industrial or agricultural ventures.

Cultural familiarity combined with the stable political environment, preferential policies and promises of reform induced many overseas Chinese to invest in small and medium-sized ventures. Investment by overseas Chinese not only accounts for the lion's share of total foreign investment in China (as high as 60–80 percent over 1983–96) but has induced other investors to follow. Since the late 1990s, more and more overseas Chinese scientists and engineers began to return back to work in science laboratories or to set up IT, alternative energy, biotechnology, and electronics companies. Many of these companies have gone public in the US and Hong Kong. The presence of the Chinese diaspora also helped many multinationals to set up subsidiaries or R&D laboratories in China.

China has gained from the presence of its diaspora in terms of both capital and local market awareness.[121] The Chinese in countries such as Indonesia, Thailand and Malaysia have a combination of capital and strong local connections. China's special economic zones (SEZs) were initially located close to Hong Kong and Taiwan where many Chinese had emigrated. The first wave of FDI was thus from the overseas Chinese. It concentrated in coastal areas on lower-quality manufacturing for export such as toys, clothes and shoes. Laws were introduced to give special privileges to overseas Chinese such as reduced land use fees, fewer restrictions through taxes and other special incentives. A quarter of the overseas Chinese who have left China in the last 30 years have returned home.

The diaspora opened up export markets initially to Hong Kong and East Asia, and once the FDI inflows accelerated and growth picked up other investors began joint ventures. The overseas Chinese business networks were larger and more active even than Indian networks, often taking advantage of weak legal systems and opaque regulatory structures to open up supply and distribution and operating licenses.

African Diasporas

Information on the activities of Sub-Saharan African diasporas in relation to their home countries is rather piecemeal. There are, as we have seen, at least 18 million first-generation migrants. About one-third of the total are resident in Europe and North America and, as in the case of India, a relatively high percentage have college degrees. The top five African recipients of diaspora investment have been Nigeria, Kenya, South Africa, Uganda and Ghana.[122] The relatively high skills of the African diaspora put them in principle in a similar category to the Asian diasporas.[123] There remains great scope for diaspora networks to support public projects and set up professional networks to share information with contacts in the homeland.[124]

Ethiopians in the US

The Ethiopian diaspora, based largely in Washington, DC, comprises a fifth of the foreign-born population from Sub-Saharan Africa living in the Washington area, totaling about 28,000. It is one of the most active African diasporas in the US, putting continual pressure on its government. There have been annual Ethiopian business conferences in New York or Washington since 2006.

According to the US Census Bureau, the Ethiopian immigrant population in the US grew from 7,500 in 1980 to 137,000 in 2008. In addition, about 30,000 native-born US citizens claim Ethiopian ancestry. Compared to other immigrants, Ethiopian-born immigrants aged 25 or older tend to be better educated, with 59 percent having had some level of college education or higher. Only 8 percent have less than high school education, 23 percent have bachelor's degrees and 12 percent have professional or graduate degrees.

The Ethiopian diaspora differs from those of India and China in several ways.[125] For example, it originally arrived largely as refugees from civil war in the 1970s and this factor has not been consistent in many diasporas with voluntary return or investment in the home country. However, the high level of education and high proportion in salaried jobs (in health care, educational, professional, managerial and retail services) has helped to promote investment interest.

Although one study in urban areas of Ethiopia has found that less than 6 percent of remittances to the country go towards investments, savings or the acquisition of assets, anecdotally many members of the diaspora have started to establish ventures in their home country, including food processing, manufacturing, IT, leasing of machinery, hotels, Internet cafes, retailing and real estate.[126] A restaurateur used capital and expertise from operating her DC restaurant to open a small hotel in Addis Ababa. An Ethiopian realtor has promoted upscale housing development for returning immigrants and richer locals.

Ethiopian immigrant business networks are supported by organizations such as the Ethiopian-American Chamber of Commerce, the Ethiopian Professionals Association Network, the Ethiopian Business Association and the Ethiopian Community Development Council. Ethiopian Diaspora Business Forums were held in Washington, DC in 2008 and 2009. The Ethiopian government up to 2006 offered diasporans special legal status, tax breaks and other investment incentives to promote return entrepreneurship, issuing between 1992 and mid-2009 over 1,800 investment licenses to Ethiopians living abroad, more than a third in the US. Still, the tendency must not be exaggerated. Diaspora investment in the past decade has accounted for only about 10 percent of total investment in Addis Ababa, the capital, according to the Ethiopian Investment Agency.

The government has asked leading members of the diaspora to organize a forum for policy input, and has launched the Diaspora Trade and Investment Center and a diaspora knowledge network. The government is working with the diaspora in the health and IT sectors, including bringing medical specialists to Ethiopia. A directorate general for diaspora affairs has been set up to support investment and trade related issues, a research department on diaspora investments, and a department to assist with issues such as relocation, family reunion and property adjudication. The country has established the Ethiopian Origin ID card that entitles any member of the diaspora to the same treatment as Ethiopian citizens, including the right to invest in all sectors except the financial sector, and the right to import, tax-free, capital goods to start up investment projects.

Nigerians and Ghanaians in the UK

The Nigerian diaspora has emerged since independence in 1960 in Africa, North America and Europe.[127] As in the case of India, Nigerians principally went to Britain, especially following the Biafran secession and civil war in the late 1960s. In 1971, about 28,000 Nigerians lived in England and Wales (according to the UK Census). The next major wave of emigration was in the 1980s and currently according to the census the Nigerian population in Britain is close on 100,000.

The Nigerian diaspora network in Britain includes business associations representing the country and ethnic religious and regional organizations represent sectional and communal interests. Sectional interests have tended to act for or against the "common" diaspora interest in parallel with ethnic and other groups. The diaspora also has pan-African interests through, for example, the African Foundation for Development (AFFORD).[128] According to the Nigeria Investment Promotion Commission each year some 2,000 Nigerians trained outside the country return home to seek employment or business opportunities. Political groups include the pro-democracy United Democratic Front of Nigeria–Abroad and the National Democratic Coalition Abroad. The two organizations have jointly organized two "world Congresses of Free Nigerians" in Washington and London. There are also the Nigerians in the Diaspora Europe (NIDOE) and "Dunamis Impact."

Ghanaians have also particularly moved to Britain.[129] The Ghanaian diaspora is one of the largest West African communities in Britain. It was initiated at the time of independence in 1957 and expanded because of political problems at home after 1981. By 2001 according to the census the population was 56,000, of which a substantial proportion was skilled, particularly in the health sector. There is an extensive network including more than 100 cultural, social, professional, ethnic, welfare and political associations in Britain.[130] There are also several small Ghanaian hometown associations. The diaspora is politically engaged, with active UK branches of the main Ghanaian political parties, encouraged by the Ghana government. In 2002, a Ghanaian

Dual-Citizenship Regulation Act was passed and discussions have taken place to allow a diaspora vote in national elections.

The UK Ghanaian diaspora is active in development projects raising funds for schools and clinics and medical laboratories. A health-insurance initiative for relatives in Ghana has been launched by some Ghana-based financial institutions. In 2003, an exhibition fair was held in London to link Ghanaians with businesses and services in Ghana. Another initiative has been the Non-resident Ghanaian Fund for investment.

Diasporas and Political Influence Back Home

The influence of the diasporas back home is bound up in their acquisition of economic, political, institutional and business experience and knowhow in their host country, as well as their communal and ethnic backgrounds. These skills, which Kapur and others have described as "social remittances" are an important precondition for a major diaspora contribution to development.[131] Migrants acquire social remittances through education, training, learning on the job and absorption of work ethics, values and attitudes as well as involvement in host country local politics.[132]

At the same time, the departure of educated citizens from their home countries may weaken home political institutions and therefore increase the influence of those that emigrated. This tendency may be enhanced if remittance income from emigrants reduces incentives to political action at home; but in the long run openness to migration is considered to have generally contributed to improved institutional quality at home (as measured by indicators of democracy and economic freedom). This is made more likely if emigration has a "brain gain" effect by stimulating demand for education in the home country.

Earlier diasporas have been the political training ground for many if not most of the world's most influential developing country leaders. These included the first modern era nationalists such as Lenin, Gandhi, Nehru, Chou En Lai, Ho Chi Minh, Nkrumah, Kenyatta, Banda and Nyerere, and this process has continued all the way through to quite recent returnees such as President Ellen Sirleaf Johnson of Liberia. Leaders of several stateless diasporas including Kurds, Kashmiris and Sri Lankan Tamils have struggled towards political recognition abroad. Malawi's Banda practiced as a medical doctor in London in the 1950s. The experience of living abroad was empowering simply because it provided a perspective on the complexities and divisions within the colonizing society that could not be perceived or understood within the colonized society where the colonizers projected themselves as a monolithic, irresistible force.

Expatriate votes are of concern to many countries with sizable diasporas. As described, several countries in Africa have granted dual nationality and voting rights to diaspora members. Overseas nationals such as in the case of Turkey and Israel have returned home to vote or voted in large numbers at overseas embassies. Some governments have started to actively welcome political participation by their diaspora, as in the case of India. Dual citizenship and nationality is expanding and in some cases special forms of representation in governments have been established. In 1990, Croatians abroad were rewarded for their support to Fanjo Tudjman with 10 percent of the seats in parliament.[133] In July 2010, Peruvian presidential candidate Keiko Fujimori visited Paterson, New Jersey to court diaspora votes in advance of the April 2011 election, promising to push for representation of the diaspora in Peru's congress.[134] Equally, diaspora leaders can cause destabilization – as in the case of Ethiopia, Kosovo and Kashmir.

The website *Mwakilishi.com* published an article in February 2011 entitled "Kenyans in Diaspora Want Stake in Local Politics." It read:

> A new political wave of Kenyans in the diaspora is set to ripple across the country in the run up to 2012 general elections. With all the money and resources, the group has vowed to consolidate their numbers to create a formidable force to take over power from the current leadership. Under the banner Kenyans in Diaspora for Change, the movement hopes to bring together all the diaspora organizations to chart the way forward ahead of the coming elections. Already, five groups – the Kenya Community Abroad, New Vision Kenya, Kenya Global Unity, the Diaspora Movement of Kenya and the Kenya for Change – have expressed willingness to unite. … A spokesman said, "We will field candidates for governorship, senators and civic candidates in their respective regions. … Most governments have left us out. We are now organizing ourselves as never before to kick out these leaders."[135]

Among the many countries with government ministries dedicated to the diaspora are India, Syria, Haiti, Georgia and Bangladesh. The Ministry for Overseas Indian Affairs runs a three-week "Know India" internship program among second- and later generation migrants.[136] The government of Mali has designated its diaspora "the 9th region of Mali." Through the High Council of Malians Abroad, members of the diaspora in over 50 countries feed their ideas back to the government. Research suggests that the success of government overtures depends on how seriously they have undertaken the initial research before setting up a diaspora agency, the resources committed, the avoidance of bureaucratic rivalries and the incorporation of diaspora plans into national development planning.[137]

Do Diasporas Have a Common Purpose?

The power of the diaspora is associated with the experience of how rich societies operate, i.e. social remittances. This is a key to the diaspora as a potent force. However, in many cases it is not a homogeneous force and it is not the case that diasporas always act in common. In fact, class, caste, ethnicity and other conflicts on home soil are sometimes replicated outside the country. In some cases, the diaspora exists in exile largely because of opposition to a regime (for example, in Iran, Sri Lanka, Somalia, Ethiopia and Nicaragua) and may hold back on support until that regime changes. In other cases, support for the home government is riven by strong group rivalries. For example, the clan rivalries that are at the heart of Somalia's chronic instability are replicated in the Somali diaspora. On the other hand, the Israeli and Armenian diasporas have shown relatively strong cohesion. There are thus differences between conflict-generated "push" diasporas and economic migrant "pull" diasporas, but there are also social divisions in both.

In 2004 CasteWatchUK was launched to raise awareness of caste-based discrimination occurring in the UK within the Indian diaspora. CasteWatch assists groups such as the Dalit Solidarity Network, which represents the 200 million so-called "untouchables" in India. On the other hand, the refugee-origin Ethiopian diaspora in the US is split between supporters of the EPRDF government and a range of opposition movements and secessionist groups (especially from the south), who send delegations to brief their respective communities in Washington and to solicit their support.[138] Using a wide range of organizations, newspapers, websites and radio and television shows, different Ethiopian communities have lobbied for specific interests including human rights in Ethiopia. Interestingly, however, when a border war erupted with Eritrea in 1998 the various interests came together to support the government.[139]

So the diaspora is not necessarily a solid community gathering its resources to ride to the rescue of the home country. Nevertheless, it is reasonable to suppose that emigration changes attitudes, the more so as younger generations migrate, and that, at least outside conflict-generated exile, the changed attitudes result in greater energy and direction towards the provision of public goods in the home country. For example, women who were excluded from public and business affairs in their home countries, such as from Somalia, have taken advantage of their emancipated status to start businesses. Even in diasporas divided by conflict circumstances can create a common approach, as in the case of the Ethiopian war with Eritrea. As we have seen, there are significant incentives for a diaspora member free of traditional ties to get involved in political action.[140]

Why Are They Important? Who Owns Diaspora Resources?

Members of the diaspora are in many cases first-generation émigrés who have living memories of their homeland and allegiance to it. They feel a need to help out and to ensure that their own contribution is spent wisely. They have "ownership" and accountability. This is the sense in which diaspora investment has a higher potential impact than general foreign investment via the market.

Ordinary individuals with ownership are more likely to be effective in transferring attitudes, values, norms and expectations than alien professionals. They can help foster a culture of entrepreneurship in countries where it is not a traditional approach to business.[141] Many members of diasporas see themselves, and to some extent are seen, as retaining a legitimate role as contributors to policy or as opinion formers. As investors, they may require a lower-risk premium for investing in their home country than the market as a whole and are probably more likely to invest in production for the home market. They therefore behave more like a home investor. Indeed, in some senses diaspora funding may be regarded as domestic funding.

Unlike foreign aid, diaspora inflows (remittance, reverse capital flows and others) are also not a complex, tied and conditional flow of resources arriving fragmented into numerous pools of funds, sets of rules and reporting requirements. They do not come through a non-transparent giving process into an unaccountable receiving process at the behest of a market-blind bureaucracy on both sides, funneled through state organizations or charitable entities. Depending on various factors like income, skill levels, time away, the politics of their home country and economic prospects, the people of the diaspora may see their home country as a critical destination for their savings. They are sending money to "their country."

There need to be reality checks, as we have discussed on several occasions. Remittances go largely into consumption, and the totality of private current flows, even including an element of returned capital, may not be enough to fuel a very large increase in rates of investment, unless concentrated in a few countries. Secondly, there are social and political divisions that often prevent a diaspora community acting with a single voice on public goods investment. Then the distribution of remittance flows is unequal between countries because it is weighted towards the middle- and upper-middle-income migrants and their families, and so it is not necessarily poverty focused. The money may also belong disproportionately to specific groups, classes, castes or elites, some of whom exported capital previously.

But leaving aside these caveats, all of which have significance in particular contexts, the central issue here is the *national identity of the resources* that flow in. This factor alone has a significant bearing on the incentive system surrounding the use of these resources for economic development. Capital and income in the hands of a country's indigenous people involves a different structure of obligation and accountability than that prevailing under foreign aid, and to some extent also that prevailing under market-based foreign investment by international companies. The alienation of government officials who spend their days processing donor offerings does not occur when the aid is private.

In addition to the importance of who owns the resources, there are several other factors that contrast diaspora remittances favorably with foreign assistance. Firstly, they directly increase the purchasing power of the population without needing programming intermediaries, complex politically driven decision environments and other elements of transaction cost. Secondly, despite some evidence of remittances being used to replace work effort in some countries or regions, cash from people who are committed to using it wisely has been more likely to be spent on things that are needed, including both consumption and investment; in other words, a portfolio choice aimed at what are perceived as good opportunities. Thirdly, the cash is automatically monitored by the sender in his or her own interests without elaborate and costly monitoring and evaluation infrastructures.[142] Fourthly, the cash may arrive along with the technical knowhow of its sender (technological, marketing, governance legal, etc.). Finally, a substantial and apparently increasing proportion of diaspora money does go into various types of productive investment, education, health, real estate and small business, and into financial intermediation, in other words to many of the same destinations that foreign aid is ideally intended to go but often does not.

"Real cash flows" are also different from aid flows in that aid consists of a mix of soft and hard resource inputs of indefinite and ambiguous value. What is formally defined as aid, as we have seen, consists of the donor's aid administration costs, technical assistance, training, capacity building, conditional economic adjustment and budget support, specialized vertical funds and capital projects, sometimes overvalued by the high prices of services prevailing in the home market of the donor. In comparison to this alphabet soup of resources, the flow of diaspora cash is homogeneous, without strings, outside government control and directly increases the market power of individual economic agents and may in this sense be regarded as *high-powered money*.

What Should an Aid Donor Do about Migration?

A very large number of donor-supported organizations, agencies and departments specifically to support and study migration have come into existence in the past few years, through the World Bank, UN, ILO, bilateral aid agencies and through numerous independent think tanks worldwide.[143] Numerous US and European universities house departments and research programs dedicated to migration issues, often funded by donor-agency research grants. As mentioned, initiatives have been started by the International Organization for Migration; for example, the Migration for Development in Africa program (MIDA) which was started in 2001. The UN has a program called "Transfer of Knowledge through Expatriate Nationals (TOKTEN)."[144]

Donors agencies have decided that the diasporas are an important resource, an important conduit for development initiatives and an important source of advice for the donors themselves because of their local knowledge and their understanding of what is likely to work in development. What should be the role of such donor agencies?

Given the main thesis of this book on the problems of the aid relationship, it stands to reason that the donor–diaspora relationship also needs some clear thinking. In particular, from the potential diaspora recipients' point of view, it is not entirely clear what public interest (of the recipient country) is being served by intervention in an ongoing, buoyant private-sector activity. Further, it is problematic insofar as donors tend to view their relationship with the diaspora in the same terms as their general aid effort, as a paternalistic, even charitable one, a view that may be encouraged by elements of the diaspora who are rent seekers looking for donations rather than entrepreneurs taking risks and seeking rewards from investments in their home countries.

One influential US voice seems to look at the diaspora relationship as part of the traditional aid relationship, with systems of rewards and punishment.[145] There seems to be an assumption that the donor has the power to do good for the diaspora, that the diasporas are waiting for the donors to develop a partnership with them, and that the donor must determine which agency deserves assistance. In this view the donor is in charge and is looking to the diaspora to "fit in" with the donors" programs. The donor's role should be to: "listen" (especially to the weaker members whose voices are less heard); "support" the rights of diasporas; "train" diaspora groups in how donor agencies work; "evaluate" programs of diaspora engagement to identify best practices; "share information" on the donors goals so that the diaspora can fit in with these goals in advocating home government action. For their part, "donors should be strengthening their own capacities to listen and respond (when appropriate) to diaspora advocacy."[116] A recent publication jointly by the IOM and MPI takes a similar position. While humbly admitting that diasporas were taking initiatives "long before the international community took notice," it then develops a "strategic action plan" for recipient governments.[117]

In this context, a principal US government initiative is the USAID sponsored "diaspora marketplace" which amongst other things organizes diaspora conventions.[118] Many other donor agencies including the World Bank are also currently staging conventions and conferences as a centerpiece of their engagement strategy. But it is questionable why a bona fide diaspora entrepreneur (as opposed to an aid-opportunist) needs multiple, expensively staged pep rallies about investment, while it is certain that he or she does need markets, customers and a friendly bank manager. For this individual, there are decreasing returns with each successive conference while, increasingly, the event beneficiary becomes the donor agency itself who chalks up another developmental event to encourage its principals.

In November 2011, the World Bank announced a "Consultation on Knowledge Partnership on Migration and Global Development." The partnership, they stated, would provide a multidisciplinary platform for debate and conduct pilot capacity building to evaluate and mainstream policy choices. It would be "a resource for policy makers, the member agencies of the Global Migration Group (GMG), regional development banks, donors, and different organizations involved in mainstreaming migration and remittances into national development plans, country strategies, and projects/programs on migration and remittances."[149]

Is this emerging donor interpretation of the role that the donors can play valid? The discussion of this book suggests that it may not be. Instead, the attitude of donors to the diaspora seems to be at risk of developing into something parallel to the flawed donor–government model.

Chapter 6

"NEW AID": NEW WAYS TO PROMOTE AND FINANCE DEVELOPMENT?

If there is any consensus today about what strategies are likely to help the development of the poorest countries it is this: there is no consensus.

Joseph Stiglitz (2005)[1]

Non-alienating and Alienating Aid

Before moving towards a conclusion we can turn our attention once again to the efforts of the aid donors following the "New Start" endorsed by the Paris and other international conferences in the first decade of the 2000s. Does this New Start in the end at least have the potential to make foreign aid effective?

At the start of this book it was suggested that aid might be reclassified into two more categories – alienative and non-alienative. Assistance in general can have negative effects but certain types of assistance tend to be the more negative, especially within the soft category of aid. The latter tend to be more intrusive, longer term and have negative effects on capacity, motivation and "buy-in." These were called "type B." Non-alienative assistance on the other hand tended to be more instrumental, focused on gaps in capability, shorter term and less likely to have the negative effects. These were called "type A." The issue here is one of process and effective development assistance. That is, it is as much to do with the "process" by which assistance is delivered as the product that is delivered.

One illustration of the dichotomy between type A and type B, alluded to before, is the choice between "technical assistance" and "capacity building," the latter of which became in the 1990s a kind of mantra in most aid programs. As we have seen, the first approach was considered to have failed in the 1980s apparently because it was too narrowly based and short term, involving filling gaps in skills within existing organizations. Richard Jolly, a leading development thinker, proclaimed that the majority of TA programs had "outlived their usefulness."[2] Instead, the donors shifted to a more intrusive, total-quality-management type of support to organizations. But the results seem to have been no better in many countries, and have probably cost more. As mentioned in Chapter 3, the World Bank's evaluators gave poor marks to many capacity building programs including decades of assistance to the Zambian and Malawian civil services.

Capacity building remains the central philosophy. The DFID Multilateral Aid Review of 2011, for example, rated as worst performer out of 40 organizations the

Commonwealth Secretariat. One of the reasons for their displeasure was the piecemeal nature of its assistance, placing individuals in organizations to do discrete jobs, as opposed to the more holistic approach. Yet for many organizations specific, well-targeted technical assistance may be the most effective. Indeed it may be concluded that neither the micro nor the macro approach has worked but the second has not only not worked but has arguably performed even worse than the alternative to which it was supposed to be superior.

As we have seen, the way aid is delivered has not been critical for large countries where aid is a relatively very small component of national income; however, for smaller aid-dependent poor countries the method by which foreign assistance has been delivered has been critical. If aid is a key element in social and institutional development, then its negative features become proportionately more critical. For poor, aid-dependent countries the key is to find a way to deliver aid that is consistent with the capacity and need to make decisions and take responsibility.

Table 6.1 draws up a stylized, perhaps extreme, illustration of type-A and type-B assistance for capacity building. Some of the key "ownership" factors that have been discussed earlier are taken into account, including systemic factors such as aid fragmentation and specific project-related factors such as who is the designer and how is the assistance paid for.

Type A is a local initiative, simpler, more like a commercial contract (with a cash payment by the recipient), contracted within the country and subject to approval by and accountable to a local authority, managed by a local agency, with conditions related mainly to contract performance. Type B is externally conceived and implemented by a donor consortium, contracted outside the country, bypasses local legislative approval, goes to non-government agencies as a grant, is managed by a donor-contracted agent, is subject to detailed monitoring and evaluation, and has detailed government and sector performance conditions.

Type B is an externally implemented yet more intrusive intervention than type A, requiring a larger footprint in the recipient country once it has been implemented, even though at the planning stage the country authority is largely out of the picture. It develops lower local buy-in at the preparation stage while it is more heavy-handed and demanding of local buy-in at the operational stage, when that buy-in is less likely to be forthcoming, partly because of lack of participation at the start.

Taking "type A" as the model and advisory services (software) as the product, New Aid would be structured around the purchase of international services by governments or their agents on a quasi-commercial basis. It could involve contracts, payments, and the minimum of transaction cost. Very broadly, assistance funds, or donor subsidies, would be designed to be obtained through a competitive process from pooled donor resources against a matching or semi-matching payment for service from the government or its designated buyer. It would be up to the purchasers to procure services according to needs that they define and according to their own rules for contracting and procurement, and subject to their own evaluations.

In this model the donor agency's footprint would be reduced significantly and, again very broadly, would become one of agreeing country subsidy rates, managing

Table 6.1.

Project activity	Example of type A – Non-alienative capacity building assistance	Example of type B – Alienative capacity building assistance
Product	Technical advice to existing government department or agency	Capacity-building program for government department or agency
Originated by	Potential recipient based on identified need, often as part of wider national or regional programs	Aid donors (multiple) with limited local collaboration
Designed by	Potential recipient organizations	Aid donors (multiple) with limited local collaboration
Programmed by	National authorities or individual organizations	As part of broader external assistance initiative
Budget arrangements	Passed through national, local government or non-government formal budgetary processes as part of specific or blanket approval	Budget allocated directly to agency or project without formal approval by legislative body, singly or as part of package
Paid for by	Local agency with own budgeted funds supplemented by aid contribution	100 percent grant funded directly by participating donors
Contractual arrangements	Subject to commercially oriented contract between recipient organization and service supplier for work to be done	Tendered by aid donors and awarded outside recipient country, with direct payment from donor agency to contract holder
Managed by	Local organization with intermittent outside reporting	Donor agency plus local hired staff through project management unit set up outside government
Reporting to	Local organization management, board or oversight organs	Donor agency with token participation of national/sub-national government agency
Performance requirements	As per contract	Detailed performance criteria based on input, output and outcome targets
Conditions	Related to contract performance	Related to contract, government and macroeconomic management performance

funds and providing information on the kinds of assistance that can be purchased. At a given interval the donor would audit the program and review the justification for further assistance funding.

Mistakes would be made by the recipient country. Learning by doing would be required over some time. Many types of assistance would still be needed and would be purchasable, and this would require that the purchasers learn what resources are available and develop an awareness of what exactly they want. If governments want subsidized assistance in international procurement, management and implementation of capital projects, drafting of laws and regulations, organizational reform or agricultural strategy, it would be up to them to secure the required local and foreign funds. If they wanted advice on tax collection, budgeting, how to phase out foreign aid, or how to negotiate with the diaspora, they would be free to purchase these services. Governments and agencies would move to a process of buying and contracting assistance and incorporating the services purchased within their operations. They would also themselves judge whether the services have been worthwhile. Obtaining of expertise would not require signing on to complex, risky, externally formulated institution building programs, strategies, plans and evaluation processes.

New Aid's New Methods

A number of new approaches to development assistance have been proposed in the past few years, in the context of the Paris and other international declarations.[3] Let us look, albeit rather cursorily, at how far a selection of the principal approaches to the conduct and financing of development assistance might rate against an objective of non-alienating assistance and the aid delivery model sketched out above.

Output-based aid

Output-based aid (OBA) was adopted in the first decade of the 2000s, initially by the World Bank and British DFID through the Global Partnership for Output-Based Aid (GPOBA). OBA is a method that is intended to ensure results on the ground by tying funding to agreed performance. It is a type of performance based funding (PBF). The method has been employed in health care, water, transport, energy and to a small extent education. According to the World Bank, since GPOBA was first launched in March 2002 it has identified 131 projects with a value of around US$3.5 billion, mostly in Latin America and the Caribbean. By 2010, the actual portfolio consisted of 31 grant agreements worth US$125 million. GPOBA's website describes its task as building a "robust sample of pilot projects from which to draw lessons and develop best practice."

The projects involve targeting community services through direct payments to providers or customers. The assistance can be provided in the form of vouchers for payment or direct payments to service providers. The provision of transparent subsidies tied to monitorable results on the ground is undoubtedly an advantage from the donor point of view since it provides a way for the donor agency to be accountable to its principals. The service provider bears the risk of non-payment if it fails to perform and the assistance is better targeted than traditional input-based aid. Some advantages also accrue to the recipient from the performance-based approach if it encourages better performance. For example, any health-service provider that enters the scheme might receive a subsidy according to the number of patients it serves, and the patient or client gets a choice of service provider.

However, a number of criticisms have been made. As is common with grant schemes, the subsidy may be directed to existing providers, including providers who do not need subsidies but have an access advantage over new applicants who may lack information or up front finance. It may also be difficult to find the population that needs to be targeted, leaving a lot of leakage into non-needy groups. The transfer of risk to the service providers may not work in countries where such service providers are highly risk averse. These factors may discourage new service providers. Thus "additionality" may be weak.

Close targeting and the associated administration and monitoring of OBA also inevitably incurs high project design and management costs. Yet despite close monitoring payments for services may be gamed and both providers and recipients find ways of colluding to increase subsidies beyond their needs. The use of vouchers also results in additional administrative costs.

A more systemic criticism of OBA is that success at the micro level may obscure the need for sector initiatives. In the case of health care this might mean clean water and family planning. OBA can also be a form of under-the-radar privatizing of basic services through donor projects, which may otherwise be regarded as part of the public goods responsibility of governments. The creation of a private market for a public good also requires a sound regulatory environment, a reliable and motivated service provider, and regulated tariffs. By focusing on direct delivery OBA also bypasses the government budget. Finally, it is notable that the GPOBA program, which is the central thrust of the OBA initiative, still regards itself after nearly 10 years as a "pilot program," a distinction that allows it to claim a public goods role and avoid too much scrutiny.

Where does OBA stand on the alienation count? On the negative side, in most cases it is designed and programmed by the donor since it is a specialized instrument responding to donor rather than government concerns. The requirement for proof of performance is potentially intrusive, generally requiring heavyweight ongoing management, especially in setting up and operating a monitoring and evaluation system. Project management contracting is probably done largely by the donor with a non-domestic agency, because OBA requires specialist independent expertise. The commitment and disbursement of funds is outside any local budget apparatus. On the positive side the service is paid for against partial reimbursement.

On balance the relative alienation rating for OBA looks to be poor.

Cash on delivery

In 2010 the Center for Global Development announced cash-on-delivery (COD) aid, which may be regarded as another example of the genre performance-based funding (PBF).[4] Like PBF, COD is designed to reduce the principal–agent problem as well as hopefully to ensure effective projects. It is supposed to increase the accountability of donor governments to their own taxpayers. Hopefully it might also increase the accountability of recipient governments to their taxpayers, and each side's accountability to each other. Like OBA it has advantages over traditional input funding because by funding outputs only (or in the COD case, longer-term "outcomes") it is linked to a certain level of performance. COD aid also claims improvements on the PBF model since it would involve medium-term contracts (at least 5 years) between governments and donors and would use agreed "simple" performance indicators. Otherwise a recipient government would be left to do whatever it wanted to meet the objective and win the funds.

But there seem to be practical drawbacks. It is difficult to identify performance indicators that are few and simple and that also provide adequate information for monitoring effectiveness. There will also be difficulties in attributing the outcome to the assistance activity if, as is the intention, other donors adopt the system and receive similar commitments against performance. A funding recipient could "transfer" achievements (for example, numbers of students passing a test or number of clinic visits) from another project when it comes time to audit the program or get the cash. That is, it seems easy to game the system by pledging the same results to different donors, precisely because the indicators are few, simple and based on long-term outcomes which are usually difficult to attribute.

While the COD procedure claims not to need monitoring and evaluation there are in fact to be annual verifications by donor-contracted auditors, a usually costly and intrusive exercise. There is a "time consistency" problem, which will limit local accountability because officials may not care about foreign money that might be available in 5 years' time for an assistance decision made today. Further, if such a system was to run for several years with many donors and numerous projects the delivery times and the starting times may run into each other and the aid money will no longer be associated de facto with output or outcome but with input, just as it has always done. So perhaps for perverse reasons there is not a time-inconsistency problem as recipients juggle multiple COD payments to try to fund programs up front. Finally, the desired transparency may be reduced with multiple COD programs and continuous media announcements of funding and achievement with little citizen capacity to verify or understand.

According to our previous arguments aid is currently ineffective not because it is provided up front but because, *inter alia*, it has very high transaction costs and lacks buy-in, and the recipients who have access to it act rationally by gaming the system to secure free money for the least effort. Trying to engineer incentives to use aid wisely in such conditions appears to be doomed to failure.

If these criticisms are valid then COD aid will not address empowerment or accountability, except for accountability of donors to their own governments.[5] The combination of "audit now and get paid in 5 years' time" could be worse than the traditional system because it introduces an element of long-term intrusion and even distrust. And ultimately it does of course complicate further the multiple channels and procedures required for foreign assistance even within the US aid program.

Where does COD stand on the alienation ratings? On the positive side the specific development activities to be funded (but not the overall program concept or design) originate with and are programmed by the potential recipient. Since aid funding is on a reimbursement basis the initiation of the program also has to go through a budget process in the recipient country. Arrangements for contracts, payments and management all have to be indigenous. On the negative side, the use of local budgetary processes may be circumvented when a number of COD programs telescope into each other, and the payments for the last project's outputs (or outcomes) may become in effect the payments on the next project's inputs. The monitoring and reporting process is potentially arduous when donors look for proof of what really happened. Finally, although there is a strong element of local design and buy-in in individual subprojects the buy-in to the COD project overall also depends on how far local agencies were involved in its conception.

On balance the relative alienation rating for COD looks to be moderate.

Foundations, funds and challenge funds

During the early 2000s foundation and fund mechanisms have become a frequent method of providing assistance. The British DFID introduced challenge funds as a way to direct grant money straight to activities on the ground rather than through government intermediaries. The funds work through competitive proposals or business plan competitions evaluated by panels of experts, and matching grants are disbursed either up front or on achievement of performance targets. DFID's Financial Deepening Challenge Fund in Kenya funded the M-PESA project, discussed in Chapter 3, through a grant to Vodafone. Another example is the Africa Enterprise Challenge Fund, which is supported by multiple donors to the tune of US$100 million. It provides grants to any viable private company that is thought to alleviate poverty including multinationals in agriculture, financial services, renewable energy, media and information. The fund has been very popular, receiving over 1,500 applications in its first 3 years but of these only 40 grants have been awarded worth US$32 million, over the whole continent.[6]

A small-scale variant of these are matching grant or innovation funds that have been employed in many countries.[7] These funds are usually input-based (to the extent that they commit funds at startup) although the actual payments might be spread out. They are not usually contingent on performance by grantees. While the grants are targeted and simple in concept the fund operation is often complex and requires external management to oversee compliance, selection, delivery and evaluation. A further problem is, as usual, gaming. There may be duplication of proposals to different funds; grantees can self-select if information and access are uneven, and proposals can be staged by experienced grant seekers to attract donations, sometimes using assistance jargon to "speak the same language" as adjudicators.[8] Thus, additionality is often weak as existing businesses obtain free funds that they do not need.[9]

The World Bank's Development Marketplace is a form of challenge fund, this time funding very small (grassroots) innovative ideas. Each year it organizes global and regional competitions and since 1998 it has awarded about US$54 million to over 1,000 projects. In 2008, a development market was conducted for the Euro-African diaspora in 2008 whereby the winners of grants also got free technical assistance for a year.

Where do challenge funds stand on the alienation ratings? On the positive side, like OBA and COD, the individual activities to be funded originate with the potential recipients. Further, if the grants are partial then a price has to be paid for the services and some type of local budget process (public or corporate) has to procure funds and contracts for procurement of goods and services are made by the individual businesses.

Furthermore, if grants are input based then unlike COD or OBA fund recipients will not need to submit to external monitoring or audits.

On the negative side, while the individual subprojects are originated locally the overall project design may be complicated and may have fiduciary requirements requiring an outside fund manager contracted by the donor. This can lead to lack of understanding and local accountability when problems arise such as eligibility disputes and contractual breaches. The fiduciary concerns about applicants gaming the system or about misrepresentation also tend to result in a complicated monitoring and evaluation system being required by the donors to oversee the project as a whole.

On balance the relative alienation rating for challenge funds and foundations in general looks to be moderate.

The US Millennium Challenge Fund

The Millennium Challenge Fund (MCF) is another version of the fund and foundation approaches, but it operates at the country level through government programs – a "challenge to governments" in effect. It thus represents a scaled up version of the project level funds, less well targeted but possibly with a better chance of constructive systemic outcomes. On its unveiling shortly after the Monterrey Donor Conference in 2002, the MCF was heralded as a completely new way of delivering aid. The US pledged to fund it through new aid money of up to US$5 billion per annum. Despite its promise, however, the MCF disbursed only US$7.5 billion in its first 8 years (about 20 percent of its target). It took over a year to make its first country awards, largely because of delays in the congressional authorization and appropriations process.

The MCF mechanism requires that potential recipient countries apply for funds based on a country program. The MCF board examines the country's performance on 17 publicized policy indicators, mainly of good governance and development readiness. It then selects compact-eligible countries. The country is then expected to identify "its priorities for achieving sustainable economic growth and poverty reduction" which it develops "in close partnership with an MCF team." Countries that meet all of the up-front conditions can then access funds relatively freely with few additional requirements. But the country has to develop donor-required artifacts such as "fiscal accountability plans" and it has to set up a "MCA accountable entity" to oversee implementation. Its use of funds is closely monitored through independent fiscal agents appointed by the MCF.

The MCF provides eligible countries with grants known as compacts and threshold programs. Compacts are 5-year grants for countries that pass the eligibility test. (By 2011, 23 countries passed with an average grant of about US$300 million.) Threshold programs involve much smaller grants (of average US$25 million) to countries that come "close to passing these criteria and are firmly committed to improving their policy performance."[10] The MCF has also introduced "second stage thresholds" for countries that have not quite made it from threshold to compact. Countries remain eligible as long as they stay above the requisite, publicly known, performance thresholds, and selection may be possible with less rigorous, transitional, conditions.

The Millennium Challenge Corporation which runs the MCF was set up as a lean body of about 300 staff with no field presence and no role in preparing, implementing, supervising or evaluation of programs. However, it uses USAID staff for these purposes. It also hires fiscal agents and consultants under contract to manage the program and in practice it has had to get involved in helping countries prepare programs appropriate for adjudication.

Where does the MCF stand on the alienation ratings? On the positive side it meets a lot of the criteria for type-A assistance. Firstly, once a country has been approved (having passed the various *ex ante* tests) it has a relatively free hand to use the funds. Local buy-in is also helped because US congressional earmarking, which severely restricts the allocation of USAID funds, does not apply to the MCF. The country program is, at least in principle, originated, designed, managed, budgeted and accountable to local bodies, and there is a minimal donor field presence if we ignore the use of USAID personnel. In principle the approach avoids the undermining of government accountability.

On the negative side, the small donor footprint has proved difficult to sustain given the demands of the US Congress for performance auditing. There is still a need for evaluations in order to be performance based. These are perhaps relatively mild negatives. However, the potential MCF beneficiary countries have to pass the series of graduated policy and performance tests imposed by the US. While these are *ex ante* conditions, in the event that a country wants to maintain eligibility for a follow-up grant, they would take the form of ongoing conditionality.

On balance the relative alienation rating for the Millennium Challenge Fund looks to be moderate to fair.

Global health funds

The series of worldwide funds which have started up in the health sector within the past few years have incorporated some of the New Aid principles. There are up to 90 funds; among the largest are GAVI and GFATM, both of which provide funds greater than many major aid agencies. GAVI claims to have committed US$4 billion to the health programs of 75 developing countries for the period 2000 to 2015 through a new way of raising money known as the "Advance Market Commitment," whereby the donors commit money to guarantee the long-term price of vaccines. The GFATM has since 2002 approved funding of US$21.7 billion for more than 600 programs in 150 countries providing AIDS and tuberculosis treatment and insecticide-treated bed nets.

The funds are disbursed through a process similar to the MCF that includes the screening of country-level (health ministry) proposals by a technical selection committee. In the case of the GFATM proposals are submitted through country coordinating committees. Like the MCF these funds aim for a hands-off, demand-led approach, with a minimal local presence. The global fund programs are implemented through partnerships with other development organizations and claim to finance only programs developed by the recipient countries themselves in coordination with their civil society and the private sector, and to hold recipients accountable to standards that require programs to reach specific targets monitorable by the public. Nevertheless, gaming of the GAVI system has occurred, such as inflation of the numbers who have received vaccines, in order to increase grant eligibility.[11]

These funds have tended to exacerbate aid fragmentation, as we previously showed, through the verticalization of the aid infrastructure. Reduced donor fragmentation through cross-country pools of funds is offset by increased sector fragmentation as these giant funds try to work alongside country funds. They also have separate funding proposal and allocation processes, delivery systems and budgets with weak integration into the broader country health system.[12]

The global funds are said to have caused disarray within some health systems, crowding out basic preventive health care in place of assistance to specific diseases. They are thus thought to be poor partners with other agencies even where they rely on other agencies to implement their programs. The DFID Multilateral Aid Review gave GAVI and GFATM high marks in general, but not for their partnership behavior. It states:

> In some cases … the global funds' procedures can result in high transaction costs for recipients, and undermine the country-led approach and/or interfere with national fiscal processes. Many global funds rely on other multilaterals to act as implementing agencies. This means that problems with partnership behaviour in other parts of the multilateral system become a problem for the global funds as well.[13]

Where do the global funds stand on the alienation ratings? On the positive side, the country programs are in principle initially centered on locally developed concepts, project designs, and contractual and budget arrangements, and therefore there is significant local ownership of the programs. There are not heavy conditions imposed or demands made on the recipients in project management monitoring and evaluation.

On the negative side, projects have been originated by donor consortia; verticalization has further fragmented health sector assistance, increasing the systemic problem of multiple processes, funding requirements and reporting structures. It has also tended to crowd out other programs, obliging them to compete for funds and personnel. Finally, as with the MCF the small footprint "on-the-ground" is misleading as it relies on outsourcing to other executing agencies.

On balance the relative alienation rating for the vertical health funds looks to be moderate.

Budget support

Another emerging development assistance vehicle is budget support funding (BSF). As previously mentioned, general budget and sector program support as a percentage of total aid commitments has risen rapidly. By 2007, it accounted for about a quarter of total aid to Africa, most of the increase being attributable to sector programs.[14]

BSFs are channeled by design through a country's budget as though they were domestically raised revenue and in so doing they strengthen budget processes and accountability. Some BSFs are also disbursed on the basis of performance targets but usually targeting is weak because the outcomes of the funding cannot be attributed, so there is a fiduciary risk which can then lead to heavy conditionality in the area of public finance management, and in monitoring and evaluation. This may require a judgment on how far potential recipients can be trusted to deploy the funds appropriately, based on the extent to which they have a functional legislative and budgetary system. Compared to structural adjustment lending, which was also a type of budgetary support, the BSF avoids broad conditionality, but in practice the judgment about the competence of the potential recipient's budgetary system could be an onerous condition.

Where do BSFs stand on the alienation ratings? On the positive side the development activities that they fund can be entirely conceived, designed, programmed, budgeted, contracted and paid for by local agencies; furthermore, once disbursed by the donor they are not usually subject to ongoing conditions. One evaluation report on BSFs gives generally favorable assessments for capacity building and aid harmonization in most countries studied.[15] On the negative side, because of the fiduciary worries of donors, large-scale transfers without upfront controls on their allocation can result in heavy monitoring and evaluation which increases the donor footprint in the country.

On balance the relative alienation rating for the BSFs looks to be moderate to fair.

Conditional Cash Transfers

Last but not least another New Aid vehicle is that of the Conditional Cash Transfer (CCT) programs. Since they were first introduced in the early 1990s interest in CCT programs has surged. The first programs were introduced in Mexico's Progresa project to rationalize several food subsidy schemes for the poor. The project started with about 300,000 households in 1997 and expanded to 5 million by 2009 under the name of "Oportunidades." Brazil followed with the Bolsa Escola and the Guaranteed Minimum Family Income program, and other Latin American countries took up the idea. Between 1997 and 2008 these programs migrated to the Caribbean, Africa and South Asia with the help of the donors. Thus, the first programs were conceived in and by the countries that used them as a way to rationalize their own subsidy systems and the idea was then transferred to countries where they were a novelty.

CCTs are safety-net programs targeting very small amounts of cash to the very poor, generally with conditions such as improved attendance in school, visits to health centers and immunizations. Most CCT programs transfer money in the range US$5 to US$30 a year per child. The programs vary from pilot programs of a few thousand families to as many as 11 million families (in Brazil).[16] They are another form of output or performance-based funding.

CCT programs are superior in impact to food aid because they allow recipients to make choices about what they want to spend money on, including local produce. But they also incur high costs for management, especially monitoring compliance with conditions. This requires establishment of the eligibility of clients, enrolment and payment. Strong monitoring and evaluation systems are needed.[17]

As usual, they face criticism. Some programs have to use means testing and behavior testing that implicitly assume that poor families act contrary to their own interests or those of the community. Conditions on school attendance or clinic visits may be problematic if schools and clinics are inadequate.[18] In Africa, pilot programs have excluded very poor households such as those where there is underemployment but not actual unemployment and this has led to charges that the programs are mistargeted.[19]

One study concluded that African governments were willing to accept donor funds for CCT-based social protection but would not necessarily commit their own resources to them.[20] The report also found that CCTs carry high transaction costs, which may divert attention from other means of daily survival for the poorest. It was uncertain overall that the Latin American CCT models were appropriate for poor countries in Africa. A recent DFID report concludes that cash transfers increased school enrolment and use of health services and that the effects were greater in poorer countries.[21] Furthermore, despite fears, they did not reduce work effort in the recipient families, apart from child labor. But the report also agrees that there are often systemic problems such as lack of adequate medical and educational services, which are part of the overall picture but which CCTs could not themselves address.

Where do CCTs stand on the alienation ratings? On the positive side, they support the local market for food, allowing free choice of purchase for cash recipients and have had some success in improving the use of social services, which are a condition of the transfer.

On the negative side, the CCT programs in Africa (and Asia) are an imported concept, which has not received total buy-in from governments. A key reason for this is that social safety nets need to be designed on a long-term affordable basis rather than introduced piecemeal on the basis of outside experiments and budgets that may be out of proportion with the resources available to the government.[22] The programs have also had significant management costs, much of which may need to be conducted by externally contracted specialist firms.

On balance the relative alienation rating for the CCTs looks to be moderate to poor.

How Far Does New Aid Create a New Relationship?

To create a new relationship requires aid projects to incorporate designs that do not alienate the recipients. A lot of the aid ideas of the past decade or so are significant improvements in this respect. They aim (variously) at results on the ground, pooling of aid, recipient initiative, use of budgetary processes and other features that circumvent a lot of the negative and alienative aspects of development assistance. How far are they a solution? The answer is only partially, for the following reasons.

Much of the New Aid approach has been for the benefit of the donor rather the recipient. Performance-based funding aims firstly to satisfy the donor country legislators about the results of their generosity. While good performance is of course a good idea for everybody the transaction costs of externally imposed compliance monitoring and the sense of a lack of trust compromises local cooperation and buy-in. Misappropriation of aid funds is not seen by recipients as such a critical issue as it is by the donors if the recipients have little faith in the motivation for or efficacy of the funds being donated.

The continued widespread use of pilot, or experimental, projects reflects the demand for "evidence" of success. But again this principally responds to donor rather than recipient needs. "Proof of concept" is often required by outsiders who cannot make judgments about what is likely to work, and at the same time a "pilot" exposes donor performance to a lower standard of scrutiny. For their part, recipients are not happy about having to grapple with externally driven experiments in development assistance, causing more fragmentation, discontinuity and increased transaction costs as donors try out new methods.

The relative success of the challenge fund model comes from targeting of specific activities, thus reducing the principal–agent problem and simplifying accountability. But, while impact on the ground is obviously critical, bypassing government (in project-level grants) responds again as much to the donors need to show results to their own legislators as it does to the needs of the recipients and it bypasses also the building of domestic capacity. The idea behind challenge funds is thus largely inconsistent with idea behind budget support funds, but the costs of this incompatibility to the recipient are not apparently obvious to the donor. If two policy-incompatible aid instruments are offered by the same major donor, such as DFID, it increases the recipient's sense that foreign aid is experimental, piecemeal and not consistent with a coherent development strategy.

None of the new project-level vehicles can deal squarely with the systemic problems of aid fragmentation, aid dependence, nor, by definition, domestic resource mobilization. As we have discussed, while being designed to reduce aid fragmentation by pooling, the vertical health funds are seen instead to have aggravated it. Pooling of funds reduces fragmentation only if it is not simply "another pool of funds." The MCF may be a partial model of the way forward but it is still "another pool" operating alongside other US agency pools, even that of the Pentagon. The MCFs minimal footprint is also under pressure from the demands of programming monitoring and evaluation, which means that it is obliged to move away from its ideals and its funds are underutilized. In the same vein, one of the key objectives of BSFs, to pool aid programs runs into the increasing number of rival single-pool systems.

The next table provides a speculative summary of the "alienation ratings" of different types of assistance. The scores on a scale of 1 to 5 are not intended to be rigorous and they are challengeable. They are for individual projects, individual assistance operations or items of expenditure items. Scores at the overall program level would be lower because the programs are all initially conceived from outside. For example, the individual activities funded by challenge funds are at local initiative while the operational details of the challenge fund have been developed by the outside donor.

Of the seven aid vehicles, the individual projects funded under a BSF or MCF show up best in terms of the alienation rating, reflecting mainly their ability to allow

Table 6.2. Alienation rating of "New Aid" vehicles by individual project (1 = very poor; 5 = very good)[23]

Project/expenditure activity	Individual projects that are funded under:						
	OBA	COD	Challenge fund	MCF	Global fund	BSF	CCT
Local origination/concept	4	3	4	4	4	5	5
Based on local design decision	4	4	5	5	4	5	5
Local preparation/ programming	4	4	5	5	5	5	n/a
Uses local budget/appropriation	2	2	1	4	3	5	4
Payment made for services rendered	2	2	5	3	2	3	1
Local contracting of expertise	3	3	4	4	3	4	n/a
Local management of project	3	3	3	4	3	4	3
Progress report to local agency	3	3	4	4	2	4	3
Performance M&E requirements	2	1	3	3	2	2	3
Conditionality for providing funding	2	2	3	4	3	3	3
Total	29	27	37	40	31	40	27+

autonomy in conception, decision making and budgetary appropriation at the individual project level. However, as stated, all these approaches including the BSF are initially designed externally and none can address the systemic issues of aid fragmentation, dependence nor local fund mobilization such as through the tax system. Thus, while material improvements in design have occurred there are clear limits to how far they can go. The positive features of the two best vehicles (MCF and BSF) could possibly be developed into an acceptable aid instrument.

Chapter 7

ANOTHER PATHWAY OUT OF POVERTY?

You cannot eliminate official ODA; that would be crazy and unproductive.
Kevin Rudd, Australian foreign minister (November 2010)[1]

I have long believed that far from being a catalyst, foreign aid has been the biggest single inhibitor of Africa's growth. Among its shortcomings, aid is correlated with corruption, fosters dependency, and invariably instills bureaucracy that hinders the emergence of an essential entrepreneurial class.
Dambisa Moyo (2008)[2]

Private Flows and Foreign Aid

The fundamental issue that I have tried to investigate in this book is how far the people of the poorest and most aid-dependent countries can begin to move beyond their need for foreign aid and, thereby, assume or resume sovereignty over their development process. One pathway to this objective is for poor economies to incorporate diaspora resources as a complement to expanding their own. Taking account of this, one plausible solution for development assistance might be a "re-emphasis." This might mean, for example, retaining the current direction of assistance but shifting a little bit. New Aid could be repackaged to support more those private flows – moving for example from "aid for capacity building" to a new solution called "aid for remittances." Thus, the story would go that the poorest countries need to leverage the full menu of resources – both public and private, and aid needs to be there to help them to do it. This essentially is the conclusion of some observers who have looked at or are looking at the "beyond aid" scenario and it is what some donors are already trying to do, as implied in the declaration of the 2011 Busan conference.

But this solution falls short of the objective of "assuming or resuming sovereignty." A simple shift in donor effort is not what is being advocated here. The key point is that, as drivers of development, *official development assistance and diaspora resource flows are in principle mutually exclusive, not complementary.* Accordingly, the choice between ODA and private flows should not be seen as a matter of optimizing the mix of donor and diaspora assistance but rather of how to capture a historically progressive dynamic that moves the poorest countries forward, leaving behind one era and development paradigm that has been largely dysfunctional and moving into another era with a different paradigm that responds to the dysfunction and provides a prospect for success.

Aid has no business trying to channel the new direction if that direction is ultimately inconsistent with its own fundamentals. Thus, diaspora private capital and income flows will find their own way as poor economies open up to opportunity and do not require in general to be leveraged or otherwise subsidized by foreign government donations and charity and may be distorted by the process.

The key point about diaspora resources is their ownership. This is why the diaspora and those holding assets outside their home countries may represent not simply another resource but a particularly potent type of resource in comparison with that represented by foreign aid over the past 50 years. It is the type of potent resource that is essential to the emergence of the low-income countries.

But first let us try to conduct another reality check. Some observers have explicitly cautioned that private flows including remittances cannot in fact be treated as a substitute for foreign-aid flows. "Remittances should not be viewed as a substitute for development aid ... they are private money that should not be expected to fund public projects."[3]

The reason for making the direct, and favorable, comparison of diaspora with aid flows is that the diaspora flows do, in fact, potentially bring with them other key developmental inputs. And where they do not, for example where they simply increase private consumption, they are probably doing significantly more to improve the welfare of the poorest than the significant proportion of foreign-aid flows that are diverted into upscale consumption rather than basic needs. Depending on the funding source it may be that foreign training and education are effectively consumption goods.

Diaspora transfers can bring with them technical and professional skills and entrepreneurial knowhow, including knowledge of foreign business practices, legal procedures and markets, and the enhanced confidence that accompanies such knowledge, a package that some writers have referred to as social remittances. The knowhow transfer effect may be especially significant if skilled migrant workers are motivated to return to their home countries, a phenomenon that appears to have been increasing in countries such as India, China and previously in South Korea. It may be expected that skills transfer between nationals of the same country has a better chance of success that transfer across ethnic groups and cultures, subject to dysfunctional power relations.

Regarding the split of diaspora flows between consumption and investment, research, as we have seen, shows that while the large majority of remittances, especially from low-skilled migrants such as laborers, are still used for consumption by low-income families, increasingly as the average skill level of migrants rises these flows are going to education, real estate, community infrastructure, small business and financial investments. Where Africa is concerned, it is notable that its migrants to rich countries have relatively high average education and skill levels; and when it comes to reflows of flight capital, it is likely that these will go to a larger extent into investment.

In the end, perhaps the most crucial benefit of migration is psychological in character – the rise in expectations fuelled by increasing wealth and knowledge within the members of the diaspora. The key discovery of a migrant in a rich country is "I can do that too."

Leveraging the Diaspora

To develop the aid-dependent, poorest countries, in Africa, Asia and Latin America, we have argued that a change in the dynamics of the development process is essential, for all the reasons that have been examined regarding ownership, motivation, commitment, transaction costs, direction of effort, efficiency and the integrity of resources deployed. These factors are basic to the poor record of development projects, rather than the design of the individual projects themselves. The development process is one that must be taken charge of by poor country citizens, groups and individuals, wherever domiciled, who have a special interest in the country and can contribute resources to it.

The problem cannot, of course, be solved by individuals alone; it is a collective problem. But individuals are part of caste, class, communal, clan or tribal systems which significantly affect the ability of individuals to take initiatives. In this respect, we have discussed the effects of ethnic divisions on the ability of a state to act in a common public interest. We have also cited division within the diaspora due to the replication in host countries of caste relationships or political factions from the home country. Thus, diasporas may not act in common. There are differences between conflict-generated "push" diasporas and economic migrant "pull" diasporas, and there are social divisions within each. Diasporas in exile may hold back on support until there is change in the regime that they oppose. Economic diasporas may contain caste and class divisions that prevent united approaches to economic problems at home.

But despite these caveats individual action is important, and to the extent that the population of a diaspora has freed itself to some extent from the constraints of caste, gender and class simply by leaving home, and has absorbed new value systems, the individuals of a diaspora may feel more empowered than the individuals of the home country, albeit within their particular communities. Emigration changes attitudes.

Government Action to Support Migration

As we have discussed, "brain drain" has always been seen as a serious problem depriving poor countries of skilled manpower. However, it has more recently been realized that the issue is complex because the short-term losses due to the drain of skills are probably more than compensated by long-term gain in foreign resources that become available later, especially if the migrant returns. Controls on migration are therefore likely to be counterproductive in the long run. Recognizing this, a number of countries have adopted a policy of "non-interference." Others have stated that their policy was to maintain or raise emigration.[4]

A number of approaches to pro-diaspora and pro-migration policies have been tried by both home and host countries. Abandoning restrictive policies such as bonding students to remain in their home country after graduation or taxing emigrants, governments are instead encouraging skilled workers to stay by improving working conditions and providing research facilities. China, from 1995 to 2003, expanded foreign programs offered in local institutions, which resulted in lower numbers of students going abroad, and offered attractive salaries, multiple-entry visas and access to foreign exchange for former citizens. Korea attracted returnees by building infrastructure, including industrial parks. The Philippines, Taiwan, Thailand and Tunisia have offered incentives, including research funding, expanded real-estate investment options and study opportunities for returnees. Taiwan's Hsinchu Industrial Park attracted more than 5,000 returning scientists in 2000 alone.[5] Thailand has offered generous research funding and monetary incentives for return.[6] On the other hand, a poor investment climate is supposed to have discouraged the return of Armenians, and prior to 1991 Indian government regulations on private business also discouraged return.

Some host countries have adopted complementary policies. Some governments, as we have seen, have adopted a proactive policy of networking and building links with the diaspora while providing incentives that encourage return migration. For example, several countries have attempted to establish initiatives with the Nigerians in Diaspora Organization (NIDO) in Europe, Asia, Africa and the Americas.[7]

An alternative to both short-term controls and the long-term improvements in the business environment at home has been to focus on actively encouraging temporary international labor mobility through guest worker programs.[8] Such an approach reduces economic and political problems in the home or host country, while allowing the international labor market to work and skills to cross borders.[9] The guest worker approach could encourage rich countries to increase migration rather than control it. Clemens has argued that rich countries should greatly raise the number of temporary work visas, tapping into the populations that want a temporary opportunity.[10] Home countries can also encourage educated emigrants to return by cooperating with host countries that have programs to promote return.

Host countries have also initiated migrant return programs. France entered into an agreement with Senegal for the voluntary return of health professionals by offering research equipment or the prospect of joint university appointments. The new mobility partnership agreements also establish circular migration schemes for professional education and expert missions by members of the diaspora. European governments have been implementing assisted voluntary return programs such as the Return of Qualified African Nationals Program. The IOM's Migration for Development in Africa (MIDA) program supports virtual return (courses and seminars online), repeat visits, investment and permanent reallocation.[11]

As we have seen, a number of initiatives have been taken to increase the political and civil roles of the diaspora communities in their home countries, encouraging both stepped-up contact and temporary or long-term return. India has created a ministry for the diaspora, which allows portable social insurance benefits, voting rights and types of dual citizenship. Many other countries in Latin America and Africa have accepted dual citizenship and voting rights, and some have allocated seats in parliament for diaspora representatives. Ethiopia has allowed migrants with foreign citizenship to hold a "person of Ethiopian origin" identification card; India has issued a Person of Indian Origin (PIO) card; and Mexico issues a *matrícula* to Mexicans living in the United States.[12]

Support to Remittances and New Financing Instruments

Apart from donor efforts to support the market for and return of migrant workers another main initiative has been to support the flows of funds from migrants in terms of cost and information provision. As we have seen, the costs of remittances have been high and have driven some of the flows into the informal market. For example, sending money to Africa and the Caribbean from Europe and the United States can cost as much as 20 percent on small amounts. Two money transfer companies, Western Union and Moneygram, control three-quarters of all remittance payout locations in Africa and most African countries restrict the type of institutions able to offer remittance services to banks.

The donors have proposed coordinated action to reduce costs, while bilaterally the government of Mexico has worked with the US on new technologies for transmitting funds.[13] Proposals have introducing electronic transfer systems, harmonizing payment systems, easing reporting requirements and enabling remittance senders to "bundle" remittances so that larger amounts are sent less frequently.[14] The United States requires remittance service providers to disclose prices and commissions and establish error resolution mechanisms for clients. IFAD issued a report on remittances in 2009 recommending reforms to regulations allowing more financial institutions to handle remittances, including microfinance institutions, especially in rural areas.[15] The World Bank has suggested a voluntary code of conduct for financial institutions handling remittances to improve banking access, and encourage microfinance institutions and credit unions to provide remittance services.

Apart from attempting to clear the way for remittance flows some governments have also investigated new financial instruments for leveraging of diaspora funds.[16] These have included investment schemes such as the Mexican government's matching grant (three-for-one) programs; better banking channels and encouraging remittance through banks; allowing home-country banks to operate overseas; enhancing the home countries' risk rating; and improving access to foreign capital by securitizing future remittances flows.[17] Other proposals are to allow deposit accounts in local and foreign currency, transnational loans to allow migrants to purchase property back home, diaspora bonds and mutual funds. There has been a rapid increase in future flow securitizations by, for example, Turkey, Mexico and Brazil, and initial sovereign investment grading of emerging economies.

Diaspora bonds are gaining increasing interest despite some failures. They represent a low cost source of finance since a "patriotic discount" may apply through the diaspora investors' greater willingness to take risks. These bonds have been issued by a number of countries. The State Bank of India issued diaspora bonds in 1991, 1998 and 2000, which raised US$11.3 billion. The Development Corporation for Israel has raised over US$25 billion mainly from infrastructure bonds since 1951. Indians living abroad stepped in to buy bonds when market demand failed and paid price premiums for development corporation bonds. The Ghana government issued a US$50 million Golden Jubilee savings bond in 2007.

Some efforts to issue bonds have met with less success. Nepal attempted a "foreign employment bond" issue and Ethiopia attempted to raise a "Millennium Corporate Bond" to finance its electricity industry.[18] However, the bonds were marketed mostly to low-skilled migrants in the Gulf rather than to the richer diaspora groups in OECD countries and interest rates in local currency were relatively low. A Kenyan infrastructure bond was marketed to the diaspora in 2011 but failed because of lingering distrust of the government and uncertainty about repayments in an inflationary economy. However, there has been a learning process. Ethiopia raised US$425 million through a second bond issue in 2011 for the Grand Renaissance Dam on the Nile.[19] A country private equity fund is also under preparation (with Ernst and Young). The project manager commented, "People like that because they see it's a business – not a charity and not public sector."[20] Diaspora mutual funds open to all investors have been launched through Liberia's Diaspora Social Investment Fund and Zambia's First Investment Fund. Nigeria floated a diaspora bond in September 2011.

As mentioned, another fund-raising mechanism is the securitization of future cash flows, which has been attempted by some banks.[21] The procedure usually involves a borrowing bank pledging future receivables through a trust fund held offshore. According to the World Bank, Telmex of Mexico completed the first securitized transaction and the main credit-rating agencies had reviewed more than 400 similar transactions by 2008, valued at US$80 billion, based on bank revenues from oil and mineral exports, airline tickets, credit-card vouchers, remittances, oil and gas royalties, and tax receipts.[22] In 1996, the African Export-Import Bank co-arranged the first securitization by a Sub-Saharan African country, a US$40 million loan to a development bank in Ghana backed by the bank's Western Union remittance receivables. Afreximbank launched a Financial Future-Flow Pre-financing Programme in 2001. It arranged a US$50 million remittance-backed facility for a Nigerian entity using Moneygram receivables in 2004 and a US$40 million remittance-backed facility for an Ethiopian bank using its Western Union receivables.

Sovereign bond ratings are also influenced by diaspora revenue flows. The major benefit occurs when a bond rating rises to investment grade, but having even a low sovereign rating may be better than none since borrowing become cheaper. Capital inflows are more diversified for rated countries, including direct investment, bank loans, bonds and equity flows. The World Bank found that out of 55 currently unrated countries, eight were likely to be above investment grade and another 18 would likely be in the "B" to "BB" category. It suggests that international community help African countries obtain sovereign ratings.[23]

A Summary of Home Government Efforts

Britain's DFID listed some of the more significant political and economic incentive programs introduced by six home-country governments to engage their own diaspora communities. The results were as follows:

Table 7.1.

Policies towards diaspora	Somalia	Nigeria	Ghana	India	Sri Lanka	China
Voting rights			D	D		
Dual citizenship			X	D		X
Representation/ministries	D			D		X
Entry concessions for diaspora with host country nationality				X		
Foreign currency accounts		D	D	X		
Incentives for diaspora FDI		D	D	DX		X
Customs/import incentives		D	D	DX		X
Property ownership	X	X	X	X	X	
Special economic zones				X		

Source: The Contribution of UK-Based Diasporas to Development and Poverty Reduction (ESRC Centre on Migration, Policy and Society [COMPAS], April 2004). Note: "D" means "in place"; "X" means "under discussion."

The report summarized activity supporting diaspora integration with the home country, particularly in areas such as property rights, trade and foreign investment incentives. Since this report was written considerably more progress has been made both in terms of financial instruments and political rights for the diaspora.

Can the Diaspora Help to Lead all Poor Countries out of Poverty?

How large, in the end, can the diaspora's contribution be and how can it be best deployed? In the case of Africa, it will be recalled that even with a relatively high rate of savings out of all private current transfers, the potential increase in the average rate of growth of African economies that could be fuelled by these transfers would be less than one half of one percent per annum. If "social remittances" are included, that is, entrepreneurial, technical skills and general knowhow learned abroad, then the value of total resource transfers would be significantly higher, but unquantifiable and probably still not transformational on their own. However, with a return of private capital the percentage could be much higher over a limited period and, accompanied by additional resources of knowhow, could be the basis for "takeoff."

Even if a large volume of capital and human resources flowed to Africa, however, such flows would be unevenly distributed between countries. Thus, while the larger diasporas of some countries could help forge a new pathway out of poverty it is questionable how the pathway would apply to those countries that apparently have few citizens overseas and small overseas assets. While Ethiopia is a very poor country, it nevertheless has a large, active and relatively prosperous diaspora; Malawi, on the other hand, is a very poor country with little in terms of either foreign held assets or a diaspora. According to the official statistics lack of foreign assets also applies to African countries such as Tanzania, Congo, Niger and Zambia. At the other extreme, Nigeria has not only large foreign assets but large current income from oil revenue and large diaspora flows.

The unevenness of diaspora flows between countries may create problems for the new pathway out of poverty. How can the capital and current flows from the private sector abroad do anything for countries without significant foreign assets? If the new pathway only applies to a few countries in Africa, for example, then there should be no reason to suppose that other countries would benefit, and the new pathway will be characterized by uneven development. For those countries with few private foreign assets, a mechanism would be needed whereby growth spreads quickly across borders; whereas it might well be that the growth of some countries will instead be at the expense of their neighbors, in a cycle of cumulative divergence. What mechanisms could be expected to accelerate the spread of prosperity?

Uneven development is not a newly discovered phenomenon. It has always characterized world development. Economic progress has to start somewhere before it spreads. There have been many types of explanation. Risking oversimplification, these include the so-called neoclassical model of growth, which regards unevenness as in principle a temporary phenomenon because factor prices, such as wages, equalize between countries as a result of competition. The time required for equalization depends on the extent to which labor, capital and technology are internationally mobile, and it may be long and discontinuous. A polar opposite explanation is based on so-called "dependency theory." This holds that unevenness is inherent in the mechanics of capitalist development and that divergence rather than convergence would occur over time as advanced economies increase their lead, leading to the pauperization of poor economies. The latter procedure could allow satellite centers of activity to grow but they would be dependent on and subordinate to metropolitan centers.

A different type of theory, originated by Kuznets and applied usually within countries, also holds that unevenness (inequality) is temporary. It is inherent in early development but declines in later development. This is because fixed capital investment is the main early driver of growth and requires a relatively large surplus, depressing wages. The resulting inequality is exacerbated by the movement of populations from low-income rural agriculture to higher income urban industry. Later on as economies mature and rural–urban migration slows, investment is directed more to building up a skilled labor force than physical capital and this reduces inequality by expanding the middle class.[24]

Another conception of unevenness is that as economies grow production tends to become concentrated geographically. Successful development involves manufacturing and service activities clustering around each other to achieve economies of agglomeration. This happens in urban areas as access to the market, skilled labor, technology, transport and other services become more important than access to material supplies. The clusters form growth poles, which can be self-reinforcing over long periods of time.[25] Only later on do diseconomies of scale set in, in the form of urban congestion.[26] In France, the United Kingdom and the United States, 75 to 95 percent of industry is localized (clustered or concentrated relative to overall economic activity).[27]

From a number of perspectives therefore unevenness and inequality are an inevitable consequence of early development. Accordingly, for some time countries like Malawi may not benefit from African poles of growth. Eventually, however, according to most conceptions the poles may be expected to have "spread effects" if they consist of efficient producers in a supportive business environment.[28] Growth in one center may encourage development in the surrounding area through a multiplier effect. Thus, for example, increased economic activity and technological advance at the core may initially stimulate demand for materials from the periphery. Over time growth would spread wealth into surrounding centers either through geographical proximity or through business linkages such that there can be parallel growth of several towns. The relative rate of growth might be dependent on the size of the towns and the distance between them.[29] Thus, rapid development in an African or Asian city may have positive effects on other African and Asian cities, albeit over time.

The progress of the first decade of the 2000s suggests that across Africa a process of the growth-pole type might be unfolding. Growth rates in some smaller towns of Ethiopia, for example, have been significantly faster than that of the capital, Addis Ababa.[30] The World Bank has recently espoused the concept as a strategy for African development. It proposes to promote several growth poles to support urban development through deploying what it calls "a critical mass of reforms, infrastructure investments and skill-building on the industries and locations of highest potential."[31] The Bank is planning growth poles in Madagascar, Cameroon, Mozambique, Gambia and the Democratic Republic of Congo.

The World Bank's five African growth pole countries however, with one exception, include none of Radelet's seventeen "fast growing African countries."[32] Nor do they necessarily include the countries with the largest diaspora resources or existing wealth inside or outside the country. Thus, Nigeria and South Africa are far more likely candidates, while on the basis of diaspora activity others might include Kenya, Ghana, Ethiopia or Senegal. For Malawi, the most likely pole of growth from which private investment may come forth would be within South Africa.

How far could the public sector guide a growth pole strategy? Not very well judging by the World Bank's seemingly politically driven choices of growth pole countries. Historically, growth poles are occurrences arising out of the effects of private sector competition. Classic cases are the clustering of the US and British motor vehicle industries around Detroit and Birmingham in the early twentieth century, or the growth of information technology in Silicon Valley in the late twentieth century. Governments had no significant role in the creation of these clusters. This therefore may not be a very good place for public-sector leadership. In Africa and elsewhere it is a case for private entrepreneurs, both inside and outside the home country, to take the initiative. Nigerian and Ghanaian entrepreneurs in conjunction with diaspora investors within a supportive business environment are more likely to spread wealth to the rest of West Africa than government programs, and the "natural pole of growth" pathway might be a way ahead.

Preconditions for Attracting Investors

While private-sector interest may spread economic activity from advanced growth poles to emerging growth poles across African countries the process also critically requires internal reforms within Africa. Central to these is economic integration through intra-African trade and investment, and this requires the strengthening of market institutions, the elimination of trade barriers, investments in infrastructure, and reduction in cross – border transport costs. These include public goods activities where governments, and aid donors, do have a role. Some of these activities are in fact those of the Aid-for-Trade Initiative, which we discussed in Chapter 1. In this respect several governments, with donor help, are promoting trade corridors such as the Bas–Congo development corridor including Angola and the two Congo Republics, designed to exploit cross-border hydroelectric power. Two other transport corridors are going ahead which will link the capital cities of Benin, Côte d'Ivoire, Ghana, Liberia, Nigeria and Togo in West Africa, and Congo, Kenya, Sudan and Uganda in East and North East Africa.

Integration also requires labor to be mobile between countries. Just as within countries, labor migration across borders assists economic growth by improving the distribution of labor and driving urban agglomeration economies. More than 60 percent of emigrants from Sub-Saharan countries move to other countries in the region. In fact, the rate of labor migration within Sub-Saharan Africa is the highest among developing regions (although it has fallen since the 1960s partly as contract mine labor has returned home), but it faces legal and procedural obstacles that are susceptible to government action.

Legal obstacles are very much a matter for government action. To enhance the regional business climate governments have to develop supportive laws and regulations, and the enforcement mechanisms such as courts, to ensure property rights, to develop supportive contracts, labor, tax and accounting laws, and to facilitate business entry, operation and exit.

Persistent economic, political and cultural divisions between African countries partly inherited from colonial times have delayed integration.[33] For several decades economic integration within Africa has been the mantra but rather than an African economic union, a series of regional economic groupings has formed, such as ECOWAS, COMESA, SADC, IGAD and EAC, to name some.[34] The launch of the African Union in 2002 as successor to the Organization for African Unity was a step forward but as yet an African economic community has not emerged. The many regional economic groupings and free-trade areas may have made economic union more rather than less difficult because each grouping has tended to develop vested interests. Apart from the geographical inheritance, unification has been delayed by factors such as the different starting points of individual economies, compensation for tariff removal, delay in harmonization of tariffs, taxes and trade rules, and lack of consultation with the private sector.[35] There has also been problems resulting from aid fragmentation as some donors have supported one economic grouping such as SADC, while others support COMESA, leading to competition for aid money.

Recently signs have proved more promising, with efforts under way to unite the 26 countries of COMESA, EAC and SADC in a free-trade area by 2014. Nevertheless, given the laborious, multi-decade progress and the ongoing political complications that impede economic integration it is more likely to proceed *de facto* where private investors identify national and inter-country business opportunities and demand public support, rather than where governments, and donors, sign impressive-sounding but non-actionable declarations of intent.

Aside from the public-sector initiatives to improve the business environment, private investors must drive regional development. The main role for governments is to get out of the way after freeing the borders, removing barriers to trade and investment, and introducing necessary regulation. Whereas the long series of government declarations have moved regional policy forward at a glacial pace, the possibilities of rapid integration look better with determined action by risk taking indigenous investors, foreign and local, who want to tap into regional markets.

The Role of the Donors in the New Pathway

As we have seen, there has been much anecdotal information compiled by organizations like the World Bank and the MPI about donor support to diasporas as a vehicle for foreign aid, and a proliferation of new agencies. There have also been doubts about the way this support is being applied, on similar grounds that have been raised for aid as a whole.

A 2008 EIU report on remittances seems to exemplify the ambiguities of donor support for diaspora engagement. It advises that public intervention in the area of remittances must be handled with care.

> Any attempt to control the amount, restrict the destination, prescribe the use of, regulate the transfer of, require certain modes of transmission of, or tax remittances, are only likely to drive them into already well-established informal channels where they are impossible to track.[36]

But the report then proceeds to advocate "permanent" programs to build the capacity of the "different players" in the process. This includes "a complete package of education, including financial literacy, mentoring, guidance in business development and identification of projects."[37] The report goes on to say that organizations that wish to support collective remittances must a) help migrants to organize themselves through empowering them to communicate with each other, to break down their isolation; and b) help them to increase their membership, improve their fundraising practices and develop capacity for project management and promotion through training, and mentoring.

Thus, on the one hand, the report starts out with a caution to foreign donors and governments and, on the other hand, it sets out a long-term program of public intervention on the basis that migrants are "isolated" – something that seems either implausible or unimportant considering the explosive increase in diaspora activity.

In similar vein the Council of Europe asked for a "policy initiative" at country and European Union level, recognizing diasporas as strategic actors in the implementation of the migration and development projects. They would support diasporas by "gathering information about their development related activities and documenting them, formulating policy options and strategies and proactively playing a predominant role in the practical implementation activities."[38] There should, says the report, be directives that make mandatory the collaboration and coordination of the donor agencies and the diaspora organizations.

The World Bank is pursuing methods of supporting the diaspora through a plethora of new institutions. In February 2010 an announcement stated:

> it is time to create an international body – an International Remittances Institute – that would monitor the flows of labor and remittances and oversee policies to make them easier, cheaper, safer, and more productive … a global institution is necessary to monitor and facilitate sizeable flows of people and money.[39]

The Bank launched this entity with US$2 million of EU funding to "strengthen the capacities of all actors (African governments, banks, remittance senders and recipients and so on) to better use remittances as development tools for poverty reduction." Other initiatives include the World Bank's "Future of Remittances" Program, which claims that it will instill best practices in remittance markets, and a Multilateral Trust Fund which was established in 2009 with US$10 million to "enhance knowledge on African remittances through thematic and sectoral studies." Most recently in November 2011 the organization announced its "Consultation on Knowledge Partnership on Migration and Global Development."[10]

Well intentioned as these initiatives might be, the entire discussion of this book suggests that they are likely to have little impact, responsive more to the push of institutional proliferation rather than the pull of value-adding activity. Our story has been one about the disempowerment and disincentives brought about by such assistance. How could this affect the diaspora? The involvement of external donations and subsidies risks distorting an already dynamic private-sector driven process by introducing the wrong incentives.

Aid diverts attention into securing of free money with the accompanying transaction costs. Rather than bona fide entrepreneurs it can attract aid-opportunists who are less willing to assume commercial risks but are willing to navigate the obstacle course of project formulation and preparation required to secure free money. This might be described as *bastard entrepreneurship*. In contrast, the investment process must be one that is driven by indigenous private individuals and corporate entities negotiating business risks and learning from failure as well as success. Another Migration Policy Institute report on diaspora entrepreneurship states appropriately that the most important resources of the entrepreneur are ingenuity and persistence.[11]

The donor community became fully aware of the significance of remittance flows only after they had already grown to a significant size, and the very rapid increase in flows has taken place despite the many publicly claimed obstacles. Private individuals have used their ingenuity and persistence, despite the cost and regulatory obstacles, to get funds back to their home countries, and they have succeeded very well. Thus, while some public support such as intervention to negotiate lower remittance costs with the banks might have helped, it is debatable to what extent there is otherwise a large "public goods" element to the promotion of these private transfers, and the infusion of publicity, donations and bureaucratic entanglements into this process carries the risk of damaging an ongoing process through, among other things, re-legitimizing government authority over private business.

Given the doubts about the value of aid the "new pathway out of poverty" is likely to require that the donors move into the background, to make way for both efficient governments and new initiatives from private business both at home and from the diaspora. A move into the background will imply a much more carefully thought out role and a much smaller donor footprint, aimed at providing support according to the expressed need of recipients. Any support that is given to the diaspora must avoid re-imposing the dysfunctional power relationships of traditional development aid.

Chapter 8

EXIT STRATEGY – REPLACING FOREIGN ASSISTANCE

Aid does work: it has brought real and profound benefits to poor people and increasingly so in recent years. …
The dead aid thesis makes a valid point but should not define how we view development.
Tony Blair speaking at the Center for Global Development, 17 December 2010

The Paris declaration fails to recognize the central paradox – that aid in itself undermines both state capacity and accountability.
Jonathan Glennie (2008)[1]

Some Elements of an Aid Disengagement Strategy

The experience of 50 years of aid shows that the donor countries in collaboration with the recipients must define far more clearly exactly where and how they can add value. They started to do something like that during the first decade of the 2000s at Monterrey, Rome, Paris, Accra and Busan; but after nearly 10 years of New Aid, the achievement has been small and the full implications of important changes in the dynamics of the international order have apparently not yet been absorbed.

One key implication of the new dynamic is that aid resources and diaspora resources are not necessarily complementary and may instead be to some extent mutually exclusive, with diaspora resources superseding aid resources. The surge in private transfers across the world and a growing partnership between the diasporas and many home countries may be a historic opportunity for a new impetus to development without aid, in Africa and the poorer countries of South Asia and Latin America. With the help of private current and capital transfers Sub-Saharan Africa may now be capable of drawing in as much as US$100 billion a year in private investment resources over a short to medium term take off period, without counting the non-indigenous market based foreign investment which has been worth up to an additional US$30 billion a year. These amounts dwarf foreign aid flows.

Aid-recipient countries should be vigilant about excluding assistance that does not add value, either technically or in terms of social development. They should limit the presence of those aid agencies that are not capable of playing a role in this respect. The rich countries may, of course, always be needed to help in emergencies such as earthquakes, floods, famines and epidemics, but they should refocus and reduce long term economic aid, especially soft aid. Where advisory services continue to be justified they should follow a hands-off, minimal-footprint approach allowing the maximum local financial and administrative accountability with far fewer individual donor agencies in each country.

An outline of some key actions, not necessarily in priority order, over the medium term for an aid-recipient national government seeking an exit from the aid relationship might look like the following:

1. Conduct through the legislature a full review of foreign aid, its costs and its benefits, and define a typology of foreign aid that can add value.
2. Develop a medium- to long-term development-without-aid strategy for the country with targets for phase-out and restructuring of assistance programs.
3. Develop new instruments for residual foreign aid consistent with the increased use of domestic and diaspora resources and set up new procedures for residual aid.
4. Work with donor agencies to close or restructure aid programs over a stipulated period and reduce them to a minimal physical footprint within the country.
5. Continually develop and strengthen the general investment climate and incentive programs for local and foreign businesses including legal and regulatory reform, infrastructure development and access to finance.
6. Intensify contact with the diaspora while relaxing political, regulatory and financial impediments to diaspora involvement in the home economy.
7. Develop policies such as citizenship rights to encourage the regular temporary or permanent return of migrants with high-level skills and capacity to invest.
8. Facilitate business contacts with African "growth pole" countries, using all available public and private channels, including regional organizations, to promote cross-border trade and investment.
9. Develop tax and regulatory instruments to encourage formalization of private foreign payments including remittances and capital return.
10. Launch medium- to long-term programs for tax reform and increase tax effort and capacity in tax policy, analysis and collection.
11. Develop and introduce new financial instruments to mobilize foreign savings such as development bonds and other incentive vehicles for financing investment.
12. Continually monitor the need for residual external assistance and the related funding gaps, based on requirements for specific goods, services and skills.
13. Develop recruitment facilities such as web portals that advertise nationally and internationally for specific foreign technical, economic and policy skills to be used within central and local government and in non-government sectors under a reorganized approach to foreign assistance.
14. Upgrade public appropriation and budgetary procedures for purchase of foreign goods and services as part of packages of government/donor or public/private assistance.
15. Restructure government departments and budgets to operate with significantly reduced external assistance, and implement redundancy and retraining schemes for government officials formerly responsible for foreign-aid programs.

The arguments and actions set out above call for a radical reorganization of the way aid is received as well as a rethink on what is included in it by recipient governments and legislatures. At the purely country level, three principles of a strategy for residual aid are required. The first is the creation of genuine demand-driven programs based on country needs, partly paid for in the commercial market for international services, and not encouraged, fostered or drafted by aid agencies. The second is the reduction of the aid footprint within the country by shrinking and closing aid agencies, and drastically reducing the fragmentation and associated transaction costs of aid. The third is domestic resource mobilization, including the restoration of taxation, increased tax effort and the channeling of tax revenue into the budget to purchase the foreign goods and services required under development programs. This is, par excellence, a job for a reinvigorated executive and one which may in turn reinvigorate the legislature. Residual foreign assistance delivery must be channeled so that it no longer undermines the budgetary system.

Country Assistance Funds: A Possible New Aid Artifact

Taking off from the "three principles," at the country level one approach which could contain the minimum critical ingredients for a non-alienating aid program could be in the form of a *country assistance fund* or a *multi-country assistance fund*. Such a vehicle could work on the basis of a combination of features of the Millennium Challenge Fund and budget support fund models, but with much reduced conditionality and monitoring, and a reduction in the aid footprint both through less resident staff and less supervision. The following is a possible, but indicative, twelve-step process.

1. A single or multi-year country proposal broken down into projects would be presented to an aid donor or a consortium of donors; for very large projects (e.g. infrastructure) individual project proposals could be presented.
2. Several proposals could be put forward simultaneously or in sequence, and the funding would be on a rolling basis so that under- or overspending would not be an impediment to further funding.
3. The donor or donor group would make a decision on the amount of funding for each program, if any, based on indicators of country performance, defining an average percent of cost to be born by the recipient which would vary according to country income level; for single large projects such as in infrastructure, cost-sharing arrangements would need to be designed case by case.
4. A national or local parliamentary, legislative or directive body would consider and approve or reject the donors' offer of funds and its cost and expenditure parameters.
5. If and when approved by both sides, a contractual agreement would be signed with the government setting out the expenditure parameters and the funds disbursed to the country, which would be in the form of budget support.
6. A notice about the agreement, funds, timing, intended uses and disbursement would be published by the recipient government in all relevant media on an intermittent basis.
7. The uncovered funding component would be met by the local agency purchasing services or goods through local cash resources authorized through a formal public

or private budgetary or appropriation process; for single large projects and large goods purchases, special procedures would apply so that the funds could be incorporated into wider financing arrangements.

8. The agency (public or private) receiving the (partial) funding according to the expenditure agreement would be independently responsible for identifying potential suppliers of goods and services and for purchasing them on the regular national and international market on commercial or other available terms.

9. The recipient agent would provide the relevant expenditure reports to the responsible government department who would maintain records according to its usual practice.

10. The government would monitor expenditure and evaluate project performance according to its usual practice, either through a specialized evaluation unit or through general resources such as a public accounts office.

11. According to a timetable, the donor would ask for a report on expenditure and new country performance indicators, in order to appraise future requests for funds.

12. The donor would determine the justification for a follow up grant which would only be approved on satisfactory fulfillment of the contractual agreement.

Such an instrument could still face gaming, fraud and mismanagement, but these should be addressed on an *ex post* basis through decisions on follow-up funding. That is, the sanction vis-à-vis fraud would be the cessation of funding unless a government makes acceptable representations for its continuance. There would not be ongoing monitoring and evaluation of individual projects by donors. A donor's involvement would be a) the initial evaluation of country performance, b) agreeing the aid package and signing the agreement, and c) the expenditure review on completion.

A minimal footprint instrument such as this could be accompanied by the withdrawal of aid-agency staff and resources on the ground and a major reduction in project programming, management and evaluation by both bilateral and multilateral agencies. Programming expertise could be purchased by the recipient government on the international market if necessary. This would also result in some reduction in the intellectual content of foreign-aid work. It would become largely a task of managing funds on specified criteria and procedures to meet specified objectives.

From the point of view of a multilateral agency such as the World Bank, this narrow profile would result in particularly far-reaching organizational change. The World Bank would have to become reactive to country requests, responding to programs developed entirely by the countries and their paid advisers.

One inevitable objection to the minimal footprint approach will be: "how will poor countries with low governmental capacity (despite 50 years of foreign aid) be able to put together proposals and identify the expertise they require?" Leaving aside post-crisis environments where, as stated, outside help might be essential, the general answer is that they will purchase all the expertise they require, according to their own plans, on the national or international market with a combination of their own funds and donor funds. An advance fund for project preparation could be included in the agreed donor assistance program, against a partial payment from the country in question. Among the wide range of expertise needed and purchased on the national or international market could, if it seemed appropriate to the government, be help for the programming of its assistance requests, expertise to negotiate on behalf of the government with its own diaspora; or, if the government considered such help was warranted, expertise to assist the government to plan the phase-out of aid. There are already numerous markets for expertise located on the Internet, which could be rapidly adapted to the new, broader international market for expertise with recipient country agencies, and not aid agencies, as buyers.

Another objection will concern the perennially difficult political action of "cutting off" aid on the basis of an unsatisfactory *ex post* assessment of how the money has been spent. This is a problem of organizational vested interests and inertia as much as it is about politics, and it is reflected in the self-perpetuating nature of aid agencies that we have discussed. It is possible that this could be solved through the reduction of the donor's "aid footprint." Such a solution might work through: a) a greater separation of the aid function from the foreign affairs and diplomacy function of government, and b) the consequent relegation of aid more to a technical level activity with specific publicly known criteria for continued disbursement. By this means the political importance of aid might be reduced and decisions on aid continuance separated to the degree possible from political calculations.

Other questions that will be raised center on how this new "instrument" would relate to the multitude of other new instruments reviewed in Chapter 6. Will it not be "just another instrument"? The answer is that this approach is merely an expression of the minimal footprint concept. The question will be how to introduce the concept in such a way that it is possible to successfully phase out, or successfully incorporate, other instruments.[2] In some cases phasing out would require major rethinking, as in the case of credits provided by the World Bank and regional development banks, which are partial grants repayable over time. World Bank budgetary support would need to be matched or partially matched by additional budgetary contributions from the recipient country. In some cases the "new concept" may be incompatible with current ideas – such as COD – since the new concept does away with heavy monitoring and evaluation and is not based on delivery but rather on a) a trust relationship and b) a view of overall country performance. It is the recipient country that would concern itself with outcome and impact and it would be the donor that judged the country's claims *ex post* with a view to continuing or winding down the country aid pool.

Global and Other Public Goods (GPGs): Where Development Aid Might Be Essential

In Chapter 1, I pointed out that it was not reasonable to claim a general failure of aid but rather that its failures were in certain countries and sectors, in certain circumstances. I end with another qualification, the case of global or regional public goods.

As is widely recognized, the public sector, including foreign aid, is most likely to be effective in assisting development in areas where private business has little involvement either because its costs are higher than the costs to society (for example, pollution which the private actor has no monetary incentive to reduce) or its expected benefits are lower than the benefits to society (for example, health benefits of vaccinations where the profits to private business are not enough to justify increasing production of vaccines). These circumstances, where the private sector is not willing to act but where a public benefit ensues from action, provide the basis of public interest and public goods.[3] Such goods can be national, wherein action by a government is essential and unique, as in the development of the legal system and judiciary, or they can be global such as climate change adaptation, environmental improvement or global health action where a government will only be willing to act in common with other governments.

Donor agencies have increasingly if belatedly been turning attention to this area, for example in the case of environmental agreements at conferences in places such as Kyoto, Hokkaido and Copenhagen. The British DFID has started a program based around a Clean Energy Investment Framework and Climate Investment Funds. The World Bank launched a Prototype Carbon Fund in 1996 followed up a series of further funds.[4] Such activities go alongside the other examples of international collective action on climate change, global health, high yielding plant varieties and pest control. In the category of justifiable international collective action are also certain information services such as the monitoring of macroeconomic and financial systems, and provision of information where it is not easily obtainable by an individual country or because it requires a collective view.[5]

Other examples of global, regional and national public goods that may be beyond what individual governments and private firms are willing or able to invest in on their own are large-scale infrastructure projects such as regional electricity generation and distribution. These have commonly required inter-government, government–donor, and/or international public–private partnerships. Cross-border infrastructure is essential in Africa, especially because of the geographical fragmentation of the continent while at the same time that very fragmentation renders cross-border investment more difficult.[6] While infrastructure development may be appropriately in the public domain there is also extensive experience built up over the past 20 years of partnerships between the public and private sector, whereby private investors are prepared to come forward with public funding or guarantees that lower risk to the point where private investors are willing to proceed.

A growth-pole strategy in Africa might also provide a justification for public-sector investments including infrastructure such as industrial parks. These had some success in countries such as South Korea in the 1960s and 1970s. Many countries have tried to establish special economic zones (SEZs) on the model of China's program in Shenzhen and other coastal cities along the Yangtze River. This type of initiative, however, has to be approached cautiously. The mere establishment of a zone is likely to produce little unless it is supported by the right policies and active private-sector interest. In India up to 1991 success was limited[7] and in Africa likewise up to now.[8] Much investment on zones, parks and estates has been based on over-optimistic assumptions about private interest, and has set up enclaves with weak linkages to the local economy.[9]

There thus needs to be caution with the GPG agenda both to ensure that there really is a private-sector failure to be compensated for, and that the design of the public intervention effectively compensates for or attracts private initiative. Kapur points out that that little analysis been done to help international organizations rank GPGs in order of their relative contribution to global welfare, and "this analytical hiatus … allows them to press for private interests in the guise of GPGs."[10] In this context, the World Bank has carried out some well-justified global action such as its carbon funds, but it has also pursued less justifiable projects in the guise of public goods.[11] Donor countries and organizations also have to confront the "policy inconsistency" that allows expenditure on a global public goods objective such as "aid for trade," but blocks the removal of the global public "bad" – that is, protection of domestic production through barriers on export of sugar, rice and other products from the poorest countries.

Leaving aside these cautionary points, the traditional method of conceiving and designing projects from outside, i.e. donor-owned and driven, may be relevant in the case of global or regional public goods that are beyond the scope of national governments, because there is not necessarily a sovereign authority available to take ownership of them. The natural "owner" of such projects may be a global organization. In this area therefore there may be a residual justification for international donors to take the initiative using an approach that circumvents local procedures and capacity. There may equally be a justification, or an urgency, in the case of global necessities such as vaccinations, for circumventing local budgeting mechanisms and for allowing pure grants with no appropriation of local funds for co-payments. However, when global initiatives are disaggregated to national level, in the form for example of action by national health services, the rules of country ownership, and country capacity are more likely to be applicable if effectiveness is to be achieved.

The comparative advantage of multilateral institutions such as the World Bank and regional development banks is with global or regional programs, while the global scale of such organizations also makes them ill suited to national and especially sub-national programs. Yet the World Bank has lent money since the start on a country or sub-sovereign basis and its global public goods role has thus been retarded. Sub-sovereign lending in particular is likely to lead it away from global public goods and towards involvement in smaller scale projects requiring close attention on the ground, which it is unable to deliver cost-effectively.

Intentions and Consequences

At the start of this book I pointed out that aid motivation was a critical factor in development assistance effectiveness. This is because if motivations are inconsistent with developmental objectives then there is no reason to suppose that any improvement will occur, despite the best efforts of Paris and Busan. If a donor government's agenda is simply to "plant the flag" or achieve commercial gain, then it will not be interested in domestic capacity, ownership or accountability. Many governments do indeed have these motivations uppermost and will not participate genuinely in reform of development assistance. In the US different motivations arise within the same administration. USAID and the US Department of Defense have different conceptions of the purpose of assistance and differing motivations to provide it.

The problem, however, is more complicated than this. What I have tried to show is that, even where intentions are good, i.e. developmental and consistent with improving domestic capacity, accountability and ownership, they have often been misdirected, have often failed and in the present aid model will continue to fail in the poorest countries. Good intentions have not been able to meaningfully affect the inherent break in accountability on both the donor side and the recipient side of foreign aid, fundamentally because of the flawed rich country–poor country aid relationship. On the one hand, the voting and taxpaying public in the donor country have almost no idea of and no control over the money that goes out and do not know whether it does any good; on the other hand, the voting and taxpaying public in the recipient country have little idea about the money that comes in and no control over it, are not asked how to spend it and have scant interest in the results overall. This would be a recipe for failure in any situation.

The aid donors at Rome, Paris and Accra adopted an agenda of "more and better aid."[12] The Paris agreement asked for a) country ownership, whereby developing countries must take the lead; b) better alignment, whereby donors must align themselves with national development strategies institutions and procedures; c) aid harmonization, to lower transaction costs; d) management for results; and e) mutual accountability. Despite the length of time and all the statements of intent the OECD's own 2011 report on the progress of the Paris and Ghana declarations gave a very poor assessment. The report on the Paris Declaration stated: "only one out of the 13 targets established for 2010 has been met." The one target was to "strengthen capacity by co-ordinated support" whose fulfillment would appear to require increasing the number of donor conferences.[13]

From years of observation, even the public officials in poor countries who stand to gain from aid programs and who support their continuation for that reason do so with misgivings because they feel a sense of alienation from a system which provides so little in terms of their commitment of time and intellect, and which diverts them from work building their own communities. Yet they are captured by a system that provides them with careers, social status and pensions. This is a conflicted situation that provides the wrong signals to the donors. Thus, commitment to aid programs is often ambivalent and the lack of ownership that so puzzles and frustrates the donors is rationally explained. The bulk of the individuals affected are competent people who are simply unprepared to assume accountability for a system in which they have little faith. As Brautigam and Knack put it, "political elites have little incentive to change a situation in which large amounts of aid provide exceptional resources for patronage and many fringe benefits."[14]

As mentioned right at the start of this book, the value of the losses in international trade by poor countries due to trade barriers overwhelms the nominal value of foreign aid. Taking into account the potential of the diaspora as well as a resurgence of general FDI, foreign aid will become increasingly unimportant. Its demise will be accelerated by its enormous systemic and transactions costs. Taking into account all private resources foreign aid worldwide has fallen to 10 percent or less of the worldwide package of inflows, far below historic levels. This has not, however, been because of any far-sighted decision by the donors to rationalize their activities. On the contrary, the number of donors, agencies and projects has continued to rise relentlessly, further increasing the transaction costs of aid. Equally, likely reductions in aid from 2011 have nothing to do with enlightenment about aid ineffectiveness but respond simply to the sudden fiscal crises that have beset most OECD countries since 2009. The decline in the relative share of aid is a result of the emergence of the private sector under its own rules.

Finally, after 50 years of poor results many of the poorest developing countries may have the opportunity and resources to start saying goodbye to the aid business as it is currently practiced. This certainly applies to Asian and Latin American countries and may also apply to African countries such as Ethiopia, Kenya and Ghana, in addition to the mineral-rich economies like Nigeria, Gabon and Botswana. Ellen Sirleaf Johnson of Liberia, the most aid-dependent country in Africa, stated at a seminar in Washington, DC in June 2011 that her goal was that Liberia should be free of aid in 10 years. Why should these countries, many of which have themselves supplied large numbers of their own skilled citizens to the outside world, continue to subject themselves to the anomalies, bureaucracy and sheer waste of time often associated with foreign assistance as it has been practiced?

Chapter 9

POSTSCRIPT

There are two organizations based in India. One is "3ie," the international aid evaluation center set up in 2009, aid-funded, with close links to academia, spending over ten million dollars each year on research to try to find out, after 50 years, what works in development assistance. The other is "TiE," the Indus Entrepreneurs, a privately funded diaspora organization supporting investors in the high technology sector. The names and locations are similar, but nothing else. The first is an artifact of development aid that is reinterpreting past decisions on public donations and the second is an artifact of diaspora initiative which is addressing the needs of future wealth creation.

The country of my childhood, now Malawi, has received US$13 billion in aid since independence (US$22 billion in today's prices), averaging well over 20 percent of its gross national income over the past 20 years. It is being assisted by about 40 official multilateral and bilateral aid agencies and approximately 200 foreign non-government organizations. In an average year it hosts several hundred donor missions. It faces similar or worse problems than it did at independence half a century ago: income levels well below the average for the poorest countries, emphasis on the same (and inappropriate) agricultural products (e.g. tobacco), a lack of infrastructure, a severe public health problem, population pressure and a lack of governance capacity.

The country's budget is funded to a significant extent from outside. The resulting vulnerability was clear in 2011 as the British government suspended aid to the government on grounds of mishandling of the economy and abusing human rights. In March 2012, the US Millennium Challenge Corporation also suspended aid on grounds of failure to meet standards of good governance after the arrest of some opposition politicians. The then president, Mutharika, stated that if donors wish to withdraw their assistance to Malawi, they can "leave and go." Aid was resumed in 2012 essentially after a promise of good behavior from the new president, Joyce Banda which included getting rid of the government vehicle fleet. The British and US governments were entitled to put their money wherever they thought it would be used best, and they may have been correct about human rights. But this episode was still a reflection of the almost craven state of Malawi's reliance on external donations.

The government of Malawi is excessively focused on managing aid programs. The total aid it receives is considerably larger than the amount of tax it raises. It has received large amounts of capacity-building assistance, including assistance to public financial management which the World Bank has itself evaluated as achieving little or nothing over many years; its parliament is often bypassed on development decisions while its executive arm cannot be adequately accountable for them.

After nearly half a century, Malawi is still in effect a client state, no longer a "protectorate" of the British Crown but instead to a significant extent a client of the international donors. Whereas once its leaders and people had to answer to a colonial government, they now find themselves having to answer to a collection of foreign governments and non-government agencies for a multitude of overlapping programs of variable quality all intended to help poor people but answerable to rich people in other countries. The poor state of the economy of Malawi has been blamed on its neo-patrimonial social system, reinforced initially by the autocratic rule of the first president, Hastings Banda. But the impact of very large inflows of foreign cash over several decades must be significantly to blame for sustaining this situation.

If Malawi is something of an outlier example, from the point of view of the billion people in the poorest countries development aid in its present form has still to a great extent failed to deliver. For the rest it has hardly played a material role. There is no evidence to show that development aid has achieved its self-proclaimed goal of ending poverty, nor any likelihood that it ever will as it is currently organized and practiced. There are ways that it can provide useful technical solutions and it can be reorganized to improve its effectiveness, but on the evidence of 50 years and even with optimistic estimates of its growth impact there is no likelihood that it can push the poorest countries on to a growth path to match those of the entrepreneurially driven economies of Asia. Foreign development aid is simply not the kind of instrument that can achieve such a goal. To paraphrase Peter T. Bauer, outside donations do not develop societies. The energy has to come from the inside. Only in the area of global public goods where individual societies and governments cannot be the owners, and where international assistance may have a legitimate and even irreplaceable role, might Bauer's generalization not apply.

Determined action by developing country governments is needed to carry out a well-planned short- to medium-term phase-out or reorganization of foreign aid, especially the software component, replacing it by non-alienating, genuinely demand driven and value adding programs paid for in part in cash through formal budgetary processes. If this enterprise is accompanied by sensible policies to improve the business environment, mobilize local resources and make way for the channeling of non-subsidized foreign resources including diaspora money and skills, it will over time accelerate the development of the poorest countries, including Malawi. This endeavor has to be matched by donor action on the most egregious anti-development anomalies – production subsidies in the donating countries, barriers to trade in poor country products such as cotton, sugar and rice, and lifting of restrictions on the migration of skills.

If outside assistance is properly designed, it can help to provide specific technical solutions and public goods like the introduction of high yielding seed varieties, the eradication of river blindness or the funding of continental transport projects. But the achievement of the end of poverty will depend in the end on the resources and intentions of the people of the poorest countries, both inside and outside their borders. It will not depend on foreign donations, foreign charity, foreign strategies or foreign road maps. Among the indigenous resources that are essential is entrepreneurship, a resource that has driven all successful development. The institutional, regulatory and infrastructural necessities of development must be met through the pressure of indigenous entrepreneurs on their own governments to make changes, helped by the democratization of those governments. This is a matter of cultural and social development. We have looked at a part of this process, the emergence of diaspora investors.

Development aid has to move into the background and focus on problems where, by agreement with host governments, it can add value. Within the poorest countries which constitute 15 percent of the world's population, and in its current form, it is a broken system that borders on the scandalous, and all donor agencies are complicit in this borderline scandal, including, and perhaps especially, those that regard themselves and are regarded as being on the "cutting edge."

At the start of this book, it was emphasized that the subject under discussion was not the fundamentals of economic and social development but the role of external aid for development. In addition, I said that I meant development aid, not aid for humanitarian, security, diplomatic or commercial objectives. Yet it is the latter that probably are in the end the most meaningful to the citizens of aid-giving countries, and that conception of its objectives surely best explains why foreign aid has been so resilient in the face of long-term criticism. Indeed it explains why the US Congress or British or French parliaments renew their aid appropriations every year. Efforts to support humanitarian, diplomatic, security and trade interests are without doubt important in preserving a donor nation's interests, but they are not the same thing as support for economic development. The dominance of commercial, diplomatic and security interests is reflected in the continuing failure to harmonize aid programs. Aid is in the end more about "planting the flag" than helping other countries to become successful economic competitors. The understanding that these motives, and not the altruistic one of poverty alleviation, are what essentially determine aid policy is one good reason for the disenchantment of the governments of poor countries. Their perception of the purpose of aid from OECD countries and international financial institutions is often reduced to one of maintaining diplomatic contacts and sustaining already aid-dependent government programs.

One organization that can focus better on long-term development objectives is the World Bank. The Bank's mission statement reads: "our dream is a world free of poverty." However, for its largest shareholder, the US, the issue is not about dreams but about control. Robert Zoellick, announcing his retirement in February 2012, argued in the face of international opposition for a continued US-owned presidency because, "I think there's a benefit for this system if the United States has a sense of responsibility to and ownership of those institutions." Apparently if it cannot exercise control the US would not be interested in institutions for global development, whereas all other countries were expected by Zoellick to remain interested regardless. If this reflects the US view, it is a strategic, not a developmental, conception of aid. The new Bank president, Jim Yong Kim, a US national, was placed in office partly because of the difficulties that the international donor community still has in mounting a credible counter-argument to US diplomatic and strategic interests worldwide and even to the influence of short-term US re-election interests. These interests have little to do with aid for development.

The belief among well-meaning and informed people that aid is a way to end poverty, despite their knowledge of its multiple and conflicting objectives, is a hopeful rationalization of those objectives. The character of public support for foreign assistance needs to be understood realistically. At best, it combines the sincere humanitarian generosity of some richer people towards poor people subject to the needs of those same richer people to guard their security and commercial interests vis-à-vis those same poor people. Assistance to secure the long-term prosperity of other people in another country (at the possible risk of reducing your own long-term prosperity) is not what justifies aid in the popular perception. Famines, epidemics, conflicts and terrorism are the primary reasons for doing it. That is essentially why it continues.

The High Level Forum at Busan in December 2011 delivered a declaration, the latest product of many years of sober discussion about better aid. Following similar statements, since 2002 at Monterrey, Rome, Paris and Accra, it made numerous pronouncements about how aid effectiveness was going to be improved. It talked about the inclusion of new official and informal donors, including the BRIC nations and the private sector, into an even bigger worldwide effort; it talked more about transparency and accountability, ownership by the recipients and focusing on sustainable results. For someone who was new to the subject, these expressions of intent may have been inspiring. But after 50 years of effort, including the ten most recent years of renewed and apparently better informed effort, those expressions are not inspiring. The next high-level forum on development assistance, most likely scheduled for 2014, should have a rather different focus. It should be how to assist poor countries *to constructively disengage from development aid and mobilize indigenous resources at home and abroad.*

Foreign aid will undoubtedly be needed in the poorest countries for some time to come, that is, if it takes a market-oriented, simplified, less intrusive and less alienating form. However, new international development dynamics resulting from the emergence of the diasporas may at last be able to create an environment in which *development without development aid* can become a realistic scenario for many of even the poorest countries, in Africa and beyond.

> *External donations have never been necessary for the development of any society anywhere.*
>
> Peter T. Bauer, *Reality and Rhetoric: Studies in Economic Development* (Harvard University Press, 1984), 43.

NOTES

1. Introduction: Motivation and Perspective

1 Peter T. Bauer, *Development Aid: End it or Mend It*, International Center for Economic Growth (ICS) Press Occasional Paper (1993), 11.

2 OECD Development Assistance Committee Database (2011).

3 Throughout this book I use the terms "aid," "assistance," "foreign aid," "economic aid," "development aid" and "ODA" interchangeably unless otherwise stated.

4 The Africana Periodical Literature Bibliographic Database currently lists 113,000 periodical journal articles. See www.africabib.org.

5 Michael Clemens, a leading author on development, asks: "Why does the West see so few thoughtful, critical analyses of aid and development written and spoken by Africans?" (see *Finance and Development*, IMF, September 2009). In a more sweeping critique, Dambisa Moyo states, "Scarcely does one see Africa's (elected) officials ... offer an opinion on what should be done, or what might actually work to save the continent from its regression" (see *Dead Aid: Why Aid is Not Working and How There is Another Way for Africa*, Allen Lane, 2008).

6 A diaspora-like association made up of former British colonial officials known as "Friends of Malawi" was formed in 1969. This is distinct from the Malawi Association of nationals formed later in the US and UK.

7 Nyasaland was not always quiet. There had been previous protest activity and there was serious opposition to Britain's decision to federate Nyasaland with Rhodesia in 1953, which fuelled the independence movement.

8 Despite his surprise my father went on to serve in the cabinet of the first Government of Malawi under President Banda. He had been in the Nyasaland government most of his career since leaving the military. His memoirs depict an administrator's life, paternalistic but engaged, far removed from his experience growing up in a north London suburb. See Sir Henry Phillips, *"From Obscurity to Bright Dawn": How Nyasaland became Malawi, An Insider's Account* (I.B. Tauris, 1998).

9 One of countless examples is a paper by Homi Kharas written 50 years after the dawn of foreign aid. It asks the time-worn question: "Can Aid Catalyze Development?" (Brooking Policy Briefs, 2010).

10 The aid donor community has made efforts to "reinvent" aid at a series of conferences: in 2002 in Monterrey, in 2003 in Rome, in 2005 in Paris, in 2008 in Accra and in 2011 in Busan, South Korea. The Paris Declaration by the main aid agencies agreed a "practical, action-orientated roadmap to improve the quality of aid and its impact on development." The OECD stated prior to the Busan conference that it would provide "an opportunity to produce a broader and deeper partnership. It represents perhaps the best and last chance to create the political will to tackle the scourge of poverty" (Brian Atwood, OECD DAC Chair speaking on "The Promise of Busan," available on the website of Fourth High Level Forum on Aid Effectiveness, 31 May 2011, http://www.aideffectiveness.org/busanhlf4/).

11 I define the "aid relationship" in historical terms. In most poor countries, the "foreign-aid era" was the immediate successor of the colonial era. In Africa, the succession was sometimes relatively peaceful, such as in Malawi and Tanzania, but it could also be violent,

as in Algeria and Mozambique. The colonial era passed on part of its culture, institutions and social structure in the formation of "neo-colonial" or "neo-patrimonial" states. A neo-colonial relationship is one where a dominant society asserts, wittingly or not, economic, political or cultural means that perpetuate or extend its influence over a subordinate society. A neo-patrimonial relationship is one where an outside power legitimizes a traditional, patronage-based social system by using public resources (aid money) to form alliances among its leaders. Many donor countries (e.g. Sweden and Norway) and recipient countries (e.g. Nepal and Ethiopia) had no overt colonial history but tend to adhere to the dominant ethic of the countries that did.

12 For a detailed definition of foreign aid, see Roger Riddell, *Does Foreign Aid Really Work?* (Oxford University Press, 2007).

13 For example, after the Haiti earthquake of 2010 objections arose to the inflows of used goods. See Alanna Shaikh, "Nobody wants your old shoes: How not to help in Haiti" and "Donating stuff instead of money is a serious problem in emergency relief," *Aid Watch* (16 January 2010).

14 World Bank, World Development Indicators (2011), tables 6.14 to 6.16. The totals vary according to the definition of ODA and the inclusion of non-DAC donors and are in other ways inconsistent. The numbers are representative of the various estimates.

15 For example, see Kym Anderson, Will Martin and Ernesto Valenzuela, *Why Market Access Is the Most Important of Agriculture's "Three Pillars" in the Doha Negotiations*, World Bank, Trade Note/Policy Brief on Doha (November 2005).

16 The UN defines the 49 poorest countries (the least-developed countries) as those with per capita income of below US$900 per annum with certain human resource and economic vulnerabilities. They include 34 Sub-Saharan African countries, 10 South Asian countries (including Afghanistan, Nepal, Laos, Cambodia and Bangladesh), Haiti and some Pacific Island nations.

17 See for example Kimberly Ann Elliott, *Opening Markets for Poor Countries: Are We There Yet?* (Center for Global Development, October 2009).

18 The UN Millennium Development Goals (MDGs) aimed to: halve extreme poverty; achieve universal primary education; empower women; promote equality between women and men; reduce under-five mortality by two-thirds; reduce maternal mortality by three-quarters; reverse the spread of diseases, especially HIV/AIDS and malaria; ensure environmental sustainability; create a global partnership on aid, trade, and debt relief. See www.un.org/millenniumgoals/background.html

19 Anderson, Martin and Valenzuela, *Market Access*.

20 Antonio La Vina, Lindsey Fransen, Paul Faeth and Yuko Kurauchi, *Reforming Agricultural Subsidies: "No Regrets" Policies for Livelihoods and the Environment* (World Resources Institute, 2006). In the US, statistics are published annually on urban dwellers that access rural subsidies – the so-called urban farmers.

21 Elliott, *Opening Markets for Poor Countries*. Elliott chaired a CGD working group that proposed 100 percent duty and quota free imports from the 49 countries. See Kimberly Ann Elliott, *Open Markets for the Poorest Countries – Trade Preferences that Work*, CGD Working Group on Global Trade Preference Reform (1 April 2010).

22 Under the Africa Growth and Opportunities Act (AGOA) of 2000, 34 Sub-Saharan African countries are eligible to export to the US duty-free under 98 percent of US tariff lines. However, "tariff rate quotas" remain on sugar, and garments are subject to a ceiling unless US fabrics are used. Eighteen of the poorest countries have received a waiver of some of these rules but for other poor countries the tariffs remain.

23 Bernard Hoekman, Francis Ng and Marcelo Olarreaga, *Eliminating Excessive Tariffs on Exports of Least Developed Countries*, World Bank Policy Research Working Paper no. 2,604 (2001).

24 Kym Anderson, Will Martin and Ernesto Valenzuela, *The Relative Importance of Global Agricultural Subsidies, and Market Access* (World Bank, Development Research Group, 2005).

The authors conclude that the cost of trade barriers is greater than that of domestic subsidies because they distort production and consumption whereas domestic subsidies only distort production. Also see E. W. F. Peterson, *A Billion Dollars a Day: The Economics and Politics of Agricultural Subsidies* (Blackwell, 2009).

25 La Vina, Fransen, Faeth and Kurauchi, *Reforming Agricultural Subsidies*.

26 This initiative was launched at the Hong Kong WTO Ministerial Conference. See OECD Development Cooperation Review (2010), box 4.1.

27 For example, by compensating for the tax losses caused by dropping tariffs within poorer countries.

28 Kenneth A. Reinert, "The European Union, the Doha Round, and Asia," *Asia Europe Journal* 5, no. 3 (2007): 317–30. Reinert reviews the European Union's intervention in agricultural markets and concludes that the offers made by the EU under the Doha Round were designed precisely to avoid genuine liberalization.

29 According to Steve Radelet in *Emerging Africa* (Center for Global Development, 2010), Malawi is a "threshold country" just behind the 17 most successful African economies of the 2000s decade. However, its per capita GDP growth over 1996–2008 was still a relatively low 1.2 percent per annum.

30 OECD Development Cooperation Review (2010), table 25, and World Bank, World Development Indicators (2010), table 6.16. In 2008, the ODA/GNI measure was 21.5 percent after being as high as 28 percent in 2005.

31 In 1891, Nyasaland, then the British Central African Protectorate, had a budget adequate to pay 10 administrators, 2 military personnel, 70 Punjabi Sikhs and 85 Zanzibari porters, for a country of 1 million people. See John Reader, *Africa: A Biography of the Continent* (Vintage, 1999). The population at the 1911 census was: Africans, 969,183; Europeans, 766; Asians, 481.

32 Some research seems to find the opposite – that high growth, not low growth, tends to generate more funding, probably because international financial institutions look for more profitable projects. See Hristos Doucouliagos (Deakin University) and Martin Paldam (University of Aarhus), *Explaining Development Aid Allocation by Growth: A Meta Study* (University of Aarhus, October 2007).

33 See William Easterly, "Was Development Assistance a Mistake?", *American Economic Review* 97, no. 2 (May 2007): 328–32. He writes, "With aid, one has an even more serious problem than with other growth regressions of endogeneity of the right hand side variable – it's very likely that low growth countries got more aid because they had low growth."

2. What Is Foreign Aid, Who Does It, Why and How Much Is There?

1 See http://www.oecd.org/dac/aideffectiveness/fourthhighlevelforumonaideffectiveness.htm

2 See http://www.telegraph.co.uk/comment/letters/7958485/What-is-the-best-way-to-help-the-worlds-deserving-poor.html#

3 For a more detailed definition see Roger Riddell, *Does Foreign Aid Really Work?* (Oxford University Press, 2007), chapter 2.

4 More precisely the present value of assistance services discounted at 10 percent.

5 A useful overview can be found in *Aid Architecture: An Overview of the Main Trends in Official Development Assistance Flows*, IDA 15 background paper (World Bank, February 2007).

6 Although it has varied widely between countries, from 40 percent to 90 percent, reflecting individual donor policy.

7 The Heavily Indebted Poor Countries Initiative (HIPC) was launched in 1996 by the IMF and World Bank. In 1999, it was re-launched with broader debt relief. In 2005, to support the Millennium Development Goals, the Multilateral Debt Relief Initiative (MDRI) was launched by the G8 countries, allowing 100 percent relief on IMF, World Bank and African Development Fund debt for countries that reached an eligibility point.

8 See David A. Phillips, *Reforming the World Bank: Twenty Years of Trial – and Error* (Cambridge University Press, 2009).

9 The relative merits of big plans and little projects, advocated respectively by "planners" and "searchers" are a topic of William Easterly, *The White Man's Burden: Why the West's Efforts to Aid the Rest Have Done So Much Ill and So Little Good* (Penguin, 2006).

10 The concept of alienation that I am referring to is "powerlessness" as defined by Melvin Seeman, "On the Meaning of Alienation," *American Sociological Review* 24 (1959): 783–91. Powerlessness is where individuals (or groups of individuals) perceive that their own action cannot affect outcomes, or that the means to achieve key outcomes are under the control of other agents.

11 A more detailed discussion of the process can be found in chapter 5 of Ian Goldin and Kenneth Reinert, *Globalization for Development: Meeting New Challenges* (Oxford University Press, 2012).

12 Two rival theories of development prevalent in this era included that of Walt Rostow, *The Stages of Economic Growth: A Non-Communist Manifesto* (Cambridge University Press, 1960), who espoused the "big push" and balanced growth approach, and Albert Hirschman, *The Strategy of Economic Development* (Yale University Press, 1958), who believed that phased progress was the most realistic strategy, with leading sectors creating pressure on following sectors.

13 The term "the Washington Consensus" was coined in 1989 by John Williamson of the Institute for International Economics, to describe the liberalization programs supported by the major international financial institutions and donors.

14 Easterly, *Elusive Quest*, 133.

15 Paul Collier, "Conditionality, Dependence and Coordination: Three Current Debates in Aid Policy," in *The World Bank: Structure and Policies*, ed. by C. L. Gilbert and D. Vines (Cambridge University Press, 2000), 304.

16 World Bank Annual Report (2010).

17 *World Bank Assistance to Agriculture in Sub-Saharan Africa: An IEG Review* (World Bank, 2007).

18 Wolfensohn used his 1996 World Bank annual meetings address to pronounce corruption as a cancer on development.

19 See Nicolas van de Walle, *Overcoming Stagnation in Aid-Dependent Countries: Politics, Policies and Incentives for Poor Countries* (Center For Global Development, April 2005).

20 This is the Millennium Villages Project. The project has echoes of the failed "industrialized villages" of the 1960s (e.g. in Tanzania) which were partly modeled on the Israeli kibbutz.

21 See Justin Lin and Ha-Joon Chang, "Should Industrial Policy in Developing Countries Conform to Comparative Advantage or Defy It?" *Development Policy Review* 27, no. 5 (2009): 483–502.

22 Carol Lancaster, *Foreign Aid, Diplomacy, Development and Domestic Politics* (Chicago, 2007). Lancaster divides aid objectives into: realist, developmental, commercial, humanitarian and ideological, and motives into altruism, budgets, politics, security, fairness and global public goods.

23 The US has often influenced the geography of World Bank lending in its own political interests. This has increased assistance to the Congo, Philippines, Turkey, Iraq, Afghanistan, Pakistan and Armenia and reduced it to Chile, Belarus and Ethiopia. See Axel Dreher, Jan-Egbert Sturm and James Raymond Vreeland, "Development Aid and International Politics: Does Membership on the UN Security Council Influence World Bank Decisions?" *Journal of Development Economics* 88, no. 1 (January 2009): 1–18.

24 As exemplified in the international context by globalgiving.com, a non-profit organization acting as a vehicle for individual donations for international project assistance.

25 Bertin Martens, "Why Do Aid Agencies Exist?" in *Reinventing Foreign Aid*, ed. by William Easterly (Center for Global Development, 2008).

26 Clark C. Gibson, Krister Andersson, Elinor Ostrom and Sujai Shivakumar, *The Samaritan's Dilemma The Political Economy of Development Aid* (Oxford University Press, 2005). This book applies institutional analysis to Sweden's development agency, SIDA.

27 See Carol Lancaster, *Foreign Aid*.

28 Article 4, section 10 of the IBRD Articles of Agreement states: "The Bank and its officers shall not interfere in the political affairs of any member; nor shall they be influenced in their decisions by the political character of the member or members concerned. Only economic considerations shall be relevant to their decisions, and these considerations shall be weighed impartially in order to achieve the purposes stated in Article 1."

29 Van de Walle, *Overcoming Stagnation in Aid-Dependent Countries*.

30 The multilateral institutions include the World Bank Group, Asian, African, Inter-American and European Development Banks, European Investment Bank, sub-regional banks and up to 70 UN agencies.

31 From *Global Programs and Vertical Funds*, ODI background paper (2004) and *Aid Architecture: An Overview of the Main Trends in Official Development Assistance Flows*, IDA 15 background paper (World Bank, February 2007), box 3, 12–26.

32 Jean-Michel Severino and Olivier Ray, *The End of ODA: Death and Rebirth of a Global Public Policy*, Center for Global Development Working Paper no. 167 (March 2009).

33 Severino and Ray, *The End of ODA*.

34 In 2002, the US announced a new approach to development assistance through the Millennium Challenge Corporation. Eight years later MCC and USAID operate side by side, and other agencies have emerged.

35 David Roodman, *Aid Project Proliferation and Absorptive Capacity*, Center for Global Development Working Paper no. 75 (January 2006).

36 Riddell, *Does Foreign Aid Really Work*, cites the LSE findings, 259.

37 Samuel A. Worthington and Tony Pipa, *International NGOs and Foundations: Essential Partners in Creating an effective Architecture for Aid*, Brookings Blum Roundtable Policy Briefs (2010).

38 See Severino and Ray, *The End of ODA*.

39 World Development Indicators (2010), table 6.16, 406.

40 Based on data in Riddell, *Does Foreign Aid Really Work*, 52.

41 Proceedings of the United Nations Conference on Trade and Development (UNCTAD), 1970, Second Session, Annex 1, Decision 27(II), paragraph 7.

42 Michael A. Clemens and Todd J. Moss, *Ghost of 0.7%: Origins and Relevance of the International Aid Target*, Center for Global Development Working Paper no. 68 (September 2005).

43 Worthington and Pipa, *International NGOs and Foundations*.

44 William Easterly and Tobias Pfutze, *Where Does the Money Go – Best and Worst Practices in Foreign Aid*, working paper (Brookings Institute Global Economy and Development, 21 June 2008). The CGD Commitment to Development Index is another important initiative in this respect but it does not look at aid-agency performance as such, rather at a range of variables reflecting aid policy.

45 There is inconsistent reporting and other problems such as multiple products (e.g. the most IFIs provide both concessional and non-concessional finance).

46 William Easterly and Claudia R. Williamson, Rhetoric versus Reality: The Best and Worst of Aid Agency Practices (Development Research Institute, New York University, May 2011).

47 Easterly and Pfutze, *Where Does the Money Go*, 7.

48 The CDI results are to be found at http://www.cgdev.org/section/initiatives/_active/cdi/

49 Nancy Birdsall, Homi Kharas, Ayah Mahgoub and Rita Perakis, *Quality of Official Development Assistance Assessment* (Center for Global Development, 5 October 2010).

50 Aid quality is scored on net amount, tying, selectivity, and project proliferation; trade assistance on the effect of tariffs, non-tariff measures and subsidies; investment assistance on official risk insurance, prevention of double taxation, actions to prevent corruption and measures to support foreign investment; support to migration on ease of access to rich country jobs,

education, wage remittance, help to returnees and commitment to international agreements; support to the environment on global climate, fisheries, biodiversity and global ecosystems; support to security on internal stability and freedom from fear of external attack (action on international peacekeeping, humanitarian interventions, protecting sea lanes, weapons exports to authoritarian regimes); finally, support to technology criteria include research and development funding, and patent and copyright rules.

51 OECD Development Cooperation Review (2009), table 2, 176. Also see Severino and Ray, *The End of ODA*.

52 Van de Walle writes that in certain sectors such as relief operations, NGOs have become the dominant players (*Overcoming Stagnation*, 60). He cites one estimate that foundations and private Americans donate between US$10 billion and US$17 billion a year and these totals appear to be rapidly increasing.

53 Global Development Finance Report (2010), table 1, 1, and DAC Development Cooperation (2010).

54 For example, John Page and Sonia Plaza, "Migration Remittances and Development: A Review of Global Evidence," *Journal of African Economies* 15, no. 2 (December 2006): 245–336. They estimate that unrecorded amounts constituted 73 percent of actual remittances.

55 *Global Development Finance* (World Bank, 2011), table 13, 18. The overall total comprised about US$53 billion in debt and equity flows, US$19 billion in recorded remittances and US$34 billion in ODA.

56 Estimate of Easterly and Pfutze, *Where Does the Money Go*.

57 See World Development Indicators (2010), table 6.15, and Easterly and Pfutze, *Where Does the Money Go*.

58 The US government agencies wholly or partly devoted to foreign aid include USAID, MCC, USTDA, offices within the Defense, State, Treasury, Energy, and Agriculture Departments, and others.

59 Riddell, *Does Foreign Aid Really Work*, 205.

60 The Berg Report, *Accelerated Development in Sub-Saharan Africa: An Agenda for Action* (World Bank, 1981), argued that the number is "closer to 40,000 than to 80,000" (14). Berg writes, "It is a particularly ironic situation for countries that continue to lose many of their best trained professionals to the West."

61 Worthington and Pipa, *International NGOs and Foundations*.

62 The two sources are not strictly comparable because total ODA contains a larger capital aid share while NGO grants contain a larger emergency component. NGO aid is also probably more labor intensive.

63 Worthington and Pipa, *International NGOs and Foundations*.

64 See www.devdir.org

65 See http://ccss.jhu.edu

66 See www.//blds.ids.ac.uk/index.html

67 These are featured on the website: http://www.aeaweb.org/econlit/journal_list

68 In 2006, Madonna started a foundation called Raising Malawi. But even her celebrity status could not grapple with the complexities of a poor, aid-dependent society. In March 2011, *Aid Watch* reported that Madonna's school-for-girls project was cancelled after spending US$3.8 million. Its total cost of US$15 million would have equaled about 10 percent of the country's entire education budget and would have thereby been unsustainable. Disgruntled employees are reported to have sued the foundation. On 14 March 2012, *Rolling Stone Magazine* reported Madonna's new plan to build ten schools. But the government told Reuters news agency, "We feel like this is all about propping up her global image and not in our interest … She has no mandate to decide where she wants to build a school because she doesn't know our needs and where we want new schools" (see http://www.reuters.com/article/2012/03/13/entertainment-us-malawi-madonna-idUSBRE82C19N20120313).

3. How Far Has Development Aid Been Effective?

1 See http://www.oecd.org/development/aideffectiveness/34428351.pdf

2 Peter T. Bauer, *Reality and Rhetoric* (Harvard University Press, 1984), 45.

3 This was the "Mind the Gap" conference on impact evaluation held in June 2011, hosted by the International Initiative for Impact Evaluation (3ie), the National Institute of Public Health of Mexico, the Inter-American Development Bank and others.

4 Delio Gianturco, "A Mixed Picture on Aid," in *"Africa – Development Aid,"* *International Affairs Forum* (Spring, 2010), 16–18.

5 Roger Riddell, *Does Foreign Aid Really Work?* (Oxford University Press, 2009), 211.

6 Anjum Altaf, "Aid to Pakistan: Advocacy or Analysis?" *SouthAsianIdea* blog (21 June 2011).

7 William Easterly, "Was Development Assistance a Mistake?" *American Economic Review* 97, no. 2 (May 2007): 328–32.

8 In one meta-study S. Durlauf, P. Johnson, and J. Temple show that 145 different right hand side variables were significant as determinants of growth in various different studies. See S. Durlauf, P. Johnson, and J. Temple, "Growth Econometrics" in *Handbook of Economic Growth*, vol. 1A, ed. by P. Aghion and S. N. Durlauf (North-Holland, 2005), 555–677.

9 *Development Aid and Growth: An Association Converging to Zero*, Economics Working Paper no. 17 (Aarhus University, 2009).

10 William Easterly, *The Ghost of Financing Gap: How the Harrod-Domar Growth Model Still Haunts Development Economics*, World Bank Policy Research Working Paper no. 1,807 (1997).

11 In contrast Katherine Marshall, a long-time World Bank official writes, "The China operation stands apart in many respects, but the experience has had repercussions far beyond in setting both a model of country leadership and in showing what a country can accomplish in poverty reduction in a remarkably short time." Marshall seems to associate the World Bank's "country leadership" with China's development achievement. See *The World Bank: From Reconstruction to Development to Equity* (Routledge, 2009), 48.

12 For example, Paul Collier and David Dollar, "Can the World Cut Poverty by Half? How Policy Reform and Effective Aid Can Meet International Development Goals," *World Development* 29, no. 11 (2001); David Dollar and Aart Kraay, "Growth is Good for the Poor," *Journal of Economic Growth* 7, no. 3 (2002).

13 David Dollar and Lant Pritchett, *Assessing Aid: What Works, What Doesn't and Why?* (World Bank, 1998), 14.

14 Easterly provides a blow-by-blow account of aid and growth research in *The White Man's Burden: Why the West's Efforts to Aid the Rest Have Done So Much Ill and So Little Good* (Penguin, 2006), 38–57.

15 R. Rajan and A. Subramanian, "Aid, Dutch Disease, and Manufacturing Growth," *Journal of Development Economics* 94, no. 1 (2011): 106–18.

16 Arndt et al. find that an increase in the aid share in GDP of 10 percentage points raises growth by about 1.3 percent per annum. See Channing Arndt, Sam Jones and Finn Tarp, "Aid, Growth and Development: Have We Come Full Circle?" *Journal of Globalization and Development* 1, no. 2 (2010).

17 Michael A. Clemens, Steven Radelet, Rikhil R. Bhavnani and Samuel Bazzi, "Counting Chickens When They Hatch: Timing and the Effects of Aid on Growth," *The Economic Journal* 122, no. 561 (2012): 590–617.

18 William Easterly, "Can the West Save Africa?" *Journal of Economic Literature* 47 (June 2009): 373–447 (390).

19 Michael Clemens et al., "Counting Chickens."

20 Steven Radelet, *Emerging Africa: How 17 Countries Are Leading the Way* (Center For Global Development, 2010). The 17 are Botswana, Burkina Faso, Cape Verde, Ethiopia, Ghana, Lesotho, Mali, Mauritius, Mozambique, Namibia, Rwanda, Sao Tome and Principe,

Seychelles, South Africa, Tanzania, Uganda and Zambia. Over 5 years their average growth rate was not far short of East and South Asian economies.

21 Jeffrey Sachs, *The End of Poverty – Economic Possibilities for Our Time* (Penguin, 2005), 364.

22 Nicholas Stern, "Making the Case for Aid," in *A Case for Aid: Building a Consensus for Development Assistance* (World Bank, 2002), 24.

23 Paul Collier in *The Bottom Billion* (Oxford University Press, 2007) explains "harm" in terms of policy incoherence – the inconsistency of agricultural subsidies and foreign aid (60). The book was based on a report on aid policy commissioned by the OECD donors.

24 Collier, *Bottom Billion*, 100. "Aid does tend to speed up the growth process. A reasonable estimate is that over the past 30 years it has added around 1 percentage point to the annual growth of the bottom billion."

25 Roger Riddell, *Does Foreign Aid Really Work?* (Oxford University Press, 2007), 257; italics added.

26 Easterly, quoted in Ken Ringle, "Writing from the Inside, an Economist Says," *Washington Post*, 20 March 2002.

27 David L. Lindauer and Lant Pritchett, "What's the Big Idea?: The Third Generation of Policies for Economic Growth," *Economía* 3, no. 1 (Fall 2002): 1–28.

28 *Economic Growth in the 1990s: Learning from a Decade of Reform* (World Bank, 2005), 12.

29 Riddell, *Does Foreign Aid Really Work*, 254.

30 South Korean industrial capacity was built partly in colonial Japan up to 1945 when several hundred thousand Koreans returned with industrial skills. It also received US military and economic assistance during the Korean War. From the 1960s when outside assistance tailed off South Korea followed the Japanese export model, obtaining increasing amounts of direct foreign investment. See Larry Westphal, Yung Rhee and Garry Pursell, *Korean Industrial Competence: Where It Came From*, World Bank Staff Working Paper no. 469 (1981).

31 Based on the original "Harrod-Domar" growth model this would assume an ICOR of 3.3 to 5.0 which would imply an average to modest long-run return to investment in the economy. But see Easterly, *Ghost of Financing Gap*.

32 In the same vein see Todd Moss, Gunilla Pettersson and Nicolas van de Walle, *An Aid-Institutions Paradox? A Review Essay on Aid Dependency and State Building in Sub-Saharan Africa*, Center for Global Development Working Paper no. 74 (January 2006), 9: "Projects provide for the allocation of all sorts of discretionary goods to be politicized and patrimonialized, including expensive four-wheel drive cars, scholarships, decisions over where to place schools and roads and so on. The common practice of paying cash 'sitting fees' for civil servants attending donor-funded workshops, where the daily rates can exceed regular monthly salaries, even turns training into a rent to be distributed."

33 According to Diana Cammack in *Poorly Performing Countries: Malawi, 1980–2002* (ODI, 2004), if governments had "honestly implemented the right policies and utilized the advice given," the country would have prospered. But "a combination of lack of capacity, weak institutions, leaders' self-interest, a weak civil society and repeated donor bail-outs have permitted actions to be subverted or delayed to the point of being ineffective" (35).

34 Easterly writes in his blog *Aid Watch* (10 November 2010): "The standard model of aid, investment and growth (old-fashioned but still in use today in the World Bank, IMF and UN Millennium Project) implies that aid goes into investment one for one and then this investment raises growth. With the usual parameters, this would imply an aid effect on growth of 0.2 or higher. THAT model we can reject."

35 The watchdogs are the evaluation group, inspection panel, quality assurance group, regional quality network, internal auditor, department of institutional integrity and procurement department, an overhead that has encountered seriously diminishing returns. See David Phillips, *Reforming the World Bank: Twenty Years of Trial – and Error* (Cambridge, 2009).

36 "Satisfactory" means that it earns a positive rate of return of at least 10 percent per annum or equivalent.

37 The reorganization of the World Bank over 1997–2001 was launched by James Wolfensohn on the basis of a so-called Strategic Compact with the Board of Directors.

38 Independent Evaluation Group, *Cost Benefit Analysis in World Bank Projects* (World Bank, June 2010).

39 See Phillips, *Reforming the World Bank*. A World Bank staffer said of McNamara's social development efforts: "with a lot of this stuff it's very hard to say the project works or it doesn't work. The more we move into the social realm the harder it gets to have any kind of yardstick."

40 See *Improving the World Bank's Development Effectiveness: What Does Evaluation Show?* (World Bank, Independent Evaluation Group, October 2005). Monitoring and evaluation in the health, education and urban sectors was found to be so weak that little was known of outcomes.

41 *Cost-Benefit Analysis in World Bank Projects: Overview* (World Bank, IEG, 2010).

42 Phillips, *Reforming the World Bank*, 172.

43 *OED Reach* (World Bank, Spring 2000), 3.

44 Impact evaluation has its roots in medical trials in which a treatment group receives the product and a control group receives a placebo. It is not practical to reproduce experimental trials in some situations (for example, the impact of school meals where the placebo consists of "no food"). However a "quasi-experimental" method has been adopted which has led to an upsurge in studies.

45 Between 1980 and 2005, the World Bank's evaluation department carried out only 23 rigorous evaluations out of its thousands of projects. By 2009, it reported that 250 impact evaluations were under way. But it continued, "A review of recently closed projects in the Agriculture, Environment and Water Sectors indicated that few collected even the minimum information to assess results ... Thus, requisite information for basic quantitative analysis is still rare." *Annual Review of Development Effectiveness* (World Bank, 2009), xv.

46 *Capacity Building in Africa: An OED Evaluation of World Bank Support* (World Bank, 2005).

47 Francois Bourguignon and Mark Sundberg, "Aid Effectiveness – Opening the Black Box," *American Economic Review* 97, no. 2 (1 May 2007): 1.

48 See Paul Mosley, "Aid Effectiveness: The Micro–Macro Paradox," *Institute of Development Studies Bulletin* 17 (1986): 214–25.

49 Robert Picciotto, "Development Effectiveness: An Evaluation Perspective," in *Development Aid, a Fresh Look*, ed. by G. Mavrotas and M. McGillivray (United Nations University, 2009).

50 Easterly, "Can Foreign Aid Buy Growth?" *Journal of Economic Perspectives* 17, no. 3 (2003): 23–48 (36).

51 Ibid., 37.

52 J. Hammer and Lant Pritchett, "Scenes from a Marriage: World Bank Economists and Social Capital," in *The Search for Empowerment: Social Capital as Idea and Practice at the World Bank*, ed. by Anthony J. Bebbington (Kumarian, 2006), 63–90.

53 Scott Guggenheim, "Crises and Contradictions; Understanding the Origins of a Community Development Project in Indonesia," in *The Search for Empowerment*, 114–44.

54 Speech at the LSE, 12 October 2010. http://www.dfid.gov.uk/news/speeches-and-statements/2010/wealth-creation-speech/

55 Vodafone acquired the German cellular firm Mannesmann through a Luxembourg subsidiary, avoiding British taxes, but was eventually forced to pay £1.25 billion (US$2 billion). Nevertheless, according to the British magazine *Private Eye* (11 November 2010) the tax revenue forgiven was over £6 billion. See David Meyer, *ZD Net* blog (1 November 2010).

56 The Green Revolution was a term invented by USAID director William Gaud in 1968 to describe the increase in agriculture productivity in Asia from the use of high-yielding varieties of grains, combined with improved irrigation, management, fertilizers and pesticides. The Consultative Group on International Agricultural Research (CGIAR) was set up to act as a channel for dissemination of the findings.

57 Celia Digger, "Ending Famine, Simply by Ignoring the Experts," *New York Times* (2 December 2007). http://www.nytimes.com/2007/12/02/world/africa/02malawi.html

58 Easterly, "Can the West Save Africa?", 414.

59 Lant Pritchett and Michael Woolcock, "Solutions when the Solution Is the Problem. Arraying the Disarray in Development," *World Development* 32, no. 2 (2004): 191–212. The authors point to "discretionality" and "transaction intensity." An agricultural extension service provides advice to farmers at the discretion of the extension officer and it is transaction intensive because it is tailored to each farmer's specific needs. These two factors mean that extension officers have lower motivation.

60 Five studies from the Millennium Challenge Corporation suggest that the impact on household incomes may be very small. See William Savedoff, "The Biggest Experiment in Evaluation: MCC and Lessons for Farmer Training," *Rethinking US Foreign Assistance* blog (Center For Global Development, 12 November 2012).

61 The Bank's evaluators put their failure down to low commodity prices, poor government commitment, weak management, complexity, inflexible design and the 1973 oil price rises.

62 Ruth Levine and Molly Kinder, *Millions Saved: Proven Successes in Global Health* (Center For Global Development, November 2004).

63 Easterly, "Can the West Save Africa?", 398. Doubts about de-worming are in D. Taylor-Robinson, N. Maayan, K. Soares-Weiser, S. Donegan and Paul Garner, *Deworming Drugs for Soil-Transmitted Intestinal Worms in Children: Effects on Nutritional Indicators, Haemoglobin and School Performance* (Cochrane Library, 11 July 2012).

64 The World Bank's Annual Report on Development Effectiveness for 2009 cited primary enrolments rising from 35 percent in 1960 to 90 percent in 2005.

65 Paul Glewwe, Michael Kremer and Sylvie Moulin, *Many Children Left Behind? Textbooks and Test Scores in Kenya*, NBER Working Paper no. 13,300 (August 2007).

66 Lant Pritchett, "Where has all the education gone?" *World Bank Economic Review* 15, no. 3 (2001): 367–91.

67 Robert J. Barro and Jong-Wha Lee, *A New Data Set of Educational Attainment in the World, 1950–2010*, NBER Working Paper no. 15,902 (April 2010).

68 Ritva Reinikka and Jakob Svensson, *Explaining Leakage of Public Funds*, World Bank Policy Research Working Paper no. 2,709 (2001).

69 Paul Hubbard, *Putting the Power of Transparency in Context: Information's Role in Reducing Corruption in Uganda's Education Sector*, Center for Global Development Working Paper no. 136 (December 2007). Hubbard observes: "transparency by itself is insufficient if there is no opportunity for collective action."

70 Easterly, "Can the West Save Africa?", 404.

71 Desmond Bermingham, "Putting the 'Fast' Back into the Education Fast Track…" *Views from the Center* blog (Center for Global Development, 16 February 2010). http://blogs.cgdev.org/globaldevelopment/2010/02/putting-the-%E2%80%98fast%E2%80%99-back-into-the-education-fast-track%E2%80%A6.php

72 Riddell, *Does Foreign Aid Really Work*, 206.

73 Moises Naim, "Fads and Fashion in Economic Reforms: Washington Consensus or Washington Confusion?" *Foreign Policy Magazine* (26 October 1999). http://www.imf.org/external/pubs/ft/seminar/1999/reforms/naim.htm

74 See D. Rodrik, A. Subramanian and F. Trebbi, *Institutions Rule: The Primacy of Institutions over Geography and Integration in Economic Development*, NBER Working Paper no. 9,305 (October 2002), 22. "[D]esirable institutional arrangements," they write "have a large element of context specificity, arising from differences in historical trajectories, geography, political economy or other initial conditions."

75 Riddell, *Does Foreign Aid Really Work*, 373.

76 See global monitoring report 2006: *Strengthening Mutual Accountability – Aid, Trade and Governance*, (World Bank Development Committee, 20 April 2006), 18.

77 *Capacity Building in Africa*, 6–7.

78 *Malawi – Country Assistance Evaluation* (World Bank, 2000).

79 Lant Pritchett, Michael Woolcock and Matt Andrews, *Capability Traps? The Mechanisms of Persistent Implementation Failure*, Center for Global Development Working Paper no. 234 (December 2010).

80 Easterly, "Can the West Save Africa?", 43.

81 Moss, Pettersson and Van de Walle, *An Aid-Institutions Paradox?*

82 Nicolas van de Walle, *Overcoming Stagnation in Aid-Dependent Countries: Politics, Policies and Incentives for Poor Countries* (Center for Global Development, 2005), 73.

83 These examples are explained further in Phillips, *Reforming the World Bank*, 173–8.

84 The assistance was to BRAC bank. Like the DFID aid to Vodafone this relationship was good for institutional reputation but had negligible impact on development.

85 C. Ashley, M. Warner and J. Romano, "Directions for Private Sector Development Instruments in Africa," in *ODI Strategies for the Policy Maker* (ODI, 2005), 1, 3.

86 David Roodman, *Due Diligence: An Impertinent Enquiry into Microfinance* (Center for Global Development 2012).

87 Eric Bellman and Arlene Chang, "India's Major Crisis in Micro-Lending: Loans Involving Tiny Amounts of Money Were a Good Idea, but the Explosion of Interest Backfires," *Wall Street Journal* (29 October 2010). http://online.wsj.com/article/SB10001424052702304316404 575580663294846100.html. Another problem could have been government regulations, which allowed rapid growth but prevented diversification (e.g. deposit-taking). The state government was also committed to a competing World Bank project to fund self-help groups.

88 Roodman, *Due Diligence*.

89 The first major exit was in 2007 when the sale of 30 percent of the shares of Compartamos of Mexico, which had been providing micro-loans at high interest rates, netted IFC and others an extremely large capital gain in principle at the expense of the micro-borrowers.

90 CGAP is the Consultative Group to Assist the Poor, a multi-donor initiative to expand microfinance established in the World Bank in 1995.

91 Xavier Reille, Sarah Forster and Daviel Rozas, *Foreign Capital Investment in Microfinance: Reassessing Financial and Social Returns*, CGAP Focus Note no. 7 (May 2011).

92 Roodman cites Denis Whittle who was a World Bank official in Indonesia at the time.

93 Reille, Forster and Rozas, *Foreign Capital Investment*.

94 Roodman, *Due Diligence*, 172.

95 Ibid., 1.

96 JP Morgan was active in mobilizing capital for microfinance during the early 2000s, through for example an entity known as Blue Orchard Securities.

97 Numbers of banks increased from 119 to 800. See D. G. H. Thorpe, *A History of English Clearing Banks* (British Banking History Society, 2010).

98 Martin Wolf, *Financial Times* (13 September 2000).

99 Rosemary McGee, Josh Levene and Alexandra Hughes, *Assessing Participation in Poverty Reduction Strategy Papers: A Desk-Based Synthesis of Experience in Sub-Saharan Africa* (Institute of Development Studies, October 2001).

100 Nancy Birdsall, "Foreword," in *Reinventing Foreign Aid*, ed. by William Easterly, 39.

101 Josh Boak, "U.S.-funded infrastructure deteriorates once under Afghan control, report says," *Washington Post* (4 January 2011), 1.

102 James Dorsey, *Devex* (25 June 2012) quoted a statement by Jeremy Pam, participant in a Pentagon review of Afghanistan: "Poor donor coordination and flaws in most international development assistance models are so profound in Afghanistan that I am not sure reducing the level of aid will cause great problems because most aid has not caused great good … The international donors have been a major problem. We internationals wanted big symbolic statements. We doubled the resources and didn't care about absorption capacity." By mid-2011 the Pentagon had committed US$7 billion in Afghanistan and Iraq for development assistance (http://www.devex.com/en/news/78524/print). See G. Johnson, V. Ramachandran and Julie Walz, *The Commander's Emergency Response Program in Afghanistan:*

Refining US Military Capabilities in Stability and In-Conflict Development Activities, Center for Global Development Working Paper no. 265 (September 2011).

103 Claire Chase and Quy-Toan Do, *Handwashing Behavior Change at Scale: Evidence from a Randomized Evaluation in Vietnam*, World Bank Policy Research Working Paper no. 6,207 (September 2012).

104 See Michael Woolcock, "The Place of Social Capital in Understanding Social and Economic Outcomes," *Canadian Journal of Policy Research* 2, no. 1 (2001): 11–17.

105 Abhijit V. Banerjee and Esther Duflo, *Poor Economics: A Radical Rethinking of the Way to Fight Global Poverty* (Public Affairs, June 2011).

106 Easterly and Williamson, "Rhetoric versus Reality: The Best and Worst of Aid Agency Practices," *World Development* 39, no. 11 (2011): table 3, 62. For bilateral agencies average cost of overheads was 7.6 percent (4.5 percent was in salaries). For multilateral agencies it was 18.2 percent (7.6 percent in salaries) and for UN agencies it was 45.5 percent overall (45.1 percent in salaries).

107 See David Phillips, *Reforming the World Bank*.

108 Jennifer Brookland, "In USAID Procurement, a Game of Stop-and-Go" *Devex* (29 August 2012).

109 William Easterly and Laura Freschi, "World Bank's 'Horizontal' Approach to Health Falls Horizontal?" *Aid Watch* (10 June 2010).

110 In a *World Bank Evaluation* blog post in February 2012, entitled "How Much Do Our Impacts Cost?" Alaka Holla wrote, "we currently know very little about accurately calculating the costs of our interventions in education, health and social protection, nor have we reached much consensus on how to combine these cost measures once we have them with our estimated impacts."

111 F. Abuzeid, "Foreign Aid and the 'Big Push' Theory: Lessons from Sub-Saharan Africa," *Stanford Journal of International Relations* 11 (2009): 16–23 (23).

4. Why Has Development Aid Done So Little?

1 See http://www.cfr.org/foreign-aid/effectiveness-foreign-aid/p12077

2 Peter T. Bauer, *Dissent on Development: Studies and Debates in Development Economics* (Harvard University Press, 1972), 100.

3 Cevdet Denizer, Daniel Kaufmann and Art Kraay, *Good Countries or Good Projects? Macro and Micro Correlates of World Bank Project Performance*, World Bank Policy Research Working Paper no. 5,646 (May 2011), 24.

4 For example, Clark C. Gibson, Krister Andersson, Elinor Ostrom and Sujai Shivakumar, *Samaritan's Dilemma: The Political Economy of Development Aid* (Oxford University Press, 2005).

5 William Savedoff and Ruth Levine, *Learning from Development: The Case for an International Council to Catalyze Independent Impact Evaluations of Social Sector Interventions* (Center for Global Development, 2009).

6 Two key papers on evaluation are Michael Kremer and Esther Duflo, "Use of Randomization in the Assessment of Development Effectiveness" (93–120) and Abhijit Banerjee and Ruimin He, "Making Aid Work" (47–92), both in *Reinventing Foreign Aid*, ed. by William Easterly (MIT Press, 2008). Also see William Savedoff, R. Levine and N. Birdsall, *When Will We Ever Learn? Improving Lives through Impact Evaluation* (Center for Global Development, May 2006).

7 "A Major Step Forward on Impact Evaluation" press release (Center for Global Development, 12 June 2006).

8 According to its website, the International Initiative for Impact Evaluation (3ie) "works to improve the lives of people in the developing world by supporting the production and use of evidence on what works, when, why and for how much."

9 For an account of the debate see William Easterly, "The Civil War in Development Economics," *Aidwatchers.com* (3 December 2009).

10 Rodrik also addresses this problem: "A study lacking internal validity is surely worthless; but a study lacking external validity is almost worthless too." D. Rodrik, *The New Development Economics: We Shall Experiment, But How Shall We Learn?*, Working Paper no. 55 (Kennedy School, Harvard University, 24 October 2008).

11 Alaka Holla, "How much do our impacts cost?" *World Bank Evaluation* blog (28 February 2012).

12 Markus Goldstein provided a curious example of a related problem: "Our main counterpart in another evaluation was busy over the summer ordering his folks to dig ditches where people really didn't want them, so this guy, with whom we spent years collaborating on building an interesting policy experiment, was sacked … The new guy is not so interested in our approach. So we have to start over again – we may have a hope since his boss was on board with what we were doing – but we don't know if we should call on him yet to support us. So maybe this broader constituency building will help us out, but I am left wondering if we could have somehow built it broader." See *blogs@worldbank* (13 September 2011).

13 David Roodman cites a paper by Karlan and Zinman about evasive or untruthful responses to researchers. Evasive or untruthful responses are "often hidden from the econometricians who analyze the data, mak(ing) data collection an underappreciated art." See David Roodman, *Due Diligence: An Impertinent Enquiry into Microfinance* (Center for Global Development, 2012), 145.

14 Those who receive and those who do not receive assistance have different motivations for answering questions and poorly paid field workers are often uninterested in accuracy. Nepalese survey personnel used to joke that DATA meant "Daily Allowance and Traveling Allowance."

15 Howard White, *An Introduction to the Use of Randomized Control Trials to Evaluate Development Interventions*, International Initiative for Impact Evaluation (3ie) Working Paper no. 9 (February 2011).

16 Lant Pritchett, "Solutions when the Solution is the Problem: Arraying the Disarray in Development," in *Reinventing Foreign Aid*, ed. by William Easterly (MIT Press, 2008). He writes, "Multiple levels of interaction must be addressed simultaneously: between citizens and the government; between government and agencies; between agencies and its employees and contractors (the providers) and between citizens and providers and public authorities" (155).

17 David Mckenzie, "One Evaluation, One Paper? Getting More for Your Money," *blogs@worldbank.org* (9 January 2012).

18 David McKenzie and Christopher Woodruff, *What Are We Learning from Business Training and Entrepreneurship Evaluations around the Developing World?*, IZA DP no. 6,895 (October 2012), 155.

19 Markus Oldstein, "Is It the Program or Is It Participation? Randomization and Placebos," *blogs@worldbank.org* (June 2011).

20 The Hawthorne Study of a Western Electric facility was undertaken by Elton Mayo. The Hawthorne Effect was the distorting effect on performance that occurs if the study itself changes the respondents willingness to perform or their expectations about future roles and rewards.

21 See *blogs@worldbank* (22 September 2011).

22 Michael A. Clemens and Gabriel Demombynes, *When Does Rigorous Impact Evaluation Make a Difference? The Case of the Millennium Villages* (Center for Global Development, October 2010).

23 Albert O. Hirschman, *The Strategy of Economic Development* (Yale University Press, 1958), 5.

24 See David Ellerman, "Revisiting Hirschman on Development Assistance and Unbalanced Growth," *Eastern Economic Journal* 30, no. 2 (2004): 311–31.

25 Researcher discretion they argue is necessary to avoid the Hawthorne Effect where respondents change their responses as a result of advance notification of a survey.

See Abhijit V. Banerjee and Esther Duflo, *The Experimental Approach to Development Economics*, NBER Working Paper no. 14,467 (November 2008).

26 William Easterly, "Can the West Save Africa?" *Journal of Economic Literature* 47, no. 2 (June 2009): 373–447 (396).

27 Nancy Birdsall, "Seven Deadly Sins: Reflections on Donor Failings," in *Reinventing Foreign Aid*, ed. by William Easterly (MIT Press, 2008), 515–52 (528).

28 William Savedoff of the Center for Global Development asks in a November 2010 blog post whether "Argentina [will] be the next country to join the Evaluation Movement? … India considered establishing an independent evaluation office last year … but it looks like Argentina may beat them to the finish line."

29 E. Duflo and M. Kremer, "Use of Randomization in the Evaluation of Development Effectiveness," in *Reinventing Foreign Aid*, ed. by William Easterly (MIT, 2008), 117.

30 See for example, Giovanni Andrea Cornia, Richard Jolly and Frances Stewart, *Adjustment with a Human Face: Protecting the Vulnerable and Promoting Growth* (Oxford University Press, 1987).

31 Andrew Natsios, *The Clash of the Counter-bureaucracy and Development* (Center for Global Development, July 2010), 3.

32 Howard White, *An Introduction to the Use of Randomized Control Trials to Evaluate Development Interventions*, International Initiative for Impact Evaluation (3ie) Working Paper no. 9 (February 2011), 16.

33 See "What Works in Development? Thinking Big and Thinking Small," Brookings Institution Conference (21 January 2010).

34 For example, Dambisa Moyo, *Dead Aid* (Allen Lane, 2009).

35 Samir Amin, *Accumulation on a World Scale: A Critique of the Theory of Underdevelopment* (Monthly Review Press, 1972). Amin was associated with the "dependency school" along with others such as: Andre Gundar Frank, *Capitalism and Underdevelopment in Latin America* (Monthly Review Press, 1968), and Walter Rodney, *How Europe Underdeveloped Africa* (Howard University Press, 1981). This perspective held in part that capitalist development in the metropolitan economies undermined progress that had already been made by the peripheral economies. Frank regarded foreign aid simply as side payments to elites to help maintain the economic domination of industrialized countries.

36 Paul Bairoch, *Cities and Economic Development: From the Dawn of History to the Present* (University of Chicago Press, 1988), 58.

37 The colonial era was preceded with a relatively small gap in years by the slave trade in Africa. The first Governor of Nyasaland (then called British Central Africa), Harry Johnson, found on his arrival in 1891 that he had to deal with a continuing African slave trade with the Middle East.

38 White settlers in South Africa appropriated 90 percent of land under the 1913 Natives Land Act. See R. Hall and L. Ntsebeza (eds), *The Land Question in South Africa: The Challenge of Transformation and Redistribution* (HSRC, 2007).

39 Aylward Shorter, "Christianity in Tropical Africa," *African Affairs* 67, no. 268 (1968): 254–56.

40 Nathan Nunn, "Historical Legacies: A Model Linking Africa's Past to its Current Underdevelopment," *Journal of Development Economics* 83 (2007): 157–75.

41 Nicola Gennaioli and Ilia Rainer, "The Modern Impact of Pre-colonial Centralization in Africa," *Journal of Economic Growth* 12 (2007): 185–234.

42 William Easterly and Janina Matuszeski, "Artificial States," *Journal of the European Economic Association* 9, no. 2 (April 2011): 246–77.

43 By illustration the Kakwa in South Sudan joined the civil war against the North, and the Kakwa in Uganda (of which Idi Amin was a member) provided refuge and arms. See Roel van der Veen, *What Went Wrong With Africa: A Contemporary History* (KIT, 2004).

44 Janina Matuszeski, and Frank Schneider, *Patterns of Ethnic Group Segregation and Civil Conflict* (Center for Global Development, 9 February 2007).

45 Anthony J. Venables, "Economic Geography and African Development," *Regional Science* 89, no. 3 (August 2010): 469–83.

46 Peter Winn, *Americas: The Changing Face of Latin America and the Caribbean* (Pantheon, 1992), 83.

47 William Easterly and R. Levine, "Africa's Growth Tragedy: Policies and Ethnic Divisions," *Quarterly Journal of Economics* 112, no. 4 (November 1997): 1,203–50.

48 Paul Collier and Tony Venables, *Trade and Economic Performance: Does Africa's Fragmentation Matter?* (Annual World Bank Conference on Development Economics, 2009).

49 R. Bates, *Markets and States in Tropical Africa: The Political Basis of Agricultural Policies* (University of California Press, 1981).

50 A key study of 104 countries was Alberto Alesina, Enrico Spolaore, and Romain Wacziarg, "Trade, Growth and the Size of Countries," in *Handbook of Economic Growth*, vol. 1, ed. by Philippe Aghion and Steven Durlauf (Elsevier, 2005).

51 Robert Lensik and Howard White, *Aid Dependence: Issues and Indicators* (Expert Group on Development Issues, 1999). The authors identify five factors linking to dependency: the scale of aid flows; the excess of aid over needs; effectiveness; self-perpetuation, and power relations, but end up with a generalized definition: "a country is aid dependent if it will not achieve objective X in the absence of aid for the foreseeable future" (13).

52 World Bank, World Development Indicators (2007, 2010).

53 World Development Indicators (2011), table 6.16, 376ff. These exclude a group of highly aid-dependent countries for which figures are not available: Afghanistan, Haiti, North Korea, Myanmar, Somalia, Timor Leste and West Bank/Gaza. Thus, average dependence is a conservative estimate.

54 Jean-Paul Azam, Shantayanan Devarajan, and Stephen A. O'Connell, *Aid Dependence Reconsidered*, Center for the Study of African Economies Working Paper no. 2,144 (1999).

55 Jonathan Glennie, *What's Wrong with Foreign Aid?* (Zed Books, 2008), 114.

56 For example, Ethiopia, Gambia, Guinea, Kenya, Malawi and Madagascar (see World Development Indicators, (2011), table 4.2, 198).

57 This is according to the World Bank's "Atlas method"; on purchasing power parity measures it ranks slightly but not materially higher.

58 Paolo de Renzio and Joseph Hanlon, "Mozambique: Contested Sovereignty? The Dilemmas of Aid Dependence," in *The Politics of Aid: African Strategies for Dealing with Donors*, ed. by Lindsay Whitfield (Oxford University Press, 2009), 246–70.

59 World Development Indicators (2010), table 6.16.

60 Andrew Mwenda, *Foreign Aid and the Weakening of Accountability in Uganda*, Cato Institute Foreign Policy Briefing no. 88 (12 July 2006), 1.

61 Paul Collier, *The Bottom Billion*, 100. Collier also objects to the term dependency because it cannot be equated to household dependency. See Paul Collier, "Aid Dependency: A Critique," *Journal of African Economies* 8, no. 4 (1999): 528–45.

62 Robert Lensink and Howard White, "*Are there Negative Returns to Aid?*" Report for Swedish Ministry of Foreign Affairs (2001).

63 R. Rajan and A. Subramanian "Aid and Growth: What Does the Cross-Country Evidence really Show?" *Review of Economics and Statistics* 90, no. 4 (2008): 643–65, and "Aid, Dutch Disease, and Manufacturing Growth," *Journal of Development Economics* 94, no. 1 (January 2011): 106–18.

64 Xavier-Sala-i-Martin and Arvind Subramanian, *Addressing the Natural Resource Curse: An Illustration from Nigeria* (May 2003).

65 Todd Moss, Gunilla Pettersson and Nicolas van de Walle, *An Aid-Institutions Paradox? A Review Essay on Aid Dependency and State Building in Sub-Saharan Africa* (Center for Global Development, January 2006).

66 B. Hoffman and C. Gibson, "Fiscal Governance and Public Services: Evidence from Tanzania and Zambia," in *Proceedings of the American Political Science Association* (September,

2005). Also see Joseph Hanlon, *Mozambique: Who Calls the Shots?* (Indiana University Press, 1991).

67 Simeon Djankov, Jose G. Montalvo and Marta Reynal-Querol, "The Curse of Aid," *Journal of Economic Growth* 13 (2008): 169–94.

68 See J. Bradford DeLong and Barry Eichengreen, "The Marshall Plan as a Structural Adjustment Programme," in *Postwar Economic Reconstruction: Lessons for the East Today*, ed. by R. Dornbusch, W. Nölling, and R. Layard (MIT Press, 1993), 189–230.

69 For a discussion of this see Stephen Knack and Aminur Rahman, *Donor Fragmentation and Bureaucratic Quality in Aid Recipients*, World Bank Policy Research Working Paper no. 3,186 (January 2004)

70 Jean-Paul Azam, Shantayanan Devarajan and Stephen A. O'Connell, *Aid Dependence Reconsidered*, World Bank Policy Research Working Paper no. 2,144 (July 1999).

71 Michael Woolcock et al. (eds), *The Search for Empowerment: Social Capital as Idea and Practice at the World Bank* (Kumarian, 2006).

72 Nicolas van de Walle, *Overcoming Stagnation in Aid-Dependent Countries: Politics, Policies and Incentives for Poor Countries* (Center for Global Development, 2005), 49–50.

73 Florian Bieber, "Aid Dependency in Bosnian Politics and Civil Society: Failures and Successes of Post-war Peacebuilding in Bosnia Herzegovina," *Croatian International Relations Review* 8, nos. 26–7 (2002): 25–30.

74 Ibid.

75 Rehman Sobhan, "The Political Economy of Bangladesh's External Relations," *Daily Star*, Bangladesh (4 November 2003). http://www.thedailystar.net/2003/11/04/d311041501102.htm

76 Janine Wedel, "US Assistance for Market Reforms: Foreign Aid Failures in Russia and the Former Soviet Bloc," *Policy Analysis* no. 338 (22 March 1999). See http://www.independent.org/pdf/tir/tir_04_3_wedel.pdf

77 See Andrew Rogerson, Adrian Hewitt, David Waldenberg, *The International Aid System 2005–2010: Forces For and Against Change*, Overseas Development Institute Working Paper no. 235 (March 2004).

78 *Aid Architecture: An Overview of the Main Trends in Official Development Assistance Flows*, IDA 15 background paper (World Bank, February 2007).

79 Hidemi Kimura, Yasuyuki Sawada and Yuko Mori, "Aid Proliferation and Economic Growth: Cross-Country Analysis," RIETI Discussion Paper Series (June 2007). The authors quote Morss ("Institutional Destruction Resulting from Donor and Project Proliferation in Sub-Saharan African Countries," *World Development* 12, no. 4 (1984): 465–70): "The most important feature distinguishing foreign aid in the 1970s from earlier programmes was the proliferation of donors and projects" (465). Robert Cassen wrote: "aid projects are planted here and there in an almost haphazard way and in excessive numbers, with a variety of untoward consequences" (175), in Cassen and Associates, *"Does Aid Work?" Report to an Intergovernmental Task Force* (Oxford University Press, 1994).

80 *Aid Architecture*.

81 Stephen Knack and Aminur Rahman, "Donor Fragmentation and Bureaucratic Quality in Aid Recipients," *Journal of Development Economics* 83, no. 1 (May 2007): 176–97.

82 *Quality Of Development Assistance (QUODA)* (Center for Global Development, 2010), 12.

83 Homi Kharas, "Can aid catalyze development?" *Brooking Policy Briefs* (2010).

84 *Quality Of Development Assistance (QUODA)*, 33.

85 See for example, Mark Sundberg and Alan Gelb "Making Aid Work," *Finance and Development* 43, no. 4 (December, 2006).

86 *Aid Architecture*, 12–26.

87 Roger Riddell, *Does Foreign Aid Really Work?* (Oxford, 2009), 52–4.

88 *Aid Architecture*.

89 The executive director was Terrie O'Leary who made the statement at the end of her term. See David Phillips, *Reforming the World Bank: Twenty Years of Trial – and Error* (Cambridge, 2009), 107.

90 Steven Knack and Aminur Rahman. "Donor Fragmentation and Bureaucratic Quality in Aid Recipients," *Journal of Development Economics* 83, no. 1 (May 2007): 176–97. World Bank Policy Research Working Paper no. 3186 (January 2004).

91 William Easterly and Claudia R. Williamson "Rhetoric versus Reality: The Best and Worst of Aid Agency Practices," *World Development* 39, no. 11 (2011): 1,930–49.

92 Noam Unger, *US Government Support for Development Outcomes: Towards Systemic Reform*, Brookings Blum Roundtable Policy Briefs (2010), 1,935–7.

93 Lael Brainard (ed.), *Security By Other Means: Foreign Assistance, Global Poverty, and American Leadership* (Brookings Institution, 2007).

94 Easterly points out that in 2004, Austrian aid spent less than US$10,000 each in Cambodia, Dominica, Equatorial Guinea, and Gabon. Ireland spent US$30,000 in Botswana; and New Zealand US$20,000 in Swaziland. "When aid is this small, it's hard to believe it even covers the fixed costs of granting and receiving it, much less any operating costs of actually helping people" (13). William Easterly and Tobias Pfutze, *Where Does the Money Go – Best and Worst Practices in Foreign Aid*, Global Economy and Development Working Paper no. 21 (Brookings Institution, June 2008).

95 The directory is published at www.devdir.org.

96 For a description of verticalization see *Aid Architecture*, box 3.

97 Nicolas van de Walle, *Overcoming Stagnation in Aid-Dependent Countries: Politics, Policies and Incentives for Poor Countries* (Center for Global Development, April 2005), 47.

98 *Aid Architecture.*

99 It scored them for performance on 12 criteria. These were: a) critical role for UK aid objectives; b) critical role for international aid objectives; c) partnership behavior; d) climate change/environment; e) focus on poor countries; f) financial resources management; g) fragile contexts; h) cost and value consciousness; i) contribution to results; j) gender equality; k) transparency and accountability; and l) strategic/performance management. At the top end performance the score overall was in the good range, and at the bottom at the just satisfactory level.

100 *Multilateral Aid Review: Taking Forward the Findings of the UK Multilateral Aid Review* (DFID, March 2011).

101 The theory of principal and agent was introduced by Ronald Coase in "The Nature of the Firm," *Economica* 4, no. 16 (1937): 386–405.

102 Donald F. Kettl, *Reinventing Government: A Fifth-Year Report Card*, CPM 98-1 (Brookings Institution Center for Public Management, September 1998).

103 Jakob Svensson, "Absorption Capacity and Disbursement Constraints," in *Reinventing Foreign Aid*, ed. by William Easterly (MIT Press, 2008), 311–32.

104 Part of the solution to this according to Svensson is for donors to encourage citizens to monitor aid through report cards and tracking surveys ("Absorption Capacity," 315). This solution is well intentioned but seems to be a recipe for more assistance, perhaps through better ICT systems. The key need is not monitoring but motivation.

105 Phillips, *Reforming the World Bank.*

106 Ibid., 243.The board director was Per Kurowski from Poland. He also wrote: "we are drowned in too many written and spoken words about too many topics so that our power, as a body, is completely diluted to such an extent that we could easily qualify as the most expensive rubber stamp in mankind's history." See Per Kurowski, "On Our Own (World Bank) Governance: Board Effectiveness and the Ticking Clock," 4 January 2005, http://perkurowski.blogspot.com/2005/01/on-our-own-world-bank-governance-board.html

107 World Bank Annual Report (2011).

108 Ritve Reinikka, "Donors and Service Delivery," in *Reinventing Foreign Aid*, ed. by William Easterly (MIT Press, 2008), 179–200.

109 Steven Knack and Nicholas Eubank, *Aid and Trust in Country Systems*, World Bank Policy Research Working Paper no. 5,005 (July 2009).

110 Svensson, "Absorption Capacity."

111 There have been many cases of shell companies and bid-rigging on World Bank projects. In 2005, the Bank debarred five individuals and six firms in Albania for collusion in bidding on the "Water Supply Urgent Rehabilitation Project." In Tajikistan, several companies were established by a government minister to compete in a fake tender.

112 The OECD Development Cooperation Report (2010), 47, reported that both in procurement and financial management only a slight increase in usage had occurred in three years since the Paris conference (about 45 percent against a target of 80 percent in 54 developing countries surveyed).

113 A concise analysis of the misalignment of donor and recipient objectives is in: Claudia R. Williamson "Exploring the failure of foreign aid: The role of incentives and information," *Review of Austrian Economics* 23, no. 2 (2010): 17–33.

114 See Easterly, "Can the West Save Africa?", 429; and Stephen Knack, "Does Foreign Aid Promote Democracy?" *International Studies Quarterly* 8, no. 1 (March 2004): 251–66. Knack also found no association between aid and improvement in democracy.

115 *Review of the Poverty Reduction Strategy Paper (PRSP) Approach. Main Findings* (World Bank, Development Committee, 27 March 2002).

116 *World Bank Update: Parliamentary Newsletter* (World Bank, April 2010).

117 See Lant Pritchett, Michael Woolcock and Matt Andrews, *Capability Traps? The Mechanisms of Persistent Implementation Failure*, Center for Global Development Working Paper no. 234 (December 2010). The authors write, "For many central aspects of political, administrative and legal reform … and for the delivery of key public services (especially health and education, which require enormous numbers of discretionary face-to-face transactions) reform via cut-and-paste from a foreign setting is no reform at all."

118 Douglass C. North, John Joseph Wallis and Barry R. Weingast, *Violence and Social Orders: A Conceptual Framework for Interpreting Recorded Human History* (Cambridge University Press, 2009), 265.

119 The following appeared in the *Deccan Chronicle*, Pakistan on 6 January 2011, "Another problem with aid utilisation is that Pakistan's bureaucrats and military officers have become adept at milking the system. As soon as a foreign-funded project is in the offing, the first item to be included in the proposal is transport, preferably of the four-wheel, air-conditioned variety. The next item is invariably foreign training. … No wonder so little actually filters down to those who are supposed to benefit from this aid."

120 Nicholas van de Walle, "The Paths from Neo-patrimonialism: Democracy and Clientelism in Africa Today," in *Neopatrimonialism in Africa and Beyond*, ed. by Daniel Bach and Mamoudou Gazibo (Routledge, 2011).

121 President Kaunda of Zambia reportedly personally controlled some 50,000 jobs in Lusaka in the late 1980s. See Bates, Robert and Paul Collier. "The Politics and Economics of Policy Reform in Zambia," *Political and Economics Interactions in Economic Policy Reform*, ed. by Robert Bates and Anne Krueger (Blackwell, 1993), 387–443.

122 Daron Acemoglu, Simon Johnson and James A. Robinson, "The Colonial Origins of Comparative Development," *American Economic Review* 91 (2001): 1,369–1,401.

123 Todd Moss and Arvind Subramanian, *After the Big Push? Fiscal and Institutional Implications of Large Aid Increases*, Center for Global Development Working Paper no. 71 (October 2005).

124 See Deborah Brautigam, *Taxation and Governance in Africa: Take a Second Look*, AEI Public Policy Research no. 1 (April 2008), 1–6. She writes, "Democracies are built not only on periodic elections but also on a social contract based on bargaining over the collection and spending of public revenue" (1).

125 Nicholas Kaldor, "Will Underdeveloped Countries Learn to Tax?" *Foreign Affairs* 41, no. 2 (January 1963): 410–19 (410). He wrote: "foreign aid is likely to be fruitful only when it is a complement to domestic effort, not when it is treated as a substitute for it."

126 Todd Moss, Gunilla Pettersson and Nicolas van de Walle, *An Aid-Institutions Paradox? A Review Essay on Aid Dependency and State Building in Sub-Saharan Africa*, Center for Global Development Working Paper no. 74 (January 2006), 15.

127 Stephen Knack and Aminur Rahman, "Donor Fragmentation and Bureaucratic Quality in Aid Recipients," *Journal of Development Economics* 83, no. 1 (May 2007): 176–97.

128 There have also been contradictory results. In Côte d'Ivoire and Zambia the relationship was negative and in Ghana and Malawi positive. In Côte d'Ivoire a study of 25 years of fiscal policy showed that project aid tended to depress taxation while program aid (e.g. budget support) had a neutral effect.

129 Deborah A. Brautigam and Stephen Knack, "Foreign Aid, Institutions, and Governance in Sub-Saharan Africa" *Economic Development and Cultural Change* 52, no. 2 (January 2004): 255–85. The authors cite several studies showing negative association between aid and tax effort. 71 percent of the African countries with aid/GDP above 10 percent in 1995 had lower than expected tax effort.

130 Paul Collier, "Aid Dependency: A Critique," *Journal of African Economies* 8, no. 4 (1999): 528–45.

131 Riddell, *Does Foreign Aid Really Work*, 20.

132 Paris Declaration indicator 3 is measured by data from recipient governments on how much aid passes through their budget compared total aid to the government sector.

133 The highest reported ratio was 114 percent for the African Development Fund resulting from misreporting.

134 See Riddell, *Does Foreign Aid Really Work*, 199.

135 Among the extensive literature on corruption see S. Rose-Ackerman, *The Political Economy of Corruption – Causes and Consequences*, Public Policy for the Private Sector, Note no. 74 (World Bank, April 1996). For example, see Alessia Isopi and Fabrizio Mattesini. *Aid and Corruption: Do Donors Use Development Assistance to Provide the right Incentives?*, CEIS Working Paper no. 266 (Rome University, April 2008).

136 Andrew Balls and Edward Alden, "Wolfowitz anti-graft mission triggers World Bank strife," *Financial Times* (12 July 2005). In 2008, the Bank announced that there were 387 unresolved cases ranging from corruption to sexual harassment. With some fanfare it also disqualified a record number of private firms.

137 For example, *Transparency International 2005 Global Corruption Report*, 87.

138 See Matthew Rosenberg and Graham Bowley, *New York Times Online* (7 March 2012). They write, "as Americans pull back from Afghanistan, … the United States is leaving behind a problem it underwrote over the past decade with tens of billions of dollars of aid and logistical support: a narrow business and political elite defined by its corruption, and despised by most Afghans for it."

139 Jakob Svensson, "Foreign Aid and Rent Seeking," *Journal of International Economics* no. 51 (2000): 437–61.

140 See Alberto Alesina and Beatrice Weder, *Do Corrupt Governments Receive Less Foreign Aid?*, NBER Working Paper no. 7,108 (May 1999). Easterly found that aid unconditionally worsened governance. See Easterly, "Can the West Save Africa?", 427.

141 See "Brazen Fraud Alleged in Army Contracting," *Washington Post* (5 October 2011). Officials from the US Army Corps of Engineers were involved in a major fraud using shell companies. The fraudsters succeeding in pulling down US$20 million from one contract.

142 The official was Jim Adams, a vice president. He was offering a mea culpa for the deepening bureaucratic problems of the World Bank.

143 Some insights are provided by Rohini Pande, "Understanding Political Corruption in Low Income Countries," *Handbook of Development Economics*, vol. 4, ed. by Paul Schultz and John Strauss (Elsevier North Holland, 2008).

144 Nicholas van de Walle, *Overcoming Stagnation in Aid-Dependent Countries* (Center for Global Development, 2005), 35.

145 An account of neo-patrimonial and clientelist states is in Riddell, *Does Foreign Aid Really Work*, 357ff.

146 May Tan-Mullins, Giles Mohan and Marcus Power, "Redefining 'Aid' in the China–Africa Context," *Development and Change* 41, no. 5 (September 2010): 857–81.

147 See Deborah Brautigam, *The Dragon's Gift: The Real Story of China in Africa* (Oxford University Press, 2010).

148 *Understanding Chinese Foreign Aid: A Look at China's Development Assistance to Africa, Southeast Asia, and Latin America* (New York University, Wagner School, 25 April 2008).

149 In comparison, US aid to Africa was US$4.7 billion in 2007 and US$5.2 billion in 2008. Similar amounts came from the UK and France.

150 Thomas Lum, *China's Foreign Aid Strategies in Africa, Latin America and South East Asia* (Congressional Research Service, February 2009).

151 *China's Foreign Aid* (Information Office of the State Council, People's Republic of China, April 2011).

152 In local currency terms this was 256 billion yuan, converted at 8 yuan to the US dollar. Total funding included US$13 billion in grants, US$9.5 billion in interest-free loans and US$9 billion in concessional loans.

153 By the end of 2009, China's aid and investment was distributed to Asia (32.8 percent), Africa (45 percent), and Latin America and the Caribbean (12.7 percent). The remainder went to Oceania and Eastern Europe.

154 These projects are broadly across-sector, especially in the category "public facilities" which consist of one third of the total, and are well represented also in transport and light industry (25 percent of the total).

155 "Africa and China: Issues and Insights" conference, Georgetown University, 7 November 2008.

156 For example, Dambisa Moyo in *Dead Aid* (Allen Lane, 2008) writes, "China, on the other hand, sends cash to Africa and demands returns. With returns Africans get jobs, get roads, get food, making Africans better off. … The secret of China's success is that its foray into Africa is all business" (152).

157 Transparency remained one of the main aims of the Busan forum. Indeed, one of its claimed achievements was that the US joined the "International Aid Transparency Initiative." It is debatable however how far publication of massive volumes of data provides insights into aid performance.

5. Changing the Dynamics of Development

1 Edward V. K. Jaycox, "Capacity Building: The Missing Link in African Development," address to the African-American Institute Conference on Capacity Building, Reston, VA, 1993.

2 Francis Williams, "Harnessing Human Capital: The African Diaspora," 22 February 2009. http://www.africagoodnews.com/pan-africa/diaspora/150-harnessing-human-capital-the-african-diaspora.html

3 Gnanaraj Chellaraj, Keith Maskus, and Aaditya Mattoo, "The Contribution of Skilled Immigrations and International Graduate Students to U.S. Innovation," *Review of International Economics* 16, no. 3 (2008): 444–62.

4 See Steven Vertovec, *The Political Importance of Diasporas* (University of Oxford and Migration Policy Institute, 2005).

5 Michel Beine, Frédéric Docquier, Çağlar Özden, *Diasporas*, World Bank Policy Research Working Paper no. 4,984 (July 2009).

6 The World Bank's World Development Indicators define a migrant as a first-generation departee who remains in the destination country on a semi-permanent basis (for at least 1 year). This definition excludes both second and later generation members and seasonal workers. Thus, there is a significant distinction between "migrants" and the totality of the diaspora.

7 *World Migration Report* (International Organization for Migration, 2010).

8 Michael Clemens, *Economics and Emigration: Trillion-Dollar Bills on the Sidewalk?*, Center for Global Development Working Paper no. 264 (August 2011). He writes, "The emigration of less than 5 percent of the population of poor regions would bring global gains exceeding the gains from total elimination of all policy barriers to merchandise trade and all barriers to capital flows," 2.

9 "The Economic Implications of Remittances and Migration," in *Global Economic Prospects* (World Bank 2006), table 2.1, 27.

10 Three of the main migratory nations are European: UK, Italy and Germany.

11 S. Douglas Massey et al., "Theories of International Migration: A Review and Appraisal," *Population and Development Review* 19, no. 3 (1993): 431.

12 Williams, "Harnessing Human Capital."

13 A large number of programs have sprung up to use the expertise of migrant diasporas. For example, the *Retour aux Sources* programme run by London-based Africa Foundation Stone and ACET, the African Centre for Economic Transformation, headquartered in Ghana. SEEDA, Supporting Entrepreneurs and Enterprise Development in Africa, is run by the UK-based African organisation, AFFORD.

14 World Development Indicators (2011), table 6.1.

15 *Global Economic Prospects* (World Bank, 2006).

16 For example Michael Clemens, *A Labor Mobility Agenda for Development*, Center for Global Development Working Paper no. 201 (January 2010).

17 See William Easterly and Yaw Nyarko "Is the Brain Drain Good for Africa?" in *Skilled Immigration Today: Prospects, Problems, and Policies*, ed. by Jagdish Bhagwati and Gordon Hanson (Oxford University Press, 2009), chapter 11.

18 Satish Chand and Michael Clemens, *Skilled Emigration and Skill Creation: A Quasi-experiment*, Center for Global Development Working Paper no. 152 (2008).

19 Dilip Ratha et al., *Leveraging Migration for Africa: Remittances, Skills, and Investments* (World Bank, 2011).

20 Graziano Battistella, and Cecilia Conoco, "The Impact of Labour Migration on the Children Left Behind: A Study of Elementary School Children in the Philippines," *Journal of Social Issues in Southeast Asia* 13, no. 2 (1998): 220–35.

21 John Bryant, *Children of International Migrants in Indonesia, Thailand, and the Philippines: A Review of Evidence and Policies*, Working Paper 2005-05 (UNICEF Innocenti Research Center, Florence, 2005).

22 *Global Economic Prospects.*

23 Devesh Kapur and John McHale *Give Us Your Brightest and Your Best: The Global Hunt for Talent and Its Impact on the Developing World* (Center for Global Development, 2005), 121.

24 Kapur and McHale, *Give Us Your Brightest*, 151.

25 Albert Bollard, David McKenzie and Melanie Morten, "The Remitting Patterns of African Migrants in the OECD," *Journal of African Economics* 19, no. 5 (2010): 605–34.

26 John Gibson and David McKenzie, *The Microeconomic Determinants of Emigration and Return Migration of the Best and Brightest: Evidence from the Pacific*, Center for Global Development Working Paper no. 173 (May 2009).

27 See Kapur and McHale, *Give Us Your Brightest*, 164.

28 Dean Yang, *Why Do Migrants Return to Poor Countries? Evidence From Philippine Migrants Responses to Exchange Rate Shocks*, NBER Working Paper no. 12,396 (2006).

29 Devesh Kapur and John McHale, "International migration and the world income distribution," *Journal of International Development* 21, no. 8 (2009): 1,102–10.

30 George J. Borjas and Bernt Bratsberg, "Who Leaves? The Outmigration of the Foreign-Born," *The Review of Economics and Statistics* 78, no. 1 (1996): 165–76.

31 Gibson and McKenzie, *Microeconomic Determinants.*

32 Borjas and Bratsberg, "Who Leaves?"

33 See Kapur and McHale, *Give Us Your Brightest*, 171.

34 Ratha et al., *Leveraging Migration for Africa*, table 1.8.

35 Williams, "Harnessing Human Capital: The African Diaspora."

36 See Kapur and McHale, *Give Us Your Brightest*, 112.

37 "Outlook for Remittance Flows 2012–14," *Migration and Development Brief no. 17* (World Bank, December 2011). It should be noted however that projections have just been revised significantly upwards as a result of new information for Nigeria and Kenya. Upward revisions are also expected for other African countries. See *Migration and Development Brief no. 19* (World Bank, November 2012), 6.

38 Alexei Kireyev, *The Macroeconomics of Remittances: The Case of Tajikistan*, IMF Working Paper no. 06/2 (January 2006).

39 The World Bank reports: "Remittance flows are likely significantly underestimated: only about half of the countries in Sub-Saharan Africa collect remittance data with any regularity, and some major receivers of remittances report no data at all. … [I]nformal remittance flows, not included in the IMF estimates, could be equal to or more than the official figures for Sub-Saharan Africa." See Ratha et al., *Leveraging Migration for Africa*. Projections for Sub-Saharan Africa have recently been revised significantly upwards; see *Migration and Development Brief no. 19*, 6.

40 Lesotho's migrants are greatly underestimated because the recorded migrants exclude Lesotho's large temporary emigrant workforce. Ghana's income flows are underestimated because they are not properly accounted for by the Central Bank.

41 John Page and Sonia Plaza, "Migration Remittances and Development: A Review of Global Evidence," *Journal of African Economies* 15, supplement 2 (2006): 245–335.

42 Jacqueline Irving, Sanket Mohapatra, and Dilip Ratha *Migrant Remittance Flows: Findings from a Global Survey of Central Banks*, World Bank Working Paper no. 194 (2010).

43 *Global Economic Prospects*. Large data gaps were also found for Nigeria, Rwanda, Sierra Leone, Ethiopia and others in a) compensation of employees, b) workers' remittances by migrants resident in another country, and c) migrant transfers during migration. Small transactions through post offices and exchange bureaus are often not reported or are misclassified as exports, tourism, nonresident deposits, or direct investment.

44 "Future of Remittances" program, World Bank, October 2010.

45 Within Kenya in 2006, 58 percent of money transfers were by hand, 24 percent through the post office and money order, 11 percent by direct deposit and 9 percent through a money transfer service. See Sanket Mohapatra and Dilip Ratha (eds), *Remittance Markets in Africa* (World Bank, April 2011).

46 Albert Bolland, David McKenzie and Melanie Morten, *The Remitting Patterns of African Migrants in the OECD*, World Bank Policy Research Working Paper no. 5,260 (April 2010).

47 Based on 220 million recorded formal migrants remitting a recorded global total of US$400 billion in 2012.

48 See "The World Bank, Future of African Remittances (FAR) Program, 2010," *African Remittances* (www.africaremittances.org).

49 This sets aside the apples and oranges problem discussed earlier in trying to add up these diverse flows.

50 Dean Yang, *International Migration, Human Capital, and Entrepreneurship: Evidence from Philippine Migrants" Exchange Rate Shocks*, Discussion Paper no. 531 (Ford School of Public Policy, University of Michigan, February 2005). See also Dilip Ratha, *Leveraging Remittances for Development* (Migration Policy Institute, June 2007).

51 Devesh Kapur, *Remittances: The New Development Mantra?*, G24 Discussion Paper (UNCTAD, 2004), 6.

52 It should also be noted that the ODA amount is inflated by the inclusion of emergency aid.

53 The 2008–2009 ODA amount may also be a temporary surge resulting from crisis financing by the World Bank and other institutions.

54 Irving, Mohapatra and Ratha, *Migrant Remittance Flows*.
55 Roger Waldinger, *Between Here and There: How Attached Are Latino Immigrants to Their Native Country?* (Pew Hispanic Center, 25 October 2007). http://www.pewhispanic.org/2007/10/25/between-here-and-there-how-attached-are-latino-immigrants-to-their-native-country/
56 This is discussed by *inter alia* Kapur and McHale, *Give Us Your Brightest*, 143ff.
57 Ratha et al., *Leveraging Migration for Africa*.
58 Employee compensation mostly consists of seasonal labor or diplomats' income; migrant transfers are movements in funds from changes in residence. For an account of the data issues see Thomas Dorsey, *The Landscape of Capital Flows*, IMF Working Paper no. 08/51 (2008).
59 Dorsey, *Landscape of Capital Flows*, table 6.
60 The World Development Indicators (2011) show these countries as having received between 0 and 1 percent of GDP in remittances compared to the recorded average (itself seriously underestimated) for Sub-Saharan Africa of 2.3 percent in 2008 and 2.6 percent in 2009.
61 See Dorsey, *Landscape of Capital Flows*.
62 Paul Collier, Anke Hoeffler and Catherine Pattillo, "Africa's Exodus: Capital Flight and the Brain Drain as Portfolio Decisions," *Journal of African Economies* 13 (October 2004): ii15–ii54.
63 For a discussion see Shanta Devarajan, William Easterly and Howard Pack, "Low Investment is not the Constraint on African Development," *Economic Development and Cultural Change* 51, no. 3 (2003): 547–71. See also Valerie Cerra, Meenakshi Rishi, and Sweta C. Saxena, "Robbing the Riches: Capital Flight, Institutions, and Instability," *Journal of Development Studies* 44, no. 8 (2008): 1,190–213. The authors find that macroeconomic policy has a significant influence on capital flight after controlling for country effects and institutional quality.
64 See Paul Collier, Anke Hoeffler, and Catherine Pattillo. "Flight Capital as a Portfolio Choice". *World Bank Economic Review* 15, no. 1 (2001): 55–80. Asset recovery was identified as a key aim by the UN Convention against Corruption in 2006. The International Centre for Asset Recovery (ICAR) was established in 2006, and the Stolen Asset Recovery (STAR) initiative (World Bank and UN Office of Drugs and Crime) in 2007.
65 Dev Kar and Karly Curcio, *Illicit Financial Flows from Developing Countries: 2000–2009* (Ford Foundation, January 2011). Calculations based on the difference between sources and uses of funds in the International Monetary Fund Balance of Payments Statistics and an estimate of transfer pricing in trade.
66 Collier, Hoeffler and Pattillo, "Flight Capital."
67 Mohammed Salisu, "The Role of Capital Flight and Remittances in Current Account Sustainability in Sub-Saharan Africa," *African Development Review* 17, no. 3 (2005): 382–404.
68 Dilip Ratha, S. Mohapatra and Sophie Plaza, *Beyond Aid: New Sources and Innovative Mechanisms for Financing Development in Sub-Saharan Africa*, World Bank Policy Research Working Paper no. 4,609 (2008).
69 Léonce Ndikumana and James K. Boyce, "Measurement of Capital Flight: Methodology and Results for Sub-Saharan Africa," *African Development Review* 22, no. 4 (2010): 471–81.
70 Hippolyte Fofack and Léonce Ndikumana, "Capital Flight Repatriation: Investigation of Its Potential Gains for Sub-Saharan African Countries," *African Development Review* 22, no. 1: 4–22; see also Hippolyte Fofack, *Causality between External Debt and Capital Flight in Sub-Saharan Africa*, World Bank Policy Research Working Paper no. 5,042 (September 2009).
71 For example, Adolfo Barajas et al., *Do Workers' Remittances Promote Economic Growth?*, IMF Working Paper no. 153 (July 2009). The authors survey previous estimates and add one of their own.
72 Association is complicated because growth is positively associated with emigration and higher remittances in the longer run, while higher (countercyclical) remittances can be negatively associated with growth in the short run. Growth and remittances may also be negatively linked because of poor governance, which encourages both higher migration and

lower economic growth, or where growth occurs in another country that is a major trading partner and a major destination for migrants.

73 For example, Reena Aggarwal, Asli Demirgüç-Kunt and María Soledad Martínez Pería, "Do Workers' Remittances Promote Financial Development," *Journal of Development Economics* 96, no. 2 (2011): 255–64. The paper shows that remittances are associated with higher ratios of both banking deposits and credit to GDP.

74 Raghuram G. Rajan and Arvind Subramanian, *What Undermines Aid's Impact on Growth?*, NBER Working Paper no. 11,657 (2005).

75 See *Global Economic Prospects*, chart 5A.

76 Ghada Fayad, *Remittances and Dutch Disease: A Dynamic Heterogeneous Panel Analysis on the Middle East and North Africa Region* (Centre for the Study of African Economies, February 2010).

77 See *Building a Future Back Home: Leveraging Migrant Worker Remittances for Development in Asia* (Economist Intelligence Unit/Western Union, 2008), 10.

78 Dean Yang, "International Migration, Human Capital, and Entrepreneurship: Evidence From Philippine Migrants' Exchange Rate Shocks," *The Economic Journal* 118, no. 528 (2008): 591–630.

79 Edward Funkhouser, "Migration from Nicaragua: Some Recent Evidence," *World Development* 20, no. 8 (1992): 1,209–18.

80 Richard H. Adams, Alfredo Cuecuecha and John Page. *Remittances, Consumption and Investment in Ghana*, World Bank Policy Research Working Paper no. 4,515 (February 2008).

81 *Building a Future Back Home: Leveraging Migrant Worker Remittances for Development in Asia* (EIU/ Western Union, 2008), 8.

82 Devesh Kapur and John McHale, "International Migration and the world income distribution," *Journal of International Development*, 21, no. 8 (2009): 1,102–10.

83 Tom de Bruyn and Umbareen Kuddus, *Dynamics of Remittance Utilization in Bangladesh* (International Organization for Migration, January 2005); Pedro J. F. De Lima, *Workers' Remittances: A Lever for Economic Development?* (Development Economics Advisory Service, European Investment Bank, 2007).

84 Prachi Mishra, *Macroeconomic Impact of Remittances in the Caribbea*, IMF working paper (2005).

85 Christopher Woodruff, *Mexican Microenterprise Investment and Employment: The Role of Remittances*, Inter-American Development Bank Working Paper no. 26 (2007).

86 *Towards Human Resilience: Sustaining MDG Progress in an Age of Economic Uncertainty* (United Nations Development Programme, Bureau for Development Policy, September 2011), 124.

87 For example, David Leblang, "Another link in the chain: migrant networks and international investment," in *Diaspora for Development in Africa*, ed. by Sonia Plaza and Dilip Ratha (World Bank, 2011), 79.

88 FAR survey.

89 See discussion of this is in Aaron Terrazas, *Diaspora Investment in Developing and Emerging Economy Capital Markets: Patterns and Prospects* (Migration Policy Institute, August 2010).

90 Ratha et al., *Leveraging Migration for Africa*, 85ff., and see Table 2.3 in Chapter 2.

91 See *World Economic Outlook* (IMF, 2005), chapter 2, on workers' remittances and economic development.

92 See *Global Economic Prospects*, 125.

93 Ratha, Mohapatra and Plaza, *Beyond Aid*, 13.

94 The borrowing bank could pledge future remittance receivables to an offshore fund. The fund would issue the debt to foreign lenders/ investors. Remittance revenues could be sent to an offshore trust account which would in turn makes principal and interest payments to the lenders/investors.

95 Thomas Debass and Michael Ardovino, "Diaspora Direct Investment: The Untapped Resource for Development," *USAID* (19 May 2009).

96 Large diaspora audiences regularly attend investment forums in Somaliland to learn about opportunities despite the post-conflict environment and the patchy regulations and infrastructure of the country.

97 This is an "intellectual/scientific diaspora network" created by the Institute of Research for Development and the University of California, April 2004.

98 *Building a Future Back Home*, 11.

99 *Building a Future Back Home*, citing Sari Canyete Jotojot, Asian Migrant Centre, Hong Kong.

100 J. Edward Taylor, "The new economics of labor migration and the role of remittances in the migration process," *International Migration* 37, no. 1 (1999): 63–88.

101 World Development Indicators (2010), table 4.2, 232.

102 Hippolyte Fofack and Léonce Ndikumana, "Capital Flight Repatriation: Investigation of Its Potential Gains for Sub-Saharan African Countries," *African Development Review* 22, no. 1: 4–22.

103 See Ratha, Mohapatra and Plaza, *Beyond Aid*.

104 "Africa: Going Long On Diaspora Bonds," *AllAfrica.Com* (5 March 2012).

105 From Dilip Ratha and Sanket Mohapatra, "Harnessing the Resources of the Diaspora," table 4.1, in Ratha et al., *Leveraging Migration for Africa*. The estimates are based on assumptions about earnings of diaspora members with and without tertiary education and that savings rates of skilled and unskilled migrants are the same as in their home countries.

106 Beata S. Javorcik, Çağlar Özden, Mariana Spatareanu and Cristina Neagu, "Migrant Networks and Foreign Direct Investment," *Journal of Development Economics* 94, no. 2 (2011): 231–41.

107 These are: *Addis Voice* (London); *Africa Monitor*; *AllAfrica.com – Ethiopia*; *Capitol Ethiopia*; *EthioMedia* (US); *EthioPress.com*; *Ethiopian Reporter* (Addis Ababa); *Ethiopian Review* (US); *Ethiopian Weekly Press Digest* (Addis Ababa); *Gambella News* (Ethiopia); *Jimma Times* (Ethiopia); *Nazret.com* (Ethiopia); *Ethiopian News Portal* (US) *Urjii*; *Walta Information Centre* (US); *Zethiopia* newspaper (US).

108 From Tjai M. Nielsen and Liesl Riddle, "Investing in Peace: The Motivational Dynamics of Diaspora Investment in Post-conflict Economies," *Journal of Business Ethics* 89 (2010): 435–48.

109 *Bridge* journal was founded in 2009 to connect Somaliland and potential foreign investors. A high quality magazine *Somaliland Eye*, started in 2011 based on the UK journal *Somali Eye*.

110 Somaliland is a former British colony that agreed to unite in greater Somalia in 1961. It re-asserted independence from Somalia in 1991 but is not recognized as a sovereign state. There is a growing literature on the country as an example of self-help development. See, for example, Nicholas Eubank, *Peace-Building without External Assistance: Lessons from Somaliland*, Center for Global Development Working Paper no. 198 (January 2010). This and other research find that Somaliland's lack of foreign aid has encouraged the growth of accountable political institutions, greater tax effort, and diaspora cooperation.

111 Kuznetsov Yevgeny (ed.), *Diaspora Networks and the International Migration of Skills: How Countries Can Draw on Their Talent Abroad* (World Bank, World Bank Institute, 2006).

112 The country cases are based on various sources including: Aaron Terrazas, *Diaspora Investment in Developing and Emerging Country Capital Markets: Patterns and Prospects* (Migration Policy Institute, 2010), organizational websites, World Bank reports and other sources.

113 Abhishek Pandey, Alok Aggarwal, Richard Devane and Yevgeny Kuznetsov "India's Transformation to Knowledge-Based Economy – Evolving Role of the Indian Diaspora," *Evalueserve* (21 July 2004).

114 Sonali Jain, *For Love and Money: Second-Generation Indian Americans' "Return to India" Migration Information Source* (Migration Policy Institute, October 2010).

115 The study reports various estimates of the number of returnees, 35,000 in 2004 Bangalore alone according to the *New York Times*; 5,000 IT professionals with over 5 years experience returned between 2003 and 2005 according to the *Economist* and 32,000 according to a 2010 report by the World Economic Forum.

116 This section draws partly from Kathleen Newland and Hiroyuki Tanaka, *Mobilizing Diaspora Entrepreneurship for Development* (Migration Policy Institute, 2010).

117 See www.tie.org

118 Anna Lee Saxenian, *International Mobility of Engineers and the Rise of Entrepreneurship in the Periphery*, Research Paper no. 2006/142 (United Nations University WIDER, November 2006).

119 This is far higher than the estimate of the World Bank's World Development Indicators of about 700,000, presumably because it includes the second and later generation.

120 Draws from Kathleen Newland and Hiroyuki Tanaka, *Mobilizing Diaspora Entrepreneurship.*

121 Based on Ali Zafar, *Learning from the Chinese Miracle Development Lessons for Sub-Saharan Africa*, World Bank Policy Research Working Paper no. 5,216 (February 2010).

122 Ali Zafar, *Learning from the Chinese Miracle Development Lessons for Sub-Saharan Africa*, World Bank Policy Research Working Paper no. 5,216 (February 2010).

123 Alice Bloch, *The Development Potential of Zimbabweans in the Diaspora*, International Organization for Migration, Research Series no. 17 (2005), 81.

124 Debass and Ardovino, "Diaspora Direct Investment."

125 See also Elizabeth Chacko and Marie Price, *Migration and Co-development. The Role of the Diaspora in Development: The case of Ethiopian and Bolivian immigrants in the USA* (Department of Geography, George Washington University, 2 October 2009, and the American Community Survey, 2010).

126 D. Aredo, *Migration Remittances, Shocks, and Poverty in Urban Ethiopia: An. Analysis of Micro Level Panel Data* (Addis Ababa University, 2005).

127 *The Contribution of UK-Based Diasporas to Development and Poverty Reduction*, ESRC Centre on Migration, Policy and Society (COMPAS) Report Team (April 2004).

128 See their website www.afford-uk.org

129 See *The Contribution of UK-Based Diasporas.*

130 See www.ghanaweb.com/GhanaHomePage/diaspora.

131 Devesh Kapur, "Social Remittances and the Flow of Ideas," in *The Transnational Villagers*, ed. by Peggy Levitt (University of California, July 2001), 123. He writes of three types of social remittances: normative structures, systems of practice, and social capital.

132 Frédéric Docquier, Elisabetta Lodigiani, Hillel Rapoport and Maurice Schiff, *Emigration and Democracy*, Working Paper no. 217 (Center for International Development, Harvard University, January 2011).

133 Docquier, Lodigiani, Rapoport and Schiff, *Emigration and Democracy.*

134 Kathleen Newland, *Voice after Exit: Diaspora Diplomacy* (Migration Policy Institute, November 2010), 9.

135 Available at http://www.standardmedia.co.ke/?id=2000028476&cid=4&ttl=Kenyans%20in%20Diaspora%20want%20stake%20in%20local%20politics&articleID=2000028476

136 Dovelyn R. Agunias (ed.), *Closing the Distance: How Governments Strengthen Ties with Their Diasporas* (Migration Policy Institute, 2009).

137 Agunias (ed.), *Closing the Distance.*

138 EPRDF is the Ethiopian People's Revolutionary Democratic Party, which took power in 1991.

139 Terrence Lyons, "Diasporas and Homeland Conflict," in *Proceedings of the 16th International Conference of Ethiopian Studies* (Trondheim 2009).

140 Docquier, Lodigiani, Rapoport and Schiff, *Emigration and Democracy.*

141 Devesh Kapur, *Diaspora, Development, and Democracy: The Domestic Impact of International Migration from India* (Princeton, 2010). He writes, "Traditions of rote learning, exam-

driven or seniority-based systems of advancement, extreme deference to superiors, nepotism as a normal practice, avoidance of risk-taking, and other such cultural traits stifle entrepreneurism."

142 A discussion of the control over flows is in Nava Ashraf et al., *Remittances and the Problem of Control: A Field Experiment Among Migrants from El Salvador* (Harvard Business School, May 2010).

143 These include (without counting general population studies institutes): ILO International Migration Program, International Organization for Migration, Center for Immigration Studies (US), Center for Migration Studies (US), Centre for Refugee Studies (Canada); Centre for Research in International Migration and Ethnic Relations (Sweden); European Research Centre on Migration and Ethnic Relations (Netherlands); Institute for the Study of International Migration (US); International Center for Migration, Ethnicity and Citizenship (US); Migration Policy Institute (US); Migration Research Unit, (UK); Center for Migration and Development (US); RAND Corporation Labor and Population Program and Population Research Center (US); Refugee Studies Centre (UK); Refugees International (US); Committee for Refugees and Immigrants (US).

144 See *Policy and Institutional Coherence to Address the Relationship between Migration and Development*, Global Forum on Migration and Development background paper (Mexico 2010).

145 Newland, *Voice after Exit*. She writes, "For donors, an enabling framework is the best approach to diaspora advocacy, capable of encouraging the voice of diaspora members without rewarding their exit" (19).

146 Ibid., 20.

147 Dovelyn Agunias and Kathleen Newland, *Developing a Roadmap for Engaging Diasporas in Development: A Handbook for Policy Makers and Practitioners in Home and Host Countries* (Migration Policy Institute, International Organization for Migration, 2012), 13.

148 The ADM is a business program that aims to boost the economies of Sub-Saharan Africa through startups and established enterprises. See http://www.diasporamarketplace.org

149 See http://blogs.worldbank.org/peoplemove/consultation-on-knowledge-partnership-on-migration-and-global-development

6. "New Aid": New Ways to Promote and Finance Development?

1 See http://policydialogue.org/files/events/Stiglitz_Post_Washington_Consensus_Paper.pdf

2 Cited in Roger Riddell, *Does Foreign Aid Really Work?* (Oxford University Press, 2007), 204–5.

3 An account of new ideas in aid giving is in Andrew Rogerson, Adrian Hewitt and David Waldenburg, *The International Aid System 2005–2010: Forces For and Against Change* (Overseas Development Institute, January 2004).

4 Nancy Birdsall, William Savedoff, Ayah Mahgoub and Katherine Vyborny, *Cash on Delivery – A New Approach to Foreign Aid* (Center for Global Development, November 2010).

5 The approach seems to be the complicated product of a genuine attempt to find a way of ensuring results while being constrained by demands for proof of performance.

6 As an aside, it is unlikely that an administrative committee can seriously cater to the emerging demands of African industrial development. The fund's tiny rate of disbursement out of total proposals received suggests that prize giving by committee is far too cautious a procedure to support such a dynamic.

7 For example, see David Phillips, *Implementing the Market Approach to Enterprise Support – An Evaluation of Matching Grant Schemes*, World Bank Policy Research Working Paper no. 2,589 (April 2001).

8 Nicolas van de Walle describes this possibility as "a new form of ventriloquism" with the recipients as puppets! See *Overcoming Stagnation in Aid-Dependent Countries: Politics, Policies and Incentives for Poor Countries* (Center for Global Development, 2005).

9 Aside from process, in terms of development effectiveness these funds sometimes have a good developmental focus such as support to innovation or creation of service markets but they can have adverse effects at sectoral level if their main effect is to provide cheap money in competition with the banks.

10 See http://www.mcc.gov/pages/about

11 Devi Sridhar and Tami Tamashiro, *Vertical Funds in the Health Sector: Lessons for Education from the Global Fund and GAVI* (UNESCO, 2009). The authors write that misreporting is a problem for implementing vertical programs in the education sector.

12 Over-reporting the number of children immunized occurs through understating vaccine coverage at the baseline year or overstating vaccine coverage after the baseline year. See S. Lim, D. Stein, A. Charrow and C. Murray, "Tracking Progress Towards Universal Childhood Immunisation and the Impact of Global Initiatives: A Systematic Analysis of Three-Dose Diphtheria, Tetanus, and Pertussis Immunisation Coverage," *The Lancet* 372 (2008): 2,031–46.

13 *Multilateral Aid Review: Ensuring Maximum Value for Money for UK Aid through Multilateral Organisations* (DFID, March 2011), 54.

14 Riddell, *Does Foreign Aid Really Work*, 198–205.

15 See *Evaluation of General Budget Support 1994–2004: Synthesis Report* (IDD, University of Birmingham and Associates, May 2006).

16 Ariel Fiszbein and Norbert Schady et al., *Conditional Cash Transfers: Reducing Present and Future Poverty* (World Bank, 2009). Also, Laura Rawlings and Gloria Rubio, *Evaluating the Impact of CCT Programs: Lessons from Latin America*, World Bank Policy Research Working Paper no. 3,119 (August 2003). Coverage has ranged from 1 percent of the poorest decile in Cambodia to more than 60 percent in Brazil, Ecuador and Mexico.

17 In the flagship Opportunidades program a delay in developing a management system caused 27 percent of its targeted population to not receive any transfers in the first 2 years.

18 Guy Standing, *Conditional Cash Transfers: Why Targeting and Conditionalities Could Fail*, International Poverty Centre (IPC) Working Paper no. 47 (December 2007).

19 Anna McCord, *Cash Transfers: Affordability and Sustainability*, Overseas Development Institute, Project Briefing no. 30 (November 2009).

20 In some cases such a commitment would be excessively costly. Governments would need to spend an unsustainable 2–6 percent of GDP to achieve what the ILO defines as an adequate provision compared to the norm for Latin America of 1–2 percent.

21 *Cash Transfers Evidence Paper* (DFID, Policy Division, April 2011).

22 This is ironically the reverse of the "capacity building" approach since here donors make piecemeal contributions to something that needs a holistic approach. It might be recalled that some consider the full social safety net including universal health insurance to be too costly even for the US.

23 Where it is difficult to provide a representative rating or where the rating depends on specific project circumstances a score of "3" has been used. Where no rating is possible n/a is entered.

7. Another Pathway Out of Poverty?

1 See Christian Oliver and Chris Giles, "South Korea urges policy shift over aid," *Financial Times* (4 November 2012). http://www.ft.com/cms/s/0/512e72ba-e843-11df-8995-00144feab49a.html#axzz2GaMESBu0

2 Dambisa Moyo, *Dead Aid: Why Aid Is Not Working and How there is another Way for Africa* (Allen Lane, 2008). Cited in "Dambisa Moyo: Aid Dependence Blights Africa: The Cure is in the Credit Crisis," *Independent*, 2 February 2009.

3 Dilip Ratha writes, "In conclusion, migration and remittances can be a valuable complement to broad-based development efforts. Yet, migration and remittances (collective or individual)

should not be viewed as a substitute for official development aid as they are private money that should not be expected to fund public projects." In Dilip Ratha, Sanket Mohapatra and Elina Scheja, *The Impact of Migration on Economic and Social Development: A Review of Evidence and Emerging Issues*, World Bank Policy Research Working Paper no. 5,558 (February 2011), 21.

4 See *International Migration, Remittances and the Brain Drain in G-15 Countries*, The Summit Level Group of Developing Countries, G15 Working Paper Series, vol. 5 (January 2009). This applies to a large number of countries in Africa, Asia and Latin America.

5 Ann Lee Saxenian, "Transnational Communities and the Evolution of Global Production Networks: The Cases of Taiwan, China and India," *Industry and Innovation* 9, no. 3 (Fall, 2002): 183–202.

6 Dilip Ratha et al., *Leveraging Migration for Africa: Remittances, Skills, and Investments* (World Bank, 2011).

7 See *International Migration*.

8 Devesh Kapur, and John McHale, "What's Wrong with Plan B? International Migration as an Alternative to Development Assistance," *Brookings Trade Forum* (2006): 137–86.

9 Lant Pritchett, *Let Their People Come: Breaking the Gridlock on Global Labor Mobility* (Center For Global Development, 2006).

10 Michael J. Clemens, *A Labor Mobility Agenda for Development*, Center for Global Development Working Paper no. 201 (January 2010).

11 Ndioro Ndiaye, Susanne Melde, and Rougui Ndiaye-Coïc, "Migration for Development in Africa Experience and Beyond," in *Diaspora for Development in Africa*, ed. by Sonia Plaza and Dilip Ratha (World Bank, 2011), 231–60. The MIDA Great Lakes Project is designed to facilitate communication between institutions in Burundi, the Democratic Republic of Congo, and Rwanda and the diaspora in Belgium.

12 *Global Economic Prospects* (World Bank, 2006).

13 *Global Economic Prospects*, 135.

14 See *International Migration*.

15 *Sending Money Home to Africa: Remittance Markets, Enabling Environment and Prospects* (IFAD, 2009).

16 See Dilip Ratha, Sanket Mohapatra and Sonia Plaza, *Beyond Aid: New Mechanisms for Financing Development in Sub-Saharan Africa*, World Bank Policy Research Working Paper no. 4,609 (April 2008).

17 Dilip Ratha, *Leveraging Remittances for Development*, MPI Policy Brief (June 2007).

18 Suhas Ketkar, and Dilip Ratha, "New Paths to Funding," *Finance & Development* 46, no. 2 (June 2009).

19 See "Africa: Going Long on Diaspora Bonds," *AllAfrica* (5 March 2012).

20 Ibid.

21 Ratha et al. *Leveraging Migration for Africa*.

22 Ibid. See also Dilip Ratha, Sanket Mohapatra and Sonia Plaza, *Beyond Aid*.

23 Ibid.

24 Rabindra Bhandari, Gyan Pradhan and Mukti Upadhyay, "Another Empirical Look at the Kuznets Curve," *International Journal of Economic Sciences and Applied Research* 3, no. 2 (2010): 7–19.

25 Originally proposed by J. R. Boudeville, *Problems of Regional Economic Planning* (Edinburgh University Press, 1966).

26 Christofakis Manolis and Athanasios Papadaskalopoulos, "The Growth Poles Strategy in Regional Planning: The Recent Experience of Greece," *Theoretical and Empirical Researches in Urban Management* 6, no. 2 (May 2011): 5–20. For a seminal paper, see Paul Krugman, "The Role of Geography in Development," *International Regional Science Review* 22, no. 142 (1999): 142–61.

27 "Reshaping Economic Geography," in *World Development Report* (World Bank, 2009).

28 See Harry W. Richardson, "Growth Pole Spillovers: The Dynamics of Backwash and Spread," *Regional Studies* 41, supplement 1 (2007): S27–S35.

29 This process is explained by the so-called "gravity model" in which bilateral trade flows are determined by the size of two economies and the distance between them.
30 See John Weiss and David Phillips, "Ethiopia: Urban Services Value Chain Study," draft (World Bank, 2011).
31 Nastasya Tay, "World Bank Identifies Five Poor States as 'Growth Poles,'" Inter Press Service (7 March 2011). http://www.ipsnews.net/2011/03/africa-world-bank-identifies-five-poor-states-as-growth-poles/
32 Steven Radelet, *Emerging Africa: How Seventeen Countries Are Leading the Way* (Center for Global Development, September 2010).
33 Each African country has an average of four neighbors compared to 2.3 in Latin America.
34 ECOWAS – Economic Community of West African States; COMESA – Common Market for Eastern and Southern Africa; SADC – Southern Africa Development Community; IGAD – Intergovernmental Authority on Development; EAC – East African Community.
35 Alemayehu Gedaa and Haile Kebret, "Regional Economic Integration in Africa: A Review of Problems and Prospects with a Case Study of COMESA," *Journal of African Economies* 17, no. 3 (2007): 357–94.
36 *Building a Future Back Home: Leveraging Migrant Worker Remittances for Development in Asia* (Economist Intelligence Unit/Western Union, 2008), 27.
37 Ibid., 6.
38 *Migration and Co-development: Social Remittances of the African Diasporas in Europe: Case Studies of Netherlands and Portugal* (North–South Centre, Council of Europe, 2007), 31.
39 Dilip Ratha, "A Conversation on Migration and Development," *People Move* blog (World Bank, 1 February 2010).
40 Ratha et al., *Leveraging Migration for Africa*, 86.
41 Kathleen Newland and Hiroyuki Tanaka, *Mobilizing Diaspora Entrepreneurship for Development* (Migration Policy Institute, July 2011), 22.

8. Exit Strategy – Replacing Foreign Assistance

1 Jonathan Glennie, *What's Wrong with Foreign Aid?* (Zed Books, 2008), 98.
2 Some similar discussion is in Tom Harford, Bita Hadjimichael and Michael Klein, *Aid Agency Competition*, World Bank, Private Sector Development Note no. 277 (2004). See also Devesh Kapur and John Mchale, *What's Wrong with Plan B? International Migration as an Alternative to Development Assistance* (Brookings Trade Forum, May 2006).
3 The rigorous definition of a public good is one that is "non-rival" (i.e. it is freely available), and "non-excludable" (i.e. it cannot be provided to one person while excluding another, such as in a private sale). A good which is rivalrous but non-excludable is a common pool resource such as fish stocks. The production or preservation of such goods generally justifies public intervention.
4 The Bank has developed the carbon market first through the Prototype Carbon Fund to demonstrate how to cost-effectively achieve GHG reductions and more recently, through other funds such as the Community Development Carbon Fund and Bio Carbon Fund. See www.carbonfinance.org.
5 In the category of global information might be included the World Bank's "Doing Business" reports, although a recent evaluation casts some doubt on this. See Dinuk Jayasuriya, *Improvements in the World Bank's Ease of Doing Business Rankings: Do They Translate into greater Foreign Direct Investment Inflows?*, World Bank Policy Research Working Paper no. 5,787 (September 2011).
6 See Paul Collier and Tony Venables, "Trade and Economic performance: does Africa's fragmentation matter?" (Centre for the Study of African Economies, Oxford University, May 2008), 29–30.

7 In Korea several new government-sponsored industrial cities attracted private investors in the 1970s and 1980s. In India, regional policy up to 1991 was restrictive. State governments and banks denied support to metropolitan areas and industrial parks were located in poorer states. After the ending of these policies in 1991 resources started to move to locations closer to markets.

8 Previous attempts with industrial estates and export processing zones in Africa have been disappointing, partly for the same reason as the Indian experience before 1991. See *World Development Report* (World Bank, 2009).

9 In March 2010, the Russian president Dimitry Mevedev announced that a high-tech research and production hub, on the model of Silicon Valley, would be built in Skolkovo near Moscow. It remains to be seen whether this project beats the odds against public entrepreneurship.

10 Devesh Kapur, *Do as I Say, Not as I Do: A Critique of G7 Proposals on Reforming the MDBs*, Center for Global Development Working Paper no. 16 (October 2002). Kapur writes, "In seeking to reinvent the Bank's public image its management and staff have labeled all kinds of activities or 'networks' as GPGs, meriting involvement on the basis of the moral claims that public goods invoke, and their ready slogan-appeal to northern tax-payers" (19).

11 A country information website in Kyrgyzstan built for a project in 1998 was escalated to global status as "dgMarket" to promote the Bank as a player in the New Economy. However, the private sector was already developing such websites. The Bank's value-addition was dubious. Two private organizations formally protested its involvement. The activist Bretton Woods Project described it as "a major land-grab on the Internet." See David Phillips, *Reforming the World Bank: Twenty Years of Trial – and Error*.

12 Jonathan Glennie suggests the slogan be revised to "less and better aid." See Glennie, *What's Wrong with Foreign Aid?*, 89.

13 See *Assessing Progress on Implementing the Paris Declaration and the Accra Agenda for Action* (OECD, 2011), 15, 62. Despite the poor performance the report stated that "it is important to note that considerable progress has been made towards many of the remaining 12 targets" (15).

14 Deborah A. Brautigam and Stephen Knack, "Foreign Aid, Institutions, and Governance in Sub-Saharan Africa," *Economic Development and Cultural Change* 52, no. 2 (2004): 263.

INDEX

Information in figures and tables is indicated by the letter *f* or *t* following the page locator.